HOW TO GET THE MOST OUT OF
DOW JONES
NEWS/RETRIEVAL

HOW TO GET THE MOST OUT OF
DOW JONES
NEWS/RETRIEVAL

Charles Bowen and David Peyton

BANTAM BOOKS

TORONTO • NEW YORK • LONDON • SYDNEY • AUCKLAND

HOW TO GET THE MOST OUT OF DOW JONES NEWS/RETRIEVAL
A Bantam Book / November 1986

Cover Design by J. Caroff Associates.

*Throughout this book, the trade names and trademarks of many
companies and products have been used and no such uses are intended to
convey endorsement of or other affiliations with the book.*

ISBN 0-553-34327-0

Published simultaneously in the United States and Canada

---

*Bantam Books are published by Bantam Books, Inc. Its trademark, consisting of
the words "Bantam Books" and the portrayal of a rooster, is Registered in U.S.
Patent and Trademark Office and in other countries. Marca Registrada. Bantam
Books, Inc., 666 Fifth Avenue, New York, New York 10103.*

PRINTED IN THE UNITED STATES OF AMERICA

B   0 9 8 7 6 5 4 3 2 1

To Bos Johnson, Dorothy Johnson,
and Bill Francois—
mentors, advisers and friends.

TRADEMARKS

The following are trademarks of Dow Jones & Co., Inc.:

Barron's National Business and Financial Weekly
Corporate Earnings Estimator
Dow Jones
Dow Jones News/Retrieval
Dow Jones News Service
Dow Jones Quotes
Dow Jones Software
Dow Jones Text-Search Services
Economic and Foreign Exchange Survey
Historical Dow Jones Averages
News/Retrieval Sports Report
News/Retrieval Symbol Directory
News/Retrieval Weather Report
The Wall Street Journal
Words of Wall Street
Market Manager PLUS
Market Analyzer
Spreadsheet Link
DowPhone

CONTENTS

PREFACE

We knew something was happening when computers started appearing on the desks of our local stockbrokers.

Huntington, West Virginia, our hometown, is not exactly on the main line to Wall Street. Its business community, while effective and talented, is small and not what you might think of as a citadel of high tech. Nonetheless, there they were: personal computers linked into fresh financial information.

"Let's see what's hot about that stock," the stockbroker said, and swung the computer around on its lazy-Susan turntable. With a few keystrokes he'd logged into Dow Jones News/Retrieval, picked up the latest stock quotation, a late-breaking business story about the company that might affect the buying and selling later in the day, and even a financial analysis of the issue, all hot off the press.

It didn't take much thinking to realize it made good sense for Huntington—and the thousands of other small- and medium-sized communities—to be online. The computer information services had already demonstrated that they could help metropolitan areas and large corporations do their business better and faster. Now everyone else was learning that these online systems also could be equalizers. Suddenly, small communities, and businesses everywhere, could have access to the same information the corporate giants could reach.

It is a concept that has fascinated us for several years of writing about online information services.

Back in 1984, when we first wrote *How to Get the Most Out of CompuServe* (Bantam Books, 2nd edition, 1986), we talked about the enormous *personal* communications network available on that system and came up with the term "Micropolis" to describe the feeling of community we found there.

Then we wrote *How to Get the Most Out of The Source* (Bantam Books, 1985) to report on the remarkable reference facilities and resources that system puts at your fingertips. If CompuServe was Micropolis's town square, then The Source was certainly its library and research center.

One of the effects of those two books was that businesspeople began asking us for advice and help in using what many of them considered "their" system—Dow Jones News/Retrieval. We were invited to seminars and computer users group meetings and were stopped on the street by technologically astute businesspeople.

What they told us was, in effect, that they didn't need help in *how* to use the information; they knew how to interpret a 10-K report and balance sheets and a collection of historical stock prices. What they needed was help in *getting to* the information quickly and efficiently and setting up procedures for letting that hot financial information flow into their daily business operations.

It was an assignment we welcomed. We'd always felt a mysterious kinship to Dow Jones News/Retrieval. During the research for this book, we found out why.

Our backgrounds are in newspapers. Between us we have some 40 years invested in the newsroom, tradition which teaches that the quality of the information—its accuracy, immediacy, and relevance—is the priority of the job. Now we'd found a computer system that felt the same way. Unlike most online information services today, News/Retrieval was born not from computing, but from a publishing heritage—and no less than the top publishing tradition of the financial community. Dow Jones & Co., with nearly a hundred years of reporting excellence with *The Wall Street Journal*, considers the information it is providing electronically to be more important than the computer systems and technological wizardry that carry it.

That should be important to you, whether you're part of a large corporation or one-half of a Mom and Pop operation.

Throughout our research we found many examples of what this news orientation means to the system. For instance, Dow Jones News/Retrieval has put together a staff of editors large enough to put out a medium-sized newspaper.

This newsroom uses good old-fashioned news judgment to determine the stories you need to know, whether general news of the day or events that affect a small corner of the business world. The electronic journalists even check the accuracy of individual stock quotes before they pass them on to us online. We know of no other information service that can make that claim.

We also found an interesting attitude at DJN/R about *us*, those who visit the system via computer. Talk to the people who work in News/Retrieval's Customer Service department and you'll find that to them we're not so much "users" or "subscribers" as we are "readers" and "clients." We think you'll find it a pleasing difference if you ever have to call on their assistance.

We called on their assistance quite a lot in the preparation of this book. We'd like to thank Julie Denny and Carla Gaffney, who saw us through the project from the beginning. Also thanks to Kathy Boyle and Richard Levine, to Patricia Sullivan, Greg Gerdy, Floy Bakes, and Barb Wolf.

Quite a few people outside Dow Jones also helped bring this book together—the outstanding editors at Bantam: Jono Hardjowirogo, Kenzi Sugihara, Michael Roney, and James Walsh. Also much thanks to our agent, Katinka Matson at John Brockman Associates, Inc.

And, as always, to the home guard—our wives, Susan Peyton and Pamela Bowen.

Charles Bowen
Dave Peyton

FOREWORD

Alfred Glossbrenner
author of
The Complete Handbook of Personal Computer Communications

If you asked a hundred people, "What do you think of when you hear the words 'Dow Jones News/Retrieval Service'?" whether they had actually heard of the service or not, 87 probably would say that it has something to do with stock quotes. Perhaps five would say, "Oh yes, I use it several times a month to update my portfolio." And only three might say, "Wonderful service. There are so *many* things you can do with it besides checking on your investments."

The responses of the remaining five would be more or less evenly divided between blank stares and either "Who wants to know?" or "Have a nice day," depending on whether the survey was conducted in New York or L.A.

My point is that "Dow Jones" and stock quotes are so nearly synonymous that most people would never expect an online system bearing that name to offer anything *but* stock quotes. Most people wouldn't expect, for instance, an electronic mail system, let alone one that can deliver paper copies to non-computer-owning associates anywhere in the country in four hours. But through MCI Mail, Dow Jones can do exactly that (your letters, reports, or whatever can be laser-printed on quality bond, and you can include a facsimile of your signature and letterhead if you like).

The system also offers you access to continuously updated sports and weather reports, as well as news from The Associated Press and its own "broadtapes" from Dow Jones News Service. Stories appear on the broadtapes, and thus on your computer screen, within 90 seconds of being filed by a Dow Jones reporter.

There's a database of movie reviews covering thousands of films, from those that came out last week to those that were made in 1926—a great way to find food for your videocassette recorder.

If you don't yet have a VCR, don't worry. Dow Jones can get it for you wholesale. Or almost. By offering you access to Comp-U-Store, the system makes it easy for you to shop for, compare, and purchase more than 50,000 products—many of which are available at discounts of up to 40 percent—without ever leaving your computer.

The system has many other nifty nonfinancial features as well. But the jewel in its crown is the exclusive access it provides to the country's finest newspaper, *The Wall Street Journal.* (More people subscribe to *The Journal* than to any other paper. I freely admit that I have long been addicted to it and am perhaps a tad prejudiced. But, as the character in the shampoo commercial solemnly opines, "They say it sells the most, so I guess that's why.")

Throughout the day and night the gigantic satellite dishes that dominate the Dow Jones corporate campus in Princeton, New Jersey, collect the information that will become tomorrow's *Journal.* By 6:00 A.M. Eastern time, Dow Jones News/Retrieval subscribers can view the result of all this activity on their computer screens, for that is when the electronic full text of *The Journal,* including both the popular "Heard on the Street" and "Abreast of the Market" columns, is brought online.

Equally important, the full text of every issue since January 1984 can be called up at any time. Article summaries are available back to June 1979. And recently full text of *The Washington Post* back to 1984 also has been made available. Of course, both newspapers can be searched electronically for every story containing any one or any combination of keywords. To my mind, this feature alone is worth the price of a Dow Jones subscription. Of course, there is financial information aplenty on virtually any form of investment—information of the highest quality.

If you already own a personal computer and are even moderately active as an investor, there is little question that you should subscribe to Dow Jones.

The price of admission is low, and since there are few continuing obligations, you have very little to lose.

If you don't have access to a personal computer, the Dow Jones News/ Retrieval system may be just the excuse you've been looking for to go out and buy one. In fact, if you're an active trader, you may find that a subscription not only pays for itself, but for your computer, modem, printer, and software as well.

Dow Jones offers so much financial information that you and your computer may discover you no longer need a full-service stockbroker and can thus eliminate the commissions you are paying. You may decide instead to open an account with Fidelity Investor's EXPRESS, one of the country's largest discount brokerage services, and do all of your trading online via News/Retrieval.

Clearly, Dow Jones is far more than just stock quotes. Unfortunately, it also seems to be one of the least approachable, least friendly systems in the electronic universe. Yes, there is a manual. And yes, it is a vast improvement over the sketchy documentation early users were forced to struggle with. But, as is the case with most computer documentation, the manual is arranged like a dictionary. Dictionaries are fine if you already speak the language and know the word you are looking for, but they are not the best thing for a new user.

The best thing for a new user is without a doubt this book. What's needed is an overview of the entire system combined with background information and detailed instructions for both using and maximizing each Dow Jones feature. That is exactly what Charlie Bowen and Dave Peyton provide here. Both are professional journalists and both are blessed with a newspaperman's keen eye for the who, what, where, why, and what-does-it-all-mean of an issue, event, or online system.

As they have done with their previous works on CompuServe and The Source, they will take you in hand and guide you through the ins and outs of Dow Jones News/Retrieval. From Media General to the Securities and Exchange Commission filings on DISCLOSURE ONLINE to the summaries of Standard & Poor's Online, Current Quotes, and all of the features cited above, Charlie and Dave will show you how it's done—and how to save money while doing it—with their unique "online tours."

Whether you are a new user, a prospective subscriber, or an old hand, this book will tell you what you need to know to make the most of the incredible resources offered by Dow Jones News/Retrieval. It may well be one of the best investments you have ever made.

Chapter 1

THE INFORMATION EDGE

They tell a story about a banker who made a fortune with a single piece of information.

It seems that during a war this banker developed a reputation for always being on top of innovations in information gathering, so his competitors began to study his habits for tips on buying and selling bonds.

As the war ground on, it became apparent to everyone that a climactic battle was brewing, the outcome of which would render war bonds either worthless in defeat or priceless in victory. All eyes were on the bank: everyone knew the experts there would have the first word from the front.

Suddenly the bank sold all its bonds, and everyone followed suit, assuming that the worst had happened. The mass selling nearly brought about the collapse of the market. But then the institution—it was London's Rothschild Bank, by the way—quickly bought everything back at bargain basement rates.

The year was 1815 and it took several days for conventional communications media to bring the big news: the English had *won* the battle of Waterloo. By then it was too late for the competition. Rothschild had pulled off a historic financial coup.

And the information tool that gave Rothschild the edge? A carrier pigeon, sent from the front lines back to London with news of the battle.

With lore like that it's no wonder that businesspeople long ago learned a fact that some segments of the community just now are catching on to: timely information is not just a luxury; it's the fuel that makes business run. A single piece of data, depending on when it's received and how it's analyzed, can mean the difference between making a lot, making a little, or taking a loss.

Until a few years ago this basic need for daily business information weighed the competition in favor of The Big Guys—the corporations and large firms that could afford staffs of information gatherers and analysts to find the trends in time to act on them. Then a few years ago today's carrier pigeon—a reliable desktop business computer—came along with the promise of rearranging that old pecking order. The personal computer, especially one that is linked to other computers and remote databases, offers balance. This equalizer has little to do with a business's size or resources, but rather how that business uses the technology available to everyone.

WHO'S IN THE VANGUARD?

Today, just as in Rothschild's London of nearly 200 years ago, not everyone is on the cutting edge.

Last year a little business newsletter called "Computerized Investing" surveyed its readers about how they used their computer systems. It discovered a remarkable fact: only one in four used online information retrieval systems. In other words, three-fourths of these otherwise technologically enlightened folks used computers to store and analyze old data, but they hadn't discovered what is probably their computers' greatest potential—gathering information *instantly*, faster than any other communications medium available today.

Meanwhile, those businesspeople who are in technology's vanguard seem to agree on one detail—*the* online information utility to plug into for financial data is Dow Jones News/Retrieval. In that survey a whopping 70 percent of the investors who were online used DJN/R. In fact, so overwhelming was the consensus that number 2 garnered less than 16 percent of the audience.

But, then, that's no real surprise, is it? For more than a century the name "Dow Jones" has been synonymous with reliable business information. Everyone would expect that prestigious company to define and *refine* the technology necessary to bring you information faster and better.

Dow Jones started its electronic news retrieval system in the summer of 1977 by opening its online databases to microcomputer users. In those days it was essentially a news summary system. However, the service has been upgraded and revised a number of times since then. These days DJN/R has more than 200,000 subscribers retrieving literally millions of pieces of information, from the latest stock quotations to thoughtful financial analysis to historical data that put figures in perspective.

This book can be your stepping-stone to joining them. It will take you online and show you Dow Jones News/Retrieval from top to bottom, giving you the facts you need to customize it to work just for you. By the time our tours are over, you'll know this system the way you know your company's best sales reps, your community's top leaders, the people who do their jobs well because they go the extra mile. And in a sense that's just what Dow Jones News/Retrieval can be—an electronic version of an enthusiastic, tireless employee, just waiting for a little direction from you.

DJN/R: DATA FOR EVERYMAN

Chances are, if you're new to computer communications, you've never seen a technology quite like Dow Jones News/Retrieval. You're not too far behind. Ten years ago few of us could have even envisioned a system like this.

Consider that the last technical innovations of this magnitude were the telephone and the automobile, introduced at the turn of the century. It didn't take businesspeople long to determine that phones and cars were much more than playthings. Bringing them into the world of work changed business forever, but the change was along rather predictable lines. Using phones and cars was about the same whether you were a corporation or a Mom and Pop grocery store.

That's not the case here; Dow Jones News/Retrieval honestly is many things to many people. What the system "is" depends on what you need it to be.

For instance, if you're associated with a large business that has a staff of researchers and information gatherers, DJN/R will slip in as neatly and quietly as a bright young research assistant. It can collect the facts and figures that affect your business life, the kinds of facts your people need to do their job. And it will be modest about it, letting the staff take the credit.

On the other hand, suppose you are part of a small partnership with no plans to hire a research department. You can "hire" Dow Jones News/Retrieval to do that job. With a minimum investment of time each day, you can let the system provide all of that data the Big Guys get, plus some resources designed with you in mind: analyses from some of the top financial experts in your field, tips on how to read the signs. And news. DJN/R has a remarkable database of business news affecting hundreds of industries and thousands of individual stocks. It has reports on file that were developed anytime from 90 seconds to seven years ago.

Suppose you haven't yet made the leap into a business that you plan for yourself. Then DJN/R can be a counselor. These days many students and people planning career changes use the system to keep up-to-date on fields they intend to enter.

Similarly, would-be investors use it to hypothesize; they set up imaginary portfolios and work with Dow Jones's excellent analytical tools to test their financial savvy before committing CHC (Cold Hard Cash). Then when they're ready to take the plunge, they can even buy stock through their computers right from home.

Speaking of home, you'll find that Dow Jones News/Retrieval works around the clock. By day it can be an able assistant at the office. At home it can be your direct connection to the business world. It'll even help out with chores around the house—make travel arrangements, do online shopping—and it offers an electronic encyclopedia for students, a college guidebook, even movie reviews and a top-flight sports page.

LEARNING THE SYSTEM

As a business innovation, then, Dow Jones News/Retrieval seems to be a lot more than four wheels and an engine. It is sophisticated, powerful . . . and sometimes, unfortunately, complex.

If you've talked to your friends and associates about DJN/R, you've probably heard of the glories of this system—along with some less enchanting things. Some may have told you, for instance, that the system can be complicated and expensive if you get lost (since you're charged for each minute your computer is connected, and surcharges are added when you use some specified databases).

Well, that's true enough. That's probably why we've found that many of

Dow Jones News/Retrieval's 200,000-plus subscribers use only a fraction of the system's features, perhaps only the current and historical quotes, for instance. Many are either unaware of other news and analysis treasures online, or reluctant to spend the money and time to learn how they work.

That's where we come in. Whether you're a newcomer wanting to know what Dow Jones News/Retrieval is all about or a long-time subscriber wanting to know more about the system, we can help.

In this book we'll use a tutorial technique we developed in our earlier works for Bantam Books (*How to Get the Most Out of CompuServe* and *How to Get the Most Out of The Source*). It's an approach we call "online tours." That simply means that we've invited ourselves to accompany you on visits to the system, to be there from log-on to log-off. Along the way, we'll urge you to enter certain commands to see the major features and let us show you how to use them.

We have about a half dozen "tours" planned. And, in the chapters between the tours, we'll expand on some of the things you've seen and give you previews of some of the features coming up.

We'll start out by giving you a feel for the *structure* of DJN/R and where it keeps its various kinds of information. Then in our first tour we'll take a "fly-by" of all the sights. After that we settle down for several chapters of in-depth study of the system's marketing information—databases of market quotes and analysis tools. Then it's off to a different part of the system, where we'll look at DJN/R's news features, including how to use its amazing Text-Search Services service, one of the most powerful databases you're likely to see anywhere. Then we'll call up another kind of service—DJN/R's travel and shopping and home features. Finally, we'll look at Dow Jones's own unique software that will allow you to use information retrieved online even more efficiently.

GETTING TO KNOW THE NATIVES

But first . . .

What kind of man or woman uses Dow Jones News/Retrieval? Well, obviously that's a question that begs a generalization. Still, Dow Jones keeps in touch with its subscribers, so it's not surprising that the service has extensive demographics. For instance, a recent survey found that the "typical" News/Retrieval subscriber is:

• 39 years old, with a college degree and a household income of $52,000.

• Likely to be in a top- or middle-management job in business or the professions and be a regular personal computer user.

• Just as likely to work in a small business as in a big one.

Investments are on the minds of most of us. The value of the average subscriber's portfolio is $62,000, built through a hefty 17 securities transactions per year.

That's why the subscribers say their most-often-used DJN/R services are those that provide stock market quotes (current and historical) and breaking business news.

AND WHERE DO YOU FIT IN?

We don't know if you see yourself in that little profile or any part of it. These online information services simply evolve too rapidly for anyone to have a firm fix on the latest subscriber picture.

We do have a *feeling* that more corporate professionals are going online these days, joining the ranks that a few years ago were made up predominantly of investors. We think that the newer subscribers *probably* are likely to be more interested in computer-generated information than in computers *per se*. We believe that more of the new subscribers are women, students, and minority groups.

These changes in the subscriber base help the system evolve. For instance, throughout its history DJN/R's subscribers have consistently called for deeper and broader coverage in business and investment areas, reflecting a growing need for more sophisticated tools to do their jobs. That need has inspired Dow Jones's development of its newest features.

Meanwhile, on the other end of the spectrum, business is on the minds of most subscribers, but not all of them and not all the time. That's why Dow Jones has continued to add services designed for use in the home.

SOME ASSUMPTIONS ABOUT YOU

While we're making assumptions, we have a few to make about you. We think you probably are among one of the following three groups of readers.

• You already have your computer and the necessary software and hardware to enable it to communicate over the telephone lines with other computers, but you have never logged on to Dow Jones News/Retrieval. We hope that you've already gotten your DJN/R subscription and received your password to the system. Then we'll be able to take you on your first journey into the system and carry on right up to the techniques the old hands use.

• Or, you have your equipment and already have used the Dow Jones system. However, you're hoping to get more out of the service, to find new features, and to learn to use them faster. We'll have material for you too. Since you're already familiar with the basics of the service, you might want to just skim the next two chapters while we bring everyone else up to speed.

• Or, you may not yet have a computer but you're considering one and you're hoping to get a preview of Dow Jones News/Retrieval here. No problem. While our tours are designed for a hands-on approach to learning, there's no reason you can't follow along from an easy chair as well as by keyboard. Everything you would see on the screen during the tours is reproduced in the printed examples along the way.

We also have to assume that you already know how to make your computer communicate and that you have a communications program and whatever add-ons your specific computer needs to hook up with the telephones. If you don't feel comfortable with your system's setup, we trust you'll consult with your computer salespeople.

You also should have a modem that can transmit and receive at least at 300 baud. Many modems these days offer higher rates—1200 and 2400 baud—and they're super. For these tours, though, we suggest you use the slower 300 baud initially. That's because Dow Jones News/Retrieval, like many information services, charges a higher connect rate for the faster speeds. We think that whenever you're exploring new territory online, it makes good sense to start out slowly, saving your faster, more expensive baud rates until you are more familiar with the neighborhood. We'll have a checklist of a few more technical details in Chapter 2.

Speaking of technical information, we have to assume that you already know how to interpret most of the financial data you'll be retrieving from the system. We leave it up to you to know how to read stock reports and company statements and know what's meant by terms such as "price-earnings ratios" and "market indices." To help, we will be offering scenarios from time to time to get you thinking about how to use some of these powerful features. We'll also show you a nifty online resource for getting definitions of most major business terms.

THE BOTTOM LINE

Now let's talk money. We've already mentioned that DJN/R charges more if you're communicating at a faster baud rate. Also you should be aware that the system charges more for connections made during weekday business hours. So if you're cost-conscious, we'd suggest you plan to take our online tours in non-prime time, that is, evenings and weekends. Furthermore, some special features on the system cost more than others.

The bottom line is this: it will cost you a few dollars to travel with us online. We have about six hours of tours planned; at the minimum 300-baud rate, that'll cost about $50 (and about twice that if you decide to do your touring during prime time).

Our experience is that it's money well-spent. Taking the time to learn the system in an overview will save time and money later because you'll know where you're going.

Our goal is to help you become a self-reliant subscriber—able to find your way around efficiently, to customize the system for your needs long after we've been retired to the bookshelf, and to roll with the changes in the system.

Uh, changes?

Yes, Dow Jones News/Retrieval, like all electronic information services, is in constant evolution, with new features (and occasional revisions in old ones) coming along all the time. A few years ago, in describing another online service, we referred to the challenge of writing about such ever-changing systems as "trying to change the tire on a moving car." That analogy applies here too.

For the uninitiated, these changes can be unsettling. However, after you've finished our tours, we think you'll find it easier to adapt to the changing electronic environment. That's because you will have seen that new features often work like those you've already grown accustomed to.

So do yourself a favor. Relax and promise yourself not to cut corners while we're exploring. It won't take you long to learn the lay of land—we'll get started in the next chapter—and that's the first step to using this system like a pro.

Chapter 2

LET'S
GET
ORGANIZED

Before any good explorer sets out, he or she studies the reports of those who have gone before. This chapter is a message from your reconnaissance team, which is happy to report that it found no ogres or bottomless pits in this brave new world you're about to enter.

What it did find is that Dow Jones News/Retrieval's massive stores of information are organized in a way that makes data easy to retrieve—once you see the system's pattern and learn to use your computer as a data-grabbing tool.

We're not computer experts and don't pretend to be. Our backgrounds are in information gathering. From that perspective, we have an abiding respect for the power of computers, but we tend to see them, as you probably do, as tools rather than ends unto themselves, or, if you will, as workhorses, not unicorns.

This approach has led us to the belief that we can use online systems like Dow Jones with a minimum of technical information, just as you can drive your car without having to know how to build your own carburetor.

Having said that, we have to concede that the more you know, the easier the trip. In this chapter, then, we'll outline the little bit of computer technical information we think you need to know to make a successful connection with

Dow Jones News/Retrieval. The technical information includes facts about the system itself, your own computer, and the invisible network that links them together.

SIGNING UP: GETTING YOUR TICKET TO RIDE

Perhaps you've already signed up as a subscriber to Dow Jones News/Retrieval. If so, feel free merely to skim the next few pages while we speak privately to the newcomers.

There are a number of ways you can come together with DJN/R.

Recently Dow Jones has taken strides to offer new kinds of opportunities for those who sign up. For one thing, the service now is offered in connection with other online systems. For instance, as of this writing, subscribers to the electronic MCI Mail service have an opportunity to use Dow Jones News/Retrieval. DJN/R is also being provided in connection with some "gateway" services, that is, companies that offer access to a number of online services under a single umbrella.

Meanwhile, many subscribers still begin by purchasing a Dow Jones News/Retrieval Membership Kit at a bookstore or computer store. The kit contains a manual of commands, examples of databases, and information about logging on to the system. Also included is a folder about the signup agreement, rates, and so on.

Others come this way as a result of finding signup information in the box when they buy computer equipment, particularly modems, since nearly every modem these days is capable of linking your computer with Dow Jones via a phone line.

Or, you can subscribe simply by calling the Dow Jones Customer Service department. The number is 1-800-257-5114. (If you live in New Jersey, Hawaii, Alaska, or Canada, call 609-452-1511.)

No matter how you reach these shores, once you're signed up, DJN/R will open an account for you and provide you with your own password that gives you access to the system.

A word about that password—never tell it to anyone and never leave it lying about where someone could make a note of it. Your password is like the key to your safe-deposit box or your credit card numbers. Anyone who has it has the ability to use your DJN/R account—and run up your bill.

It's best to keep your password written on a sheet of paper and stored in a secure place with no indication on the paper as to what it is. That way, if it should be discovered accidentally, it's unlikely the person finding it will make the connection between it and your online account. And if you ever have reason to believe that someone has taken your password, call that Dow Jones News/ Retrieval customer service number immediately and make arrangements to have your password changed. Customer service will make the change for you.

Speaking of money, what does it cost to subscribe to Dow Jones? There's no simple answer to that. More than any other information service available today, the cost of using Dow Jones is dependent not only upon how long you're online but also on what services you use.

After you begin using the system, you'll receive in the mail regular statements that tell you exactly how many minutes you spent using each database.

GETTING ACCESS: THE NUMBER TO CALL . . .

Once you have your password, you're ready to dial into the system, and you'll do that by calling one of several carriers, sometimes called "packet networks." That's simply a local telephone number that links your computer to the DJN/R system in Princeton, New Jersey.

Dow Jones News/Retrieval is available on three major networks in the United States—Tymnet, Telenet, and U.S. Telecom (formerly called Uninet)— and on DataPac, the major Canadian system. These networks have hundreds of exchanges all over the country that allow your computer to link up to remote systems, including Dow Jones. Therefore you'll need to determine which network you want to use. To do that, you might want to call your computer salesperson to see if he or she knows which networks have local numbers for your community. Or you can call Dow Jones's customer service people again. They'll be glad to help.

Each network has its own unique log-on procedures and we've summarized them in the back of the book. We'll be reminding you of that in the next chapter when we log on for the first time.

By the way, at the beginning of 1986 the providers of GTE's Telenet and United Telecommunications' U.S. Telecom (Uninet) announced they planned to merge those data networks. That means that if you use either Telenet or Uninet, you should be on the lookout for minor changes in the log-on procedures as the details of the merger are ironed out.

SETTING UP YOUR COMPUTER

As we said in the last chapter, we hope you'll take your first tours of Dow Jones News/Retrieval at 300 baud, even if your modem is capable of faster baud rates. That's partly because the slower rate is cheaper, and we want you to feel free to think about what you're *seeing* rather than what you're *spending*. In addition, we think that 300 baud will make it easier initially to examine what's scrolling up the screen as it's being displayed. Once you become familiar with large areas of the system, you'll probably want to begin using 1200 baud to save time.

Also, if your hardware and software configuration allows you to get printouts of what's being displayed on the screen, by all means, use it. Reviewing the printouts later can be a valuable study aid.

And speaking of your software, Dow Jones recommends that you set your computer for this configuration:

- Full duplex.

- No parity (sometimes called "space," "off," or "ignore").

- One stop bit.

In addition, DJN/R suggests that the XON/XOFF switch in your communications program be set to off.

Now hold the phone. If all of that just sounded like Greek to you, don't panic. All communications programs work a little differently, so we can't give you specific tips here. However, all you need to do is check the manual that came with your communications software, or call your computer representatives and tell them you need help in "setting the communications parameters to connect with Dow Jones News/Retrieval." If you need to, recite that list of settings we just mentioned. That should do the trick.

By the way, if you're already a News/Retrieval subscriber and are using some of Dow Jones's software to connect with the system, congratulations—it was a good choice. For the purpose of our tours, look in your manual under the section about "terminal mode" (sometimes called "E-Z Terminal") for instructions on how to use that option. We would suggest you use terminal mode for all our online excursions.

LOOKING AHEAD: THE BIG VIEW OF THE SYSTEM

At this point you've done everything you need to do on your end to make the connection with Dow Jones News/Retrieval. You've signed up and gotten your password. You've located your local network phone number and taken a look at the log-on procedures described in the back of the book. And you've configured your communications software to conform with DJN/R's suggested settings.

In Chapter 3 we'll put all of that fine groundwork to good use when we log on for the first tour. First, though, in the rest of this chapter we'd like to give you an idea of what to expect on Dow Jones, a sort of Big Picture of the system that awaits you.

MENUS VERSUS COMMANDS

Here's a little computer jargon for you. Most online information systems are either primarily *menu-driven* or primarily *command-driven*. The concept is really rather simple.

If you've used any modem application software on your computer, you're probably already familiar with *menus*, the choices or options presented on your screen as a list. Usually the lists are numbered (1, 2, 3, etc.) or lettered (A, B, C, etc.) and you are asked to choose an option by typing in its number or letter.

In the online information world, menu-driven systems are easy for newcomers because the lists provide handy reminders of all the alternatives available at any point in the electronic visit. That's the good news. The bad news is that menu-driven systems are slow. It takes time for the remote system to transmit to your computer all the information necessary for it to display the options. It takes time for you to read them and respond. It takes more time for the system to register your response and do what you asked it to do. For the long-time subscribers of a particular online system, menus can be downright frustrating, like a harping teacher who won't realize that you've progressed enough that you don't need to have constant reminders anymore.

That's why these days most good online services provide alternatives to allow command-driven use of the system. In *command mode* you're generally given a minimum of direction. Often you enter commands, not from the bottom of a menu list of alternatives, but from a terse "READY" prompt, or maybe just a question mark. That's great, if you already know your options. However, if you're new to the territory, that can be a frightening experience, the way you might feel if you went into a new restaurant and the waiter stomped up to you empty-handed and demanded, "Whaddaya want?"

Well, if you went into DJN/R for the first time without our little pep talk here, you might feel the same way. That's because the first thing you're likely to see on the system is a no-nonsense message that says merely:

ENTER QUERY

Not very enlightening. Besides, because of the use of the word "query," it sounds as if the system might be wanting you to type in a question rather than an answer or a command.

Actually, this is an example of the kind of command-driven system that DJN/R tends to be. We say "tends to be" because the system is a kind of hybrid, the best of both the menu and command worlds.

The people at Dow Jones know that the expertise of their users spans a wide range indeed. At the same time that a five-year veteran of the system may be online zipping from database to database, there probably is a new user reluctantly opening the front door and peeking inside for the first time. Dow Jones's answer has been to try to design a system for everyone.

The truth is that behind that curt ENTER QUERY, there is a menu if you want to see it. What's more, the menu can be called from nearly anyplace in the system, in case you need to be reminded of where you are or where you want to go.

Showing you how to reach that *pocket menu* will be the job of the next chapter. For now, just note that many of the individual databases we'll be seeing are actually menu-driven. Help files for all the databases are a simple command away from nearly every level of the system.

Despite all the menus, though, the system still is weighed in favor of commands. The reason? Because experience shows that you won't need to rely on menus for very long. We've found this system so logical in its organization that we think you'll soon be bypassing the menus to go directly to the information you want through direct commands.

For example, in the early stages of your DJN/R experience you might occasionally forget the command to take you to a particular database, such as one called "Investext." When that happens, you would use the command to summon that menu (which happens to be two slashes and the word "menu": //MENU). Using that menu, you learn that the way to get to Investext is by typing //INVEST. Simple enough. So simple, in fact, that the next time you log on and want to see Investext, you'll probably type //INVEST from the first ENTER QUERY prompt, bypassing the menu and saving time and money.

It's like having the best of both systems, and we think that early on you'll grow to like it.

ENTERING COMMANDS

When we begin logging on to the system, we'll advise you what commands to enter to keep up with the tours.

About commands, remember this: they're almost always followed by a carriage return. On some computers, that's the key marked RETURN; on others, it's marked ENTER; on still others, it looks like an arrow that can't decide which way to go. In any event, it's comparable to the carriage return on the typewriter, and to DJN/R's host system it means "execute this command."

At the start of our first tour we'll be reminding you to press RETURN following a command. However, after the first few times we're going to assume you've gotten into the habit of doing that and we'll start saying simply ENTER the relevant command.

Also, in this book we generally use CAPITAL LETTERS when showing you the commands you are supposed to use, but it's not necessary for *you* to use capital letters. Dow Jones News/Retrieval sees no difference between uppercase and lowercase commands. Just use whatever feels better to you.

KEEPING THINGS UNDER CONTROL

Finally, there are some special commands available to you called *control key functions*. They literally help you control the way things are displayed on your screen when you're hooked up to Dow Jones News/Retrieval.

Most desktop computers these days have a key labeled CONTROL, perhaps abbreviated as CTRL. (Those few computer systems that don't have such a key usually allow you to simulate a control key. For example, on some computers you simulate a control key by pressing both the SHIFT and DOWN ARROW key at the same time. If you aren't sure how to create a control key on your system, check your manual or your computer store.)

When you're online, you can use a control function by pressing the control key and another key at the same time. Note that CONTROL codes are the only commands used online that do *not* require you to follow them with a RETURN.

The CONTROL codes most useful on Dow Jones News/Retrieval are:

CONTROL S: Use it when you want to "freeze" the computer display. It temporarily stops the incoming information. This is useful if the material is coming in faster than you can read it.

CONTROL Q: Use it to cancel CONTROL S and start the screen display scrolling again.

CONTROL X: On most networks, use this to "break" data transmission in most areas of the system. When you use it, you'll generally be taken back to a prompt.

CONTROL H: On some networks, use this to signal a backspace. As a practical matter, CONTROL H is not usually needed, since your keyboard probably has a backspace key and your communications program recognizes that key. However, it's good to know that CONTROL H is available if the backspace key isn't recognized.

THE NEXT STEP

There comes a time when it's clear that there's been enough talk and what's needed is action. In the next chapter we'll be taking a look at this world of information about which we've been bragging.

You're ready for it because you're armed with the only computer concepts you really need to know for the journey.

Chapter 3

GETTING ONLINE: THE FIRST TOUR

If our pitch worked in the first two chapters, you now should know enough about Dow Jones News/Retrieval to have your appetite whetted. We hope you're itching to get to a keyboard to look at it for yourself.

Our first online tour is designed to give you a bird's-eye view of the system, and a little more. In addition to giving a "fly-by" of all the major points of interest, we want to show you how to:

• Log on to the system through each of its major access lines.

• Travel from one database to another, both by menus and, more important, by the express lane of direct address commands.

• Use the important navigation commands to move about within a database.

• Find online help and the latest news about the system from Dow Jones itself.

• Log off the system at the end of the session.

In this tour, and in all the subsequent ones, if you press the keys that we ask you to press, you'll see the pages of information on your own computer screen that we present in the book. Remember, though, that there may be some differences, since Dow Jones is constantly changing, but nothing so major that you'll be confused.

SIGNING ON

Now put this book in a convenient place near your computer so you can turn the pages and follow along on the screen. This tour should take less than an hour to complete.

First you need to dial the local number for the network you are using to access the system. Once the connection is made, follow that network's procedure for connecting to the system. If you haven't already reviewed our summary of the log-on procedures for Telenet, Tymnet, Uninet, or DataPac, please do that now. See page 306 in the Online Survival Kit.

You know you have arrived at Dow Jones's front door when the system asks for your password. It will not display the password as you type. This is a security measure to guard against prying eyes.

Type in the password exactly as it was supplied by Dow Jones and press RETURN. You'll have three chances to get it right. (If, after the third time, you still aren't successful, you'll be logged off the Dow Jones system and generally sent back to the main network prompt. If you think the problem is just that you've made typing errors, try logging on again. However, if you're certain your typing was correct, check with the customer service department to make sure you have the right password.)

THE FIRST WORDS FROM DOW JONES

You know you've gotten everything right and have entered the system when you see the first Dow Jones "page," also known as the *copyright page*. It will appear a bit different from the one we present here (since obviously the headlines will have changed), but it should look much like this:

```
          DOW JONES NEWS/RETRIEVAL
             COPYRIGHT (C) 1986
          DOW JONES & COMPANY, INC.
             ALL RIGHTS RESERVED
EIGHT WOUNDED AS PRO-MARCOS
TROOPS FIRE ON CROWD IN
MANILA, SEE //NEWS OR TYPE
//MENU FOR DATA-BASE LIST.
ENTER QUERY
```

At the bottom are the words we told you about—ENTER QUERY. They are an indicator to you that you have reached the end of a *section* of information and the system is awaiting your command to let it know what you want to do next.

The commands to reach all major databases on Dow Jones begin with two slashes (//). The slashes let the system know that you're making a quantum leap to a new database. The simplicity of this command system belies its power, as we'll show you in this chapter.

Right now let's take the suggestion made at the bottom of the page now on your screen and go to the MENU, that area we mentioned in the last chapter as being a list of all the Dow Jones databases and services.

At the ENTER QUERY prompt, where your cursor now is positioned, type the two slashes and the word MENU, and press the RETURN key, like this:

```
          ENTER QUERY //MENU<RETURN>
```

Note there are no spaces between the slashes and before the database name.

When the system recognizes that command, here's what you'll see:

```
MASTER MENU

          BUSINESS & INVESTOR SERVICES

PRESS   FOR
  A       Company/Industry Data & News
  B       Quotes & Market Averages
  C       Brokerage
                    ---
                GENERAL SERVICES
  D       World News, Sports & Weather
  E       Shopping, Travel & Mail
  F       Education & Entertainment
                    ---
              USING NEWS/RETRIEVAL
  G       Getting Started & What's New
  H       Symbols You Will Need
```

As the screen explains, this is the Master Menu of services available on Dow Jones. Notice that it says press the letter A to get "Company/Industry Data and News," the letter B to get "Quotes and Market Averages," and so on.

That doesn't mean that if you press A, you'll actually receive data and news. It means you'll get a list—or menu—of databases where you can get such information.

In other words, think of the Master Menu as an index where you can find the name of a database, including the command word (or *direct address*) to type to get to that database. The Master Menu is available from nearly anywhere in the system; just type //MENU and press RETURN. It should be comforting to know it's there in case a needed command word suddenly slips your mind.

The Master Menu is also a great place to get an overview of the Dow Jones News/Retrieval system, and that's how we'll use it this time.

At the bottom of the Master Menu page, type A and press RETURN to see the list of databases that contain "Company/Industry Data and News." In a moment you should see something like this:

COMPANY/INDUSTRY DATA & NEWS

TYPE	FOR
//DJNEWS	Current Business News From Dow Jones
//TEXT	*Wall Street Journal Full-Text Version *Dow Jones News *The Washington Post
//DSCLO	Company Profiles From Filings With The SEC

Take a moment to read the descriptions of each database and note the variety of information, from current business news to specific documents from the files of the Securities and Exchange Commission. However, don't worry about trying to remember specifics about any of the databases we'll see described over the next few minutes. We'll have opportunities for closer introductions to all of them later, starting with some scenarios in Chapter 4. Besides, all the databases are also described in the back of the book.

For this tour, rather than trying to memorize database descriptions, it's more important for you to get comfortable with the mechanics of navigating the system. For instance, let's look at the format of the screen itself, specifically the top of the page. You'll see that it's telling you this is part of the Master Menu list and this particular page is one of five that provide information on databases that fall under the Company/Industry Data & News category. Three command words (that is, database names) with associated descriptions are then listed: //DJNEWS, //TEXT, and //DSCLO.

To get to the next page in this collection, press RETURN to see:

//TRACK	Automatic Retrieval Of News & Stock Quotes On Up To 125 Companies

```
//INVEST  Research Reports
          From Leading Brokerage
          And Investment Firms

//SP      Financial Information
          On Public Companies
          From Standard & Poor's
```

Three more databases appear along with their commands and brief descriptions. Remember, we told you that things change on Dow Jones, so don't be surprised if you see additions or deletions. Now, press RETURN again to see page 3.

```
MASTER MENU                          PAGE 3 OF 5

//MG    Market & Fundamental
        Data On Companies &
        Related Industries

//EARN  Consensus Earnings
        Forecasts For Major
        U.S. Companies

//MMS   Weekly Survey Of U.S.
        Money Market & Foreign
        Exchange Trends
```

You're still reading the online descriptions, right? Don't be in a hurry. You have up to three minutes to issue a command. If DJN/R does not receive a command from you within three minutes, it assumes something is wrong and the system will log you off. That's for your protection. It keeps you from racking up connection fees should something go awry and you are accidentally disconnected from Dow Jones without logging off properly.

Now, press RETURN and up comes the next page:

```
     MASTER MENU                          PAGE 4 OF 5

     //KYODO   Today's Japanese
               Business News

     //UPDATE  A Roundup of The Past
               Economic Week

     //WSJ     Summaries Of The Past
               5 Days Of The Journal

     //WSW     'Wall $treet Week'
               Transcripts, With
               Louis Rukeyser
```

Finally, let's see the last page in this section. Press RETURN for:

```
MASTER MENU                              PAGE 5 OF 5

//SYMBOL Stock Symbol Directory

//DEFINE Investment Dictionary

                    * * *

     Type the access code and HELP for complete
information on any service. EXAMPLE: //DJNEWS HELP
```

You no doubt noticed the message at the bottom about the HELP command. We'll give that a spin in a moment.

GETTING BACK ON TOP: WITH //MENU

Right now we want to get back to the *top* of the Master Menu section, that is, our location before we looked at the list of "Company/Industry Data and News" databases. There are several handy ways to do that. This time we'll get there by using the //MENU command—the same one we used in the first place to get from the copyright page to the Master Menu.

So, type //MENU and press RETURN to see the Master Menu's opening page again.

```
MASTER MENU

            BUSINESS & INVESTOR SERVICES

PRESS   FOR
  A     Company/Industry Data & News
  B     Quotes & Market Averages
  C     Brokerage
                    ---
                GENERAL SERVICES
  D     World News, Sports & Weather
  E     Shopping, Travel & Mail
  F     Education & Entertainment
                    ---
                USING NEWS/RETRIEVAL
  G     Getting Started & What's New
  H     Symbols You Will Need
```

All the databases you just saw described provide news and other information about industries and specific companies, that is, they fall under option A.

Now let's see the descriptions of some other kinds of databases, those available for retrieving stock market quotes and averages. Type B and press RETURN. That should show you something like:

```
MASTER MENU                         PAGE 1 OF 4

            QUOTES & MARKET AVERAGES

  TYPE    FOR
//CQE     Quotes On Stocks
          & Other Financial
          Instruments, Delayed
          15 Minutes & With A
          Company News Alert

//RTQ     Real-Time Stock
          Quotes With A
          Company News Alert
```

For starters, notice that the first line tells you that this time there are four pages in the list. Read the descriptions of these in the Quotes and Market Averages collection and then press RETURN to see page 2:

MASTER MENU   PAGE 2 OF 4

```
//FUTURES  Futures Quotes From
           Major North American
           Exchanges

//HQ       Historical Stock
           Quotes

//TRACK    Automatic Retrieval
           Of News & Stock Quotes
           On Up To 125 Companies

//DJA      Dow Jones Averages
           For The Past Year
```

Are you feeling overwhelmed by all the different commands you're seeing? Resist it. Remember that we'll be taking a close-up inspection of most of these databases in future tours and, like so many things about computers, the commands are much easier to remember once you start actually using and learning what they do.

When you're finished with this page, press RETURN again to get the third page of this section.

MASTER MENU   PAGE 3 OF 4

```
//SYMBOL   Directory Of Symbols
           You Will Need To Use
           Stock Quote Services

.I/DJA     Dow Jones Averages
           Updated Each 1/2 Hour

.I/ACT 01  Most Active Stocks &
           Stock Options, NYSE &
           AMEX Market Diaries,
           Closing NASDAQ Most
           Actives
```

You may notice in the menu that some of the items are preceded by periods (as in ".I/DJA" in our example). This is a special command that we will be discussing later when we visit the Dow Jones News Service.

To see the final page of this section, press RETURN one more time.

```
MASTER MENU                         PAGE 4 OF 4

.I/STK 01 Morning Market
          Comment, Filings,
          Suspensions & Other
          Stock Market News
                  * * *
  Type the access code and HELP for more
information on any service. EXAMPLE: //CQE HELP
```

BACK TO THE TOP: ANOTHER WAY

Now that we are at the end of this section, we could type //MENU as we did last time to get to the top of the Master Menu, but let's use another helpful command. The T command will take you to the *top* of the database, the place where you first arrived.

Two things about the T command:

• First, it doesn't require the two slashes. (The slashes are used only to move to a specific database.) Unlike the slashes, T is a *navigation command* used with menus inside a database. You'll be meeting a few other useful navigation commands in a few minutes.

• In addition, T (and the other navigation commands) can be used on most of the databases in the system, not just in //MENU where we are now.

So, to get to the top of the Master Menu, type T and press RETURN, and here's the now-familiar:

```
MASTER MENU

          BUSINESS & INVESTOR SERVICES

PRESS    FOR
  A      Company/Industry Data & News
  B      Quotes & Market Averages
  C      Brokerage
                    - - -
               GENERAL SERVICES
  D      World News, Sports & Weather
  E      Shopping, Travel & Mail
  F      Education & Entertainment
                    - - -
             USING NEWS/RETRIEVAL
  G      Getting Started & What's New
  H      Symbols You Will Need
```

You've noticed, no doubt, that all of the databases we've seen described so far are in the general category of Business and Investor Services. Let's finish out that group by looking at the Brokerage services. Type C and press RETURN to see:

```
MASTER MENU                          PAGE 1 OF 1
                     BROKERAGE

  TYPE       FOR
//FIDELITY Fidelity Investor's
           EXPRESS: Online
           Trading & Portfolio
           Management Service

//SYMBOL   News/Retrieval
           Directory Of Symbols
                      * * *
     Type the access code and HELP for information on
any service: EXAMPLE //FIDELITY HELP
```

At this writing, only one page of information was available in this section.

After you've looked it over, return to the top of the Master Menu, with either //MENU or the T command, then RETURN, to see:

```
MASTER MENU

          BUSINESS & INVESTOR SERVICES

  PRESS   FOR
     A      Company/Industry Data & News
     B      Quotes & Market Averages
     C      Brokerage
                     - - -
                GENERAL SERVICES
     D      World News, Sports & Weather
     E      Shopping, Travel & Mail
     F      Education & Entertainment
                     - - -
               USING NEWS/RETRIEVAL
     G      Getting Started & What's New
     H      Symbols You Will Need
```

FASTER, FASTER

Incidentally, you've just read the descriptions of what many consider Dow Jones News/Retrieval's most important databases. Those are the ones that provide the business specifics—the quotes, the analyses, the business news of the day and of days past. But, as we've indicated, DJN/R is a fairly well-rounded service, with some general-interest databases as well, the section we'll look at next.

To see the databases covering World News, Sports and Weather, type D and press RETURN, and you should find this page of descriptions:

```
MASTER MENU                              PAGE 1 OF 1

          WORLD NEWS, SPORTS & WEATHER
    TYPE     FOR
  //NEWS     World & National News

  //SPORTS   Current Scores,
             Statistics & Stories
```

```
//WTHR     Accu-Weather Forecasts
           & Ski Report
                      *  *  *
     Type the access code and HELP for complete
information on any service. EXAMPLE: //NEWS HELP
```

In other words, this is *general* news, as opposed to specific business news you saw described in the other section of //MENU.

By now you may be getting tired of the repetition of going to the top of the Master Menu each time. Well, the truth is you don't *have* to go back to the top to see the next section. The section we're seeing now is D (World News, Sports and Weather). You can go directly to section E (for a description of Shopping, Travel and Mail services) from the bottom of this page by typing E and pressing RETURN. Try it.

```
MASTER MENU                              PAGE 1 OF 2

               SHOPPING, TRAVEL & MAIL

     TYPE    FOR

   //OAG     Official Airline
             Guide: Schedules
             & Least-Cost Fares;
             Airline Reservations;
             Hotel, Motel Listings

   //STORE   Comp-U-Store: Discount
             Shopping Service
             For Buying & Price
             Comparisons
```

Now we're into the "services" area of the system—airline schedules and online shopping. As it says at the top of page 1 of this Section E, there's a second page, so press RETURN to see it.

```
MASTER MENU                        PAGE 2 OF 2

//AXP    American Express
         ADVANCE: Cardmember
         Information, Shopping
         & Travel Services

//MCI    MCI Mail: Messages
         Sent Electronically
         Or In Printed Form
                      * * *
    Type the access code and HELP for complete
information on any service. EXAMPLE: //MCI HELP
```

Wait! Don't second-guess us. Let's try a new command.

When you're reading "paged" material like this on Dow Jones, you can usually return to the previous page by using another navigation command—the R command (for "Return").

We're on page 2 now, and suppose you wanted to see page 1 of this list again. Type R and RETURN and see:

```
MASTER MENU                        PAGE 1 OF 2

           SHOPPING, TRAVEL & MAIL

    TYPE    FOR

//OAG    Official Airline
         Guide: Schedules
         & Least-Cost Fares;
         Airline Reservations;
         Hotel, Motel Listings

//STORE  Comp-U-Store: Discount
         Shopping Service
         For Buying & Price
         Comparisons
```

Remember we told you that you can use the double slash (///) commands from nearly anywhere in the system. Well, that means you don't need to be at the end of a section of information to use it. For instance, at the end of this page, which happens to be the first of two, you can type //MENU and press RETURN and you'll go to the top of the Master Menu again. Do that, please, for (once again):

```
MASTER MENU

              BUSINESS & INVESTOR SERVICES

PRESS   FOR
  A       Company/Industry Data & News
  B       Quotes & Market Averages
  C       Brokerage
                      - - -
                  GENERAL SERVICES
  D       World News, Sports & Weather
  E       Shopping, Travel & Mail
  F       Education & Entertainment
                      - - -
                USING NEWS/RETRIEVAL
  G       Getting Started & What's New
  H       Symbols You Will Need
```

Okay, time out.

From this point on we are going to assume that you'll remember without our reminding you that all commands (except CONTROL codes) are executed by your pressing the RETURN key. We're going to start saying just "enter" such-and-such command, and you'll remember that means "and press RETURN."

Now to look at descriptions of the "Education and Entertainment" databases, enter F and see:

```
MASTER MENU                                   PAGE 1 OF 2

              EDUCATION & ENTERTAINMENT
    TYPE     FOR
 //MOVIES   Reviews Of Movies
            Produced Since 1926

 //SCHOOL   Peterson's College
            Selection Service
```

```
//ENCYC     Grolier's Academic
            American Encyclopedia

//MEDX      Medical & Drug
            Reference Service
```

After you've glanced over these descriptions, check out the second page of descriptions by pressing RETURN.

```
MASTER MENU                          PAGE 2 OF 2

//DEFINE  "Words Of Wall Street"
           Dictionary Of Market
           & Investment Terms

//TEXT    * Wall Street Journal
            Full-Text Version
          * Dow Jones News
          * The Washington Post
                    * * *
 Type the access code and HELP
for complete information on any
service. EXAMPLE: //SCHOOL HELP
```

For the moment let's skip Section G of the Master Menu (Getting Started and What's New). We have some special plans for that section.

Instead, go directly to Section H (Symbols You Will Need) by entering H, and you should see this description:

```
MASTER MENU                          PAGE 1 OF 1

            SYMBOLS YOU WILL NEED

     TYPE   FOR

//SYMBOL   Directory Of Symbols
           Used In News/Retrieval
           Stock & Market
           Symbols, //DJNEWS
           Codes, Media General
           Industry Codes,
           Updated Daily
                    * * *
  Type the access code and HELP for complete
information on any service. EXAMPLE: //SYMBOL HELP
```

Incidentally, if you see commands duplicated in these sections—as with //SYMBOL, which is listed here as well as under online brokerage services— it's because several of these databases fall into more than one category. This particular database, //SYMBOL, is an important one you'll use a number of times to get the "addresses" for information about specific companies.

SOMETHING FOR NOTHING

Now, on to Section G, which is a goodie because part of it is a freebie. Enter G.

```
MASTER MENU                                PAGE 1 OF 2
             GETTING STARTED & WHAT'S NEW
   TYPE     FOR
//INTRO    Free Newsletter About
           News/Retrieval & Dow
           Jones Software, With
           Tutorials For Our
           Newest Online Services
//DJ HELP  Getting Started: A
           Short Guide To Using
           News/Retrieval
```

Take a quick look at the descriptions of these services, then check page 2 of this section by pressing RETURN.

```
MASTER MENU                                PAGE 2 OF 2
//COPYRT   News Bulletins &
           Special Announcements
//SYMBOL   Directory Of Symbols
//MCI      Use MCI Mail To Tell
           News/Retrieval What
           You Think. Send A Free
           Letter To The DJNR
           Mailbox
                     * * *
   Type the access code and HELP for complete
information on any service. EXAMPLE: //MCI HELP
```

Now, what's this about something free on Dow Jones?

Well, let's back up a page—remember the R navigation command?—enter R and that should take you back to the first page of "Getting Started & What's New."

```
MASTER MENU                          PAGE 1 OF 2
         GETTING STARTED & WHAT'S NEW
    TYPE    FOR
//INTRO     Free Newsletter About
            News/Retrieval & Dow
            Jones Software, With
            Tutorials For Our
            Newest Online Services

//DJ HELP   Getting Started: A
            Short Guide To Using
            News/Retrieval
```

The command //INTRO takes you to a special database in which Dow Jones News/Retrieval publishes a free newsletter. In other words, the meter isn't running when you're in the INTRO area.

Sounds good to us, too, so enter //INTRO (don't forget the two slashes, because we're changing databases, leaving//MENU and going to //INTRO).

In a moment the system should display something like this:

```
Welcome to //INTRO, the free
newsletter to News/Retrieval

PRESS   FOR
1       Free Time Offer In //FUTURES
2       Tutorials For New Services
3       Data Bases: Commodities News
        IN //DJNEWS G/CFT; Brokerage
        Services In //FIDELITY;
        //AXP Contest, New Services
4       Prices, Customer Information
5       DowPhone News; Bank At Home
6       DJN/R Software, Seminars,
        And Other Services: A Book
        On News/Retrieval; Answers
        To Dowline Tutorials
```

Of course, since this is a newsletter, this menu you see will be different from the one on your screen, which will contain the latest news about Dow Jones's services. If, for example, a new database has been added since this book was written, tips on using it are likely to be included here. That means you should make a note of it so you can return later to read that brief article.

Also, take note of any tutorials (learning exercises) included in the newsletter. You might want to return here later to read them as a sort of postgraduate course or continuing education seminar.

And by the way, we mentioned that the connect rates for various online features change from time to time. //INTRO is where you can come for details of those changes. Therefore it would seem that //INTRO would be a good feature to visit regularly. At least once every week or two should keep you well informed about systems changes.

The selections from this menu are numbers rather than letters, but reading them is the same as reading from the Master Menu. After choosing one of the numbered sections, you can read through to the end by pressing RETURN at the bottom of each page. At the end, you can enter T or //INTRO to get back to this menu.

Since what you see in our example and what you see on the screen are certain to be different, we won't confuse matters by taking you any farther into the //INTRO area. We'll urge you, however, to return later to explore it on your own. Remember, this area is free and therefore an excellent place to practice your navigation commands as well as to catch up on what's new.

GETTING ONLINE HELP

No matter how good you get at zipping around online information services, you can always use a helping hand from time to time. Dow Jones News/ Retrieval makes the online help easy to get to.

At the bottom of some of the screens we've toured so far you've seen suggestions for getting help. Let's try the command out to see if it works.

Perhaps you recall one note (in the "Getting Started and What's New" menu) said you could get help for using the entire News/Retrieval system (a sort of introductory help file) by typing //DJ HELP. Enter that at the bottom of the current page, and you'll see something like this:

```
            How to Use News/Retrieval
                      ---
    News/Retrieval offers over 35 services, including
stock and future quotes, news from The Wall Street
Journal and Dow Jones News Service, and a stock
quote and news tracking service.
    Other services offered are Peterson's College
Selection Service, the Academic American
Encyclopedia, Official Airline guide, Standard &
Poor's Online, INVESTEXT brokerage reports, and
a medical and drug reference.
          -PRESS <RETURN> FOR MORE-
```

What we have here is the first page of a help file on using the system. For now, we'll not go any farther into this one, but of course you can return later for a closer look at it if you'd like. Instead, we'll see how we can use the HELP command for more specific information.

Generally, you can get detailed help with any individual DJN/R database by entering two slashes, the database's name, and a space, and the word HELP. For example, let's say you needed help on using the //NEWS database. To see its help file, try this: enter //NEWS HELP. That should cause the system to respond with:

```
             The World Report
         On Dow Jones News/Retrieval

    To enter the World Report, type //News and press
the Return key.
    You'll see a front page which displays the top
five stories at the time indicated on the clock
seen on the screen.
    The clock shows Eastern time.
    To retrieve a story, type the number appearing to
the left of the headline and press return.
          -PRESS <RETURN> FOR MORE-
```

Another popular DJN/R feature we'll be exploring in an upcoming chapter is Investext, a collection of top-flight investment analyses for a wide variety of companies. To go directly to that database, you would type //INVEST. To get help with that database . . . right you are— //INVEST HELP. Enter that now and you'll see:

How To Use INVESTEXT
\---

INVESTEXT contains research reports on more than 3,000 companies and 50 industries.
    Type //INVEST (Return) for the INVESTEXT welcome screen.
    You can then press Return for a menu listing three selections: legal disclaimers, a list of more than 30 research providers, and instructions.
    Or, for an INVESTEXT company report, you may type the ticker symbol for the company you want.
             -PRESS <RETURN> FOR MORE-

There were two points to this little exercise. The obvious one was to show you that help is almost always just a few keystrokes away, meaning it's darn difficult to get lost in this system.

In addition, this was an example of what we were saying in the last chapter about Dow Jones's being easy to operate from a kind of command mode for quick access to information. There's no need to travel any long menu trails to get from one group of services to another, whether we're talking about databases or help files about databases. Entering just two slashes and the name of the database gets you to those features quickly. And for help in using the feature, just append the word HELP.

Try one more. The command for getting to Peterson's College Guides is //SCHOOL. To get help for that database, it would be //SCHOOL HELP. Enter that.

Peterson's College Guides
On Dow Jones News/Retrieval
\---

Peterson's College Selection Service offers in-depth profiles on over 3,000 universities and colleges in the U.S. and Canada.
    You can find information on specific colleges or you can search for the schools that best meet your individual needs.

```
    To access the data base, type //SCHOOL and press
Return. You will see a welcome screen offering two
selections.
          -PRESS RETURN FOR MORE-
```

Now compare that with the Peterson database itself. Enter //SCHOOL to see:

```
          PETERSON'S COLLEGE SELECTION SERVICE
                 COPYRIGHT (C) 1986
             PETERSON'S COLLEGE GUIDES, INC.

COLLEGE DESCRIPTIONS ARE SUPPLIED BY THE SCHOOLS.

THERE ARE TWO WAYS TO FIND INFORMATION:

PRESS     TO SEARCH BY

  1 COLLEGE NAME FOR DETAILED INFORMATION ABOUT
    SPECIFIC SCHOOLS

  2 YOUR INDIVIDUAL REQUIREMENTS TO FIND THE RIGHT
    SCHOOLS FOR YOU
```

Now, let's see how fast we can jump from //SCHOOL all the way over to the Investext database. Enter //INVEST.

```
                    INVESTEXT
               COPYRIGHT (C) 1986
           BUSINESS RESEARCH CORPORATION

            COMPANY AND INDUSTRY REPORTS
         FROM TOP BROKERS, INVESTMENT BANKERS
                 AND OTHER ANALYSTS

Enter stock symbol for reports on one of more than
3,000 companies.

Or type INDUSTRY for reports on one of 50
industries.
-----------------------------------------------------
PRESS <RETURN> FOR INSTRUCTIONS, RESEARCH PROVIDERS
AND LEGAL DISCLAIMERS.
```

And now, just as quickly to the Dow Jones World Report by entering //NEWS.

```
        DOW JONES NEWS/RETRIEVAL WORLD REPORT
            FRONT PAGE AT 9:14 P.M. MONDAY
                      FROM AP

PRESS FOR

1 Eight Hurt As Philippine Troops Open Fire On Crowd
  In Manila

2 Reagan, In Reversal, Urges Marcos To Yield Power In
  Philippines

3 Eastern Airlines Accepts Offer For Takeover By
  Texas Air

4 Low Temperature Of Shuttle Rocket Reportedly Known
  Before Launch

5 Reagan Answers Soviet Arms Offer
-------------------------------------------------------
PRESS N FOR MORE NATIONAL OR F FOR MORE FOREIGN
NEWS. THEN PRESS <RETURN>.
```

A NEWS BREAK

Let's stop here for a quick update on the news.

Now, of course, unless you've just entered the Twilight Zone, your screen is not displaying the headlines you see above. They were on the system in late February 1986. Nonetheless, your procedure for reading the stories is the same. Each of these numbered headlines represents a top story of the day. Enter the digit 1 to read the story associated with the first headline. When we did that, it looked like this:

```
NEWS 2/24/86                              PAGE 1 OF 5
            Eight Hurt As Philippine Troops
             Open Fire On Crowd In Manila
                          ---
     MANILA-Soldiers fired on a jeering crowd Tuesday
near the presidential palace, where Ferdinand Marcos
was isolated in his struggle to retain power.
     Fighting was also reported near the rebel-held
government television station.
     Eight people were wounded in the shooting near the
palace and five were injured while trying to flee.
```

Note the familiar line at the top of the page on your screen and the indication of how many "pages" the story contains. As with the pages in the Master Menu, press RETURN to see page 2, then page 3, and so on.

When you get to the last page in this section, press RETURN again and you'll see that you go immediately to page 1 of story 2. In other words, you don't need to go back to the top menu to see the next story. In fact you can begin with story 1 and, by continuing to press RETURN, see all the top stories in //NEWS.

Read as many of the stories as you like this way. When you're finished, enter the T command at the bottom of any page to get back to the main //NEWS menu.

```
         DOW JONES NEWS/RETRIEVAL WORLD REPORT
              FRONT PAGE AT 9:15 P.M. MONDAY
                        FROM AP

PRESS FOR

1 Eight Hurt As Philippine Troops Open Fire On Crowd
  In Manila
2 Reagan, In Reversal, Urges Marcos To Yield Power In
  Philippines
3 Eastern Airlines Accepts Offer For Takeover By Texas
  Air
4 Low Temperatures Of Shuttle Rocket Reportedly Known
  Before Launch
5 Reagan Answers Soviet Arms Offer
 ------------------------------------------------------
PRESS N FOR MORE NATIONAL OR F FOR MORE FOREIGN NEWS.
THEN PRESS <RETURN>.
```

In addition to the commands we've already met, some databases have extra navigation commands for "local" use only. Usually, the system will tell you about these local commands on the first page of that feature. For instance, here in //NEWS, note at the bottom of this page that you can see more national headlines by entering N and more headlines from abroad by entering F.

Look first at the additional national news by entering N.

2/24/86   PAGE 1 OF 3

NATIONAL NEWS

PRESS FOR

1 Reagan Promises Governors Nothing In Meeting On
  Budget Proposals
2 Supreme Court To Decide By July If Gramm-Rudman
  Constitutional
3 High Court Roundup: Indianapolis Loses Anti-
  Pornography Case
4 Judge Backs Government Suspension Of Hospital From
  Medicare Plan
5 U.S. Tells Medicare Patients Of Their Right To
  Proper Care

There is likely to be more than one page of stories in the National News section. If you wanted to read all of them, you could enter 1 and then press RETURN at the bottom of each page to display all the stories from the first to the last. Or, you could begin with any story by typing the number associated with that headline. For example, you could be in the middle of story 2 and decide that's all you wanted to read of it and that you really wanted to see the beginning of story 3. All you have to do is enter the digit 3 at the bottom of the current page.

DIAL M FOR MENU

We're almost done for this evening, but before we log off, we'd like to show you one more navigation command—the M command, which will take you to the *previous* menu. It's useful if you are in a submenu and you want to get back to the previous menu. We can see how it works right here.

Pick out one of the stories on the National News menu that should now be on your screen and enter its number. That will give you the first page of that story. At the bottom of that page, enter M and the system will take you back to the previous menu, that is, the menu from which the current screen branched:

2/24/86   PAGE 1 OF 3

NATIONAL NEWS

PRESS FOR

1 Reagan Promises Governors Nothing In Meeting On
  Budget Proposals
2 Supreme Court To Decide By July If Gramm-Rudman
  Constitutional
3 High Court Roundup: Indianapolis Loses Anti-
  Pornography Case
4 Judge Backs Government Suspension Of Hospital From
  Medicare Plan
5 U.S. Tells Medicare Patients Of Their Right To
  Proper Care

If you entered another M at this point, you'd be taken to *this* screen's previous menu, in this case, something like this:

DOW JONES NEWS/RETRIEVAL WORLD REPORT
FRONT PAGE AT 9:15 P.M. MONDAY
FROM AP

PRESS FOR

1 Eight Hurt As Philippine Troops Open Fire On Crowd
  In Manila
2 Reagan, In Reversal, Urges Marcos To Yield Power
  In Philippines
3 Eastern Airlines Accepts Offer For Takeover By
  Texas Air
4 Low Temperature Of Shuttle Rocket Reportedly Known
  Before Launch
5 Reagan Answers Soviet Arms Offer
- -
PRESS N FOR MORE NATIONAL OR F FOR MORE FOREIGN
NEWS. THEN PRESS <RETURN>.

Take note of the difference between the T and M navigation commands:

• T takes you to the *Top* of the database you're currently visiting, whether it's //NEWS, //INTRO, //MENU, //INVEST, or whatever.

• M takes you to the *previous menu* inside a database. It's handy for stepping back from a subsubmenu to a submenu. And of course, you could continue stepping back with the M all the way to the top of the database.

Now check the foreign news headlines by entering F. It should display a list like this:

```
2/24/86                                        PAGE 1 OF 2

                    FOREIGN NEWS

PRESS FOR

1 Focus: Soviet Party Congress Faces Tough Economic
  Problems
2 Syria Refuses To Extradite Ex-Nazi Sought By West
  Germany
3 Car Bomb Kills 5, Injures 12 Near Market In East
  Beirut
4 Segregated Beaches New Target Of Protesters In
  South Africa
5 South Korean Regime, Opposition Begin Talks On
  Constitution
```

From this you could read stories by entering the digits, just as you did with the National News menu.

WRAPPING UP AND LOGGING OFF

This ends our first tour of the system and we've seen a lot. In fact, you've just used every major command you'll need to get around the system and you've seen the name of nearly every database available.

It's time to log off, and it's important you do it just the way we tell you. The command for letting the system know you are ready to disconnect is DISC, with no slashes in front of the letters. So now type:

DISC<RETURN>

You should see the system tell you the time you logged on, the time you logged off, and the date. Then you'll probably see the word DISCONNECTED.

Always use the DISC to end your online session. If you simply turn off your modem to disconnect, you're likely to be charged the additional three minutes of connect time it took the system to discover you were gone.

IN CONCLUSION

Our first tour has been full of all sorts of information, and perhaps it has left you a bit bewildered. Just keep in mind what we hoped to accomplish with this first tour—just for you to get comfortable pushing the right keys to get what you want from the system.

We hope you learned that nothing you can do on your end will cause the DJN/R computers to crash. And Big Brother isn't watching over your shoulder to check your error rate.

We showed you a number of valuable commands you'll be using often on the system including:

//MENU, the command you can use from the bottom of nearly any page in Dow Jones to take you back to a kind of index where you can find a list of databases and the commands you can use to get you there.

DISC, the command that disconnects you from DJN/R. Remember, *no* slashes. That's because DISC is not the name of a database. You use the double slashes (//) only to signal to the system that you want to go to a specified database.

You also learned three powerful navigation commands:

T, which takes you to the top (or entry level) of the database you're using. If you feel you're hopelessly lost in a maze, this command will whisk you to the top of the database so you can begin your search all over again.

R, which lets you go back ("return to") a page in a series of text pages you may be reading. If, for example, you are on page 4, enter R at the bottom of the page to see page 3 again.

M, which allows you to return to the previous menu when you are in a submenu of a database. This one is particularly good when a database may have three or four levels of menus and you are, say, in level 3 and want to go back to level 2. The M command will do that for you, whereas T would take you to the top menu.

Now that you understand these commands and how they work, you have all the tools you need to explore every database on Dow Jones. You might say the hard work is over. Now the fun of exploration can begin.

Chapter 4

AN OVERVIEW
OF THINGS
TO COME

You should feel good—you're well on your way now. You've had an overview of Dow Jones News/Retrieval, and some insights into its goals. More important at this stage, you've also learned how to navigate from one part of the system to another and how to get help on the entire system as well as its individual parts.

Now we'll start building on that knowledge. From here on, we'll zoom in closer to look at specific databases and how they work. There will be some differences in commands, but you'll find that the overall principles of operation remain the same.

Before we begin this long fact-finding mission, we'd like to huddle for some thoughts about how we want to use all the data we're going to be receiving.

First a few reminders about the upcoming chapters:

• Don't strain yourself. An energetic person like you will be tempted to try to retain—even try to memorize—all we'll be seeing in the next part of the book. Once again, you'll do yourself a disservice if you make that a goal at the expense of taking in the broad concepts. It's much wiser initially to concentrate on the overall operations of each database and, more important, whether it's useful to your life at work and home. You can always go back later to take in the finer points. And frankly, some of the databases have far more commands available than the average person needs. You'll find that, through routine use of these tools, you'll quickly become familiar with the commands you usually need.

• If you have a printer, use it. More than likely, the communications program you're using has options for getting printouts of the material being displayed on your screen. If you're not familiar with those options, take time to check your manual or consult with your computer sales representative. Printouts of these online tours we're taking may not be necessary, since they're already printed in the book. However, when you begin taking your own side trips into Dow Jones News/Retrieval, get in the habit of flipping on the printer, particularly when you're entering a searchable database. Looking over the printouts after you're off line sometimes can help you discover ways you could have saved time.

• But don't let time become the boss. We all want to save money, but, just as speeding in your automobile uses up more gasoline than driving at saner speeds, trying to rush through an online session probably will just make you more prone to time-wasting errors. If you really need to be cost-conscious, make your connections during DJN/R's off hours (evenings and weekends).

• Plan your strategies offline. That's the biggest money-saver of all. When you've finished the next chapters, you will have seen every database DJN/R had online at the time of this writing, how it works, and what kind of information it specializes in. That knowledge will put you in a perfect position to make critical navigation decisions before you ever connect with your local access number and turn on the money meter.

DOW JONES: A SET OF TOOLS

Now for the Big Secret: DJN/R is not a random collection of databases, but a set of *interrelated* tools.

Not everybody seems to realize this. As we've already suggested, we suspect that most dissatisfied Dow Jones subscribers have this characteristic in common: they've found one or two databases with which they're comfortable and they seldom venture out to see what's around the electronic corner. Perhaps they use only the Current Quotes or Historical Quotes databases, or only check on breaking business news.

Obviously, the system *can* be used that way, but we submit that those folks just aren't getting their money's worth. It's much smarter to use the resources of several related databases to home in on specific information.

In other words, you'll be head and shoulders above even some of the old-timers on this service if you come away from our excursions with this message: often several databases can be used in concert with each other—as a *system* of databases, if you will—to give you a broader picture of the information you've retrieved, so you can actually cross-reference and verify it. What we mean is that the service as a whole can be used for problem solving if you early on develop some good habits: start offline thinking about the problem and planning your strategies; and then connect to the service and go directly to relevant databases.

Dow Jones News/Retrieval itself is beginning to think in terms of linking databases. As you'll be seeing, some of its newest features make that job easier. In addition, as we were wrapping up this book, News/Retrieval was putting the finishing touches on a new database called Dow Jones QuickSearch that would gather up to seven different types of business information from a number of databases. You might want to make a note of the command—//QUICK—for a little independent study later.

For now, to get ourselves in the right frame of mind, we're using this chapter to sketch out some scenarios that show how specific problems can be solved with the databases. To prepare for that, please flip ahead to the Online Survival Kit in the back of the book. Beginning on page 309 you'll find a list that describes every database available on the system at this writing, the same ones you saw briefly described in last chapter's online tour.

As you look at the list, notice that the 35-odd databases fall into five general groups: those that help with using the system itself, those for business facts and statistics, those for business and investment analysis and forecasting, news and current events, and general information often useful for the home. A closer look shows that even within the same category, each database has its own specific applications.

For this chapter keep this list handy for reference, maybe by putting a bookmark on that page, as we now tackle some problem-solving scenarios, some taken from real life and others culled from our fertile imaginations.

Of course in this chapter we'll be talking about a number of DJN/R services that you haven't visited yet. Don't let that throw you. The descriptions in the Survival Kit will give you all the background you need to follow along as we concentrate on the *what to do* with each service. Trust us—later chapters will fill in the *how to* information on each database.

Case 1: Bob

Bob, a public information officer for a major pharmaceutical company, is in the center of things when public concerns suddenly are raised about the safety of an ingredient in a popular over-the-counter drug. The product of a competitor, XYZ Corp., has been linked to illnesses reported by certain people, and this is the second time in three years that such reports have been made in connection with this drug. However, there's much dispute as to whether the ingredient is actually to blame.

Since Bob's company also uses this ingredient in some of its products, the boss asked for a thorough analysis of the situation, including the possible impact on the company's products. In addition, he wants to know what effect the first incidents had on business at XYZ Corp., what the company did in the aftermath, what competing drug companies have done, and what the medical community is suggesting.

As Bob sees it, the questions involve three major areas that he can probe on DJN/R—news (current and historical), financial (statistical and analysis), and medical.

To start, Bob wants to get a background on the ingredient and its alleged side effects in some users, so he begins his research, not in news or financial databases, but with a database called the Medical and Drug Reference (//MEDX). That provides him with some quick reference points.

Then, to bring himself up-to-date on the latest news on the situation, he visits the Dow Jones News database (//DJNEWS) to read reports in the top news of the day. That service allows him also to check news affecting specific industry groups, so he looks in on the pharmaceutical industry categories.

After that, he's ready to begin the in-depth research, so he turns to the best online archive of news stories, a feature called the Text-Search Services. With //TEXT, he can look for specific stories all the way back to 1979, dealing with XYZ Corp., medicines in general, and the drug additive in question, as well as stories on file about his own company and others in the pharmaceutical industry group.

Bob concentrates on news from the first episodes involving the ingredient and retrieves stories that deal specifically with concerns over safety of medicines that contain it. As you'll see when we learn about //TEXT in Chapter 10, the feature allows Bob to search the Dow Jones News files as well as the backlog of stories from complete editions of *The Wall Street Journal* and *The Washington Post*.

Studying printouts of relevant stories from these two databases prepares Bob for the next challenge—determining the business effects. For instance, the news accounts provide him with the dates of important developments in the continuing story, such as when the illnesses were reported, subsequent announcements from XYZ Corp., congressional and industry statements, and so forth.

Since XYZ Corp. is a publicly traded company, Bob wants to get a quick reading on the effects of the controversy by looking at what has happened to the company's stock over the past several years. To do this, he accesses a different database, Historical Quotes (//HQ), which allows him to look at monthly and quarterly summaries of XYZ's performance over the past several years. Using the dates he retrieved from the news accounts, he even can zero in on weekly and daily reports around the dates of major events in the controversy. That gives him a feeling for how specific statements and actions by XYZ were perceived by investors.

Finally, Bob wants to see what top analysts are saying about XYZ's future in light of the newest controversy, so he moves on to the analytical databases such as the Corporate Earnings Estimator (//EARN), Standard & Poor's (//SP), and Investext (//INVEST). These services tell him what leading observers in the business think will happen to XYZ in the months ahead.

So, after perhaps less than an hour of connect time and only one phone call, Bob is ready to write a report that he can be sure is up-to-date.

Case 2: Alex

Investor Alex has just heard a hot tip—Aardvark Aviation has come up with a new device that's going to revolutionize air travel and it has industry insiders so excited that they're doing cartwheels. In fact, the rumor is that Aardvark has struck a deal with the powerful ZYX Corp., which is going to make Aardvark stock a sweet buy.

On the way to the office, Alex recalls that a few months ago he read some small item about Aardvark in *The Wall Street Journal*. Was it in the "Heard on the Street" column? And when? Logging into DJN/R, Alex heads for that Text-Search Services database (//TEXT) we just heard about; he knows the commands that will allow him to look specifically at the *Journal's* "Heard" columns. With subsequent searches, he doesn't find Aardvark, but he does find several references to ZYX. That must be what he was remembering, he decides. Among the references was a report that ZYX was working with a new unidentified development company. That's enough to make it worth pursuing.

Alex wants to know how Aardvark and ZYX have performed these days on the stock market, so he looks into Media General Financial Services (//MG) and Standard & Poor's (//SP) for detailed financial profiles, including earnings, revenues, dividends, and projections. He also checks on the latest market activity with Current Quotes (//CQE) and Historical Quotes (//HQ).

Finally, he's wondering if either Aardvark or ZYX have filed any documents with the Securities and Exchange Commission that would be a tip-off to a pending deal. That's just the kind of information a DJN/R feature called Disclosure ONLINE (//DSCLO) specializes in. As you'll find later, that database can provide Alex with detailed stock ownership information, 10-K extracts, profiles, and any new reports filed.

If questions arise from these searches, Alex might return to //TEXT or the Dow Jones News (//DJNEWS) to look at other stories about Aardvark, ZYX, or the aviation industry in general.

Finally, if he's decided to invest, he can call his broker. Or, if he is already a subscriber to DJN/R's Fidelity Investor's EXPRESS (//FIDELITY) he could order the stock online.

Case 3: Cathy

Cathy sells business equipment, specifically computer printers and photocopiers. She sees her job as more than simply answering the phone and taking orders. She knows that many clients these days hope she'll be a consultant as well as a vendor. Her challenge, then, is to try to know her major customers' businesses like an insider.

For her, a major daily resource online is Dow Jones's news database, //DJNEWS, where she can request breaking stories on specific companies. Cathy has cultivated a good relationship with the local headquarters of a major chemical company, Exxoff, and //DJNEWS gives her options to follow the news of that specific company and its competitors as well as reports from the chemical and petroleum industries in general.

Recently Cathy thinks she has spotted a trend: business in the petrochemical industry is improving, a tip-off that maybe Exxoff would be receptive to a presentation about her company's newest line of copiers. To verify her perception of this new growth, she cross-references with Media General (//MG) to look at what the analysts are predicting for the months ahead in the chemical industry group. She also looks at the Corporate Earnings Estimator (//EARN) to see if Exxoff itself is projected to follow the industry's upward trend.

Along the way, she picks up an interesting tidbit: Exxoff has recently entered into merger discussions with a small but impressive Oklahoma oil company. It takes only a moment in //TEXT, //EARN and Standard & Poor's (//SP) to get background on that firm. Then when she meets with her people at Exxoff, she can casually mention, "Hey, congratulations on the deal with that Oklahoma company. It looks like a real winner. I read in the *Journal* that. . . ." With that, not only does she demonstrate that she has a continuing interest in Exxoff's success, but she might even provide some background information on the Oklahoma company that her client had missed.

Cathy also uses the system to keep up-to-date on her *own* business. By regularly checking the Office Equipment news category in //DJNEWS, she comes across a report on a new computer printer from a major competitor. She makes a note to be sure others in her department know about this machine so that no one will be taken by surprise if a prospective client mentions it. She also makes plans to prepare some cost comparisons between her best machines and this new entry, so she'll have some ammunition if she needs it.

Finally, Cathy uses other databases to help her cultivate new clients. When she hears that a new local soft drink bottling company is moving into the area, she uses Investext (//INVEST), Media General (//MG), and other analytical resources to get background on everything from the names of the company's top officers to a description of its major successes and failures. Then when she visits the newcomers to introduce herself, she'll impress them with the fact that she's not a stranger to their business.

Case 4: Hardin

Hardin is an overworked business reporter on a middle-sized newspaper. Because of recent staff reductions, he doesn't have nearly enough help in covering all the industries in his three-state area. With DJN/R, though, he "hired" some electronic assistants.

Using a relatively new feature on the system called //TRACK, Hardin can make a one-time list of the codes for every major company in his readership area. Then with a single command every afternoon, he can pick up the latest stock quote for each business as well as any breaking news the Dow Jones News Service has learned about any of them. Some of the stories that develop from a company's headquarters miles away can be "localized" for his readers.

Hardin's also found that companies' annual reports to their stockholders often are valuable starting places for local news stories. Unfortunately, his geographic area is a little off the beaten path, so he used to be at the mercy of the headquarters' mailing him these reports early enough still to be timely. Now he uses Disclosure ONLINE (//DSCLO) to get the latest reports through his computer. //DSCLO also lets him keep abreast of new SEC filings, such as 10-K extracts, that can signal changes for a business: changes mean news.

Hardin also uses DJN/R for special research. For instance, he has a Sunday story to do on the investment opportunities in the mining industry, his region's biggest business. Investext (//INVEST) and the Corporate Earnings Estimator (//EARN) provide him with more than enough background information with which to form his questions for the local analysts he'll be interviewing.

In addition, his city editor has just come by with an assignment that could be a potential problem. A fellow staffer who just called in sick was going to interview William H. Hardnose, an outspoken media critic who's visiting the local university. The assignment now has fallen to Hardin, who now has 45 minutes to give himself background on the speaker in order to interview and write a story for tomorrow's editions. Since Hardnose isn't a local resident, the newspaper's own library has few clippings about him on file. However, both *The Washington Post* and *The Wall Street Journal* have reported a great deal about Hardnose in the past few years. In ten minutes of searching //TEXT, Hardin has pertinent articles in hand and is ready to go.

Case 5: Carla

Carla is a busy financial consultant with clients needing advice on a variety of topics, from stock investment opportunities to real estate.

For Carla, staying informed is more than following the top news of the hour through DJN/R's news feature. She needs the latest in economic indicators. Therefore, throughout her business week she regularly checks portions of the Dow Jones News (//DJNEWS) that provide economic summaries and indicators; the status of the money market; activities of the Federal Reserve Board, the Securities and Exchange Commission, and the Treasury Department; and the latest Dow Jones Averages.

Through another database, Money Market Services (//MMS), she plugs into a regular flow of data on the M-1 and M-2, the Gross National Product, indexes of personal income, durable goods, borrowing levels, employment rates, producers price and retail sales indexes, and more.

One of her clients follows high-tech stocks, and for Carla to be in a position to advise, she needs to keep track of the Japanese business scene. Japan's Economic Daily (//KYODO) provides up-to-the-minute reports from the Kyodo News Service at the start of every U.S. business day.

The important client also likes to know about investment possibilities in new companies, so Carla regularly checks *The Wall Street Journal* through //TEXT for stories about patents and new product announcements, then follows up good prospects by checking what the analysts are saying in Media General (//MG), Standard & Poor's (//SP), and Investext (//INVEST).

Another client needs to be kept up-to-date on the gold and silver markets, a perfect job for the commodities databases (//FUTURES) as well as for //MMS.

Case 6: Franklin

Not all Dow Jones News/Retrieval features are for the office alone. For instance, Franklin finally is going to be able to take the kids on an educational vacation—a tour of Washington, D.C.

To whet their enthusiasm for the trek early, they log on to the Academic American Encyclopedia (//ENCYC) to read an assortment of articles on the history and culture of the city, picking out sites that would make for interesting viewing.

To find out what's going on in Washington these days, they turn to //TEXT and look at recent issues of *The Washington Post*. They can look at specific sections of the paper for news of upcoming exhibits, displays, entertainment, and sports events.

Franklin learns he can even use the electronic copies of the *Post* to find interesting places to eat by concentrating on the paper's restaurant reviews.

And when the family's ready to make its travel arrangements, Franklin uses the Official Airline Guide (//OAG) to determine the best connections and even order tickets.

Before leaving, Franklin even checked out the weather picture with Accu-Weather's (//WTHR) databases, which provide three-day forecasts for 100 major cities, including the D.C. area.

THIS AND MUCH MORE

Of course, these scenarios only scratch the surface, but we hope this kind of mind game will help you come up with your own ideas. If you'd like to see more scenarios, there are two good sources. First, Dow Jones News/Retrieval has produced an excellent demonstration disk, "The Off-line Sampler," that provides five sample sessions of applications for the service. It's available from Customer Service for about $5.

Also, the *Dowline* magazine that you receive as a subscriber to the service frequently includes "interactive" features and tutorials that state a problem and then show how the databases can be used to solve it.

Chapter 5

GETTING BUSINESS'S RAW INFORMATION

Our tours of Dow Jones News/Retrieval now will kick into high gear. From here on we'll zero in on specific databases to learn how you can make them perform the way our imaginary cast of characters did in the last chapter.

This chapter and the next three will concentrate on the services that have made this system famous—the top-drawer financial utilities, from the ones that retrieve raw business information to the sophisticated analytical tools.

Perhaps the most basic financial data you'll ever need is a stock market quotation, so that's where we'll begin our research.

Back in the first chapter, when we profiled the "typical" DJN/R subscriber, we noted that among the most popular features to the subscriber were the databases that provided current and historical quotes. That's not surprising when you consider that quotes are valuable to such a wide range of people. The same quotes a professional investor needs for his livelihood can be used by corporate managers and salespeople to gauge the vital signs of their business and those of their competitors.

When we go online this time for our second tour, the main stops will be:

• The Current Quotes database (//CQE), a real workhorse that provides up-to-date prices on securities listed on the New York, American, Midwest, and

Pacific stock exchanges and NASDAQ over-the-counter stocks, as well as composite quotes. It can provide data on common and preferred stocks, warrants, options, bonds and government securities, foreign bonds, and mutual funds. A recent enhancement even allows you to retrieve current news about various companies while getting quotes.

• Historical Quotes (//HQ), a first-rate collection of stock information dating back to 1978, with daily, quarterly and monthly summaries available as well as quotes for any specific trading day. This is your first major resource for researching the performance of a company.

• The Dow Jones Averages (//DJA), a database of daily and historical summaries of the transportation, industrial, utilities, and composite stock indexes. The system keeps a full year's worth of reports online and you can request indexes for a specific day or a range of days.

• The Futures Quotes database (//FUTURES), with price quotes for more than 60 commodities contracts traded on North American exchanges.

Most of the daily quotes we'll see on this tour are delayed about 20 minutes from the actual prices reported at the exchanges. However, if that's too slow for you, there's another relatively new feature, Real-Time Quotes (//RTQ), which offers pricing information with no delay from the four major exchanges and NASDAQ, as well as a news alert feature.

A few things to note about these features before we log on:

First, most electronic information services these days offer some kind of stock quotation database. However, DJN/R is the only system we know that provides extra security for accuracy, an innovation you might call the "human interface." It works something like this: If a stock quote comes over the transom and it looks incorrect, a DNJ/R statistician actually checks it out with a phone call or two before passing it along to all of us.

Second, we'll be taking a good, long look at these databases on this tour. Obviously, that's partly because we want you to feel comfortable with these basic information providers. In addition, we hope to continue illustrating general tips for using the system. For instance, this tour will provide our first look at //SYMBOL, a database of vital codes and symbols you can use throughout Dow Jones News/Retrieval to obtain information about specific companies and groups of companies. It's a service you'll be using many times in the course of the book.

Finally, have a pencil and notepad beside the computer for this tour; you'll need to make a few notes as we go along.

FIRING UP THE SYSTEM

Okay, enough preview. Let's get online. Fire up the computer and log on to Dow Jones, just as you did on the last tour, calling your chosen access network and entering your password.

We're heading in the general direction of the Current Quotes (//CQE) database, but let's start by getting to know the //SYMBOL database.

At your current cursor position, the ENTER QUERY prompt at the bottom of the system's first screen, enter the command //SYMBOL. After a moment the system should display:

```
               DIRECTORY OF SYMBOLS
                 COPYRIGHT (C) 1986
             DOW JONES & COMPANY, INC.

PRESS FOR

   1 STOCK SYMBOLS
   2 COMPANY NAMES USING STOCK SYMBOLS
   3 STOCK OPTIONS
   4 MUTUAL FUNDS
   5 U.S. CORPORATE BONDS
   6 FOREIGN BONDS
   7 U.S. TREASURY NOTES & BONDS
   8 NEWS/RETRIEVAL CATEGORY CODES
   9 MEDIA GENERAL INDUSTRY GROUP CODES
  10 RECENT SYMBOL CHANGES

OR, PRESS <RETURN> FOR INSTRUCTIONS
```

Lots of options here. We want to find the stock symbols for a half dozen companies, so select the first option (enter 1 for Stock Symbols) and the system will display:

```
SYMBOL                                        STOCKS

ENTER QUERY
```

Let's get the symbol for IBM (and no extra credit for guessing that one in advance). At the ENTER QUERY prompt, enter (without the quote marks) "International Business Machines." In a second the system should respond with something like:

```
SYMBOL   STOCKS                                PAGE 1 OF 1

IBM        *INTERNATIONAL BUSINESS MACHINES
            CORP. - NY
```

```
ENTER QUERY
OR PRESS <RETURN> FOR MAIN MENU
```

Good. So "IBM" means IBM to DJN/R. Make a note of that and let's get the symbol for another company. At ENTER QUERY, enter (again, no quote marks) "Goodyear," and see the system say:

```
SYMBOL    STOCKS                               PAGE 1 OF 1

T.GT  *GOODYEAR CANADA INC. - TS
GT    *GOODYEAR TIRE & RUBBER CO. - NY
```

```
ENTER QUERY
OR PRESS <RETURN> FOR MAIN MENU
```

Two Goodyears are listed in the database. The one we want is the second one, the one traded on the New York Stock Exchange (see the "- NY" following the second listing?), so make a note of the symbol GT.

Now follow the same procedure to get symbols for four other companies and make notes on your scratch pad. At ENTER QUERY, enter General Motors and note the symbol, and then do the same for Xerox, then Lotus Development, and finally Apple Computer.

While you're gathering that information, you may see some things you're wondering about in the //SYMBOL listings. For instance:

• Some of the company names have asterisks (*) before them, as the Goodyear listings do in our example. How come? Well, that's Dow Jones News/ Retrieval's way of identifying the symbols used in another important database, Dow Jones News (//DJNEWS) which we'll be learning about in Chapter 9.

• Some of the listings you find in //SYMBOL may be preceded by a D. such as "D.AAPL." That's a symbol indicating that information about the over-the-counter stock can be found in yet another database, DISCLOSURE II, which we'll be seeing in the next chapter. For now, just concentrate on the main stock symbols.

• Finally, you may come across some symbols that are preceded by T.—such as "T.GT" in the above example. The T. means the company is Canadian, in this case, the Canadian division of Goodyear.

PUTTING //SYMBOL TO WORK

Once you have your six stock symbols in tow (they should be IBM for IBM, GT for Goodyear, GM for General Motors, XRX for Xerox, LOTS for Lotus, and AAPL for Apple), we're ready to head out for the Current Quotes database.

At the ENTER QUERY prompt, enter //CQE (remember that the "//" tells DJN/R that you're moving on to a new database).

Incidentally, the letters stand for "Current Quotes, Enhanced." If you're a long-time DJN/R subscriber, you may be used to entering //CQ (sans E); that's the older version of Current Quotes. //CQE and //CQ work the same way. The advantage of //CQE is that, in addition to giving you stock quotes, it gives you a bulletin if there is a daily news story about one of the companies you've inquired about. More about that in a few minutes.

After entering //CQE, you should see this brief message:

```
CURRENT DAY QUOTES BEING ACCESSED

ENTER QUERY
```

Clear enough. Give it a whirl. At this query prompt, enter your first symbol, IBM, and watch the system display:

```
       DOW JONES STOCK QUOTE REPORTER SERVICE
         STOCK QUOTES DELAYED OVER 15 MINUTES
        *=CLOSE PRICE ADJUSTED FOR EX-DIVIDEND
```

It then should report its latest quote for IBM. When we accessed this information, we were told:

```
STOCK  BID      ASKED
       CLOSE   OPEN     HIGH    LOW      LAST VOL(100's)
IBM    155 1/2 154 3/4 154 7/8 153 1/2 154  13206
```

Time out. Most of these columns are self-explanatory, but one of them seems to confuse some people. The CLOSE column in this display always refers to the *previous* trading day's closing price. That means that if you visit //CQE even after today's market closes, today's closing price still will be listed in the LAST column. Tomorrow that figure moves to the CLOSE column.

Hmmmm—that probably makes you wonder what time you should access //CQE to be sure of having the day's closing prices in the LAST column. All closing prices are online by 6 P.M. Eastern Time every business day.

//CQE also will check up to five stocks at the same time. To give that feature a test, enter the rest of the symbols on your list, like this:

```
    ENTER QUERY GM XRX LOTS AAPL GT<RETURN>
```

Note that there is a space between each symbol, *not* a comma.

The system, after giving that some thought, responds with something like this:

```
STOCK    BID      ASKED
         CLOSE    OPEN     HIGH     LOW      LAST     VOL(100'S)
GM       70 3/8   70 1/2   71 1/4   69 5/8   71 1/4   4311
XRX      59 3/4   59 3/4   59 7/8   59       59       2019
LOTS     25       25       25 1/8   24 1/2   25       703
AAPL     22       22 1/8   22 1/8   21 3/4   22       2870
GT       31 1/4   31 1/4   31 1/4   30 7/8   30 7/8   4628
```

What the system is showing in this chart is the last trading day's closing bid, today's opening bid, the high and low, the last price quoted, and the cumulative trading volume.

These are composite stocks, based on the activity on all exchanges. But suppose you need to know how one of the stocks, say General Motors, performed on each of the major markets that make up the composite? DJN/R can do that too. All you need to do is precede the stock symbol with the numbered code for each exchange you want the system to check. Here are the number codes:

1 for the New York Exchange
2 for the American Exchange
3 for the Pacific Exchange
4 for the Midwest Exchange

With that information, try this—enter:

1GM 2GM 3GM 4GM

That asks the system to check GM's performance on each individual exchange. Do you see a problem with that request? Dow Jones News/Retrieval does and it reports:

```
STOCK   BID     ASKED
        CLOSE   OPEN    HIGH    LOW     LAST    VOL(100'S)
1GM     70 3/8  70 1/2  71 1/8  69 5/8  71 1/8  3621
2GM     STOCK SYMBOL IN ERROR
3GM     70 3/8  70 1/2  71      69 7/8  71      116
4GM     71      70 1/2  71 1/4  69 3/4  70 7/8  593
```

Notice that the system has come up with an "error message" on 2GM; that's because the stock can't be traded on both the New York and American exchanges.

Two important points here—if you'd already known that GM is traded on NYSE and not the American, you could have entered your command as "1GM 3GM 4GM," leaving out a request for a check of the American. However, not knowing was no problem. The system didn't "crash" because of the error; it simply acknowledged it and moved on. From time to time on DJN/R you'll find an error message like this that doesn't really mean you've made a mistake—it just means no such information is available.

In a moment we'll move on to the Historical Quotes database. Before we leave here, though, you need to know that //CQE also can provide current information on other kinds of trading, such as mutual funds and government, corporate, and foreign bonds. To make those searches, you need the symbol from //SYMBOL. (If you'll recall, the main menu of //SYMBOL provided options for finding codes for mutual funds, corporate bonds, foreign bonds, and U.S. Treasury notes and bonds.) With one of those codes, you can indicate to //CQE that you're looking for data on something *other than* a common stock. You do that by attaching to the symbol a prefix from the following list:

Prefix	Means
+	Mutual Funds
/	Corporate and Foreign Bonds
#	U.S. Treasury Bonds and Notes

Let's look up the report on a mutual fund, say, Drexl Burnham, which, //SYMBOL would tell you, is DBURX. At the prompt, enter +DBURX (that is, a plus sign to indicate "mutual funds" and the symbol for the fund) and you should see something like this:

```
STOCK   BID     ASKED
        CLOSE   OPEN    HIGH    LOW     LAST    VOL(100'S)
DBURX   21.95                                   1231
```

(By the way, the net asset value per share and offering price are updated daily at 6 P.M. Eastern Time. Before that, only the net asset value is available.)

You also can use //SYMBOL to find Treasury bond symbols and look them up in //CQE (using the # prefix) as well as corporate and foreign bonds (using the single slash (/) prefix).

There's one more major use of //CQE—tracking quotes on stock *options* for "calls" and "puts" and strike dates. However, we'd like to delay that discussion for the time being. We'll return to the topic after we're off line and can stretch out in the easy chair with a cup of coffee.

TIME OUT FOR NEWS

Because Current Quotes is so popular, DJN/R's programmers have been inspired to make it even better. In 1985 that effort led to the introduction of the *enhanced* version of Current Quotes, which we've been using. //CQE (as opposed to plain old //CQ) tips you off if there's daily news about one of the companies you've inquired about. In other words, when you request a stock quote for a company, say Apple (AAPL), //CQE also checks the Dow Jones news wire. If it finds some late-breaking news about Apple, it signals you with a message like this:

```
NEWS AVAILABLE FOR AAPL 11:11am
```

(Perhaps you've already seen a message like this when you looked up quotes on the six issues we've chosen to work with.)

To take advantage of the //CQE news flash and read the latest on Apple, you'd need to enter a period (.) followed by the stock symbol, like this:

```
.AAPL
```

Actually, //CQE is a sophisticated linking of the Current Quotes database with the //DJNEWS database, which we'll be visiting at length later.

ADDING PERSPECTIVE WITH //HQ

Back to work.

The Current Quotes database is great for the latest on stocks and other securities you've been tracking for a while. However, if you're eyeing a new investment or putting together a record of the past performance of particular securities, you need some historical perspective.

That's where the Historical Quotes database comes into play. To get there, enter the command //HQ.

The system quickly takes you from the //CQE database to //HQ and you know you've arrived when you see:

```
HISTORICAL QUOTES BEING ACCESSED

ENTER QUERY
```

No surprises here. This is similar to the display we've already been using. Obviously, ENTER QUERY is waiting for you to type in a stock symbol.

//HQ can give you all kinds of perspectives—daily summaries, monthly summaries back to 1979, quarterly reports back to 1978 about any company listed on the New York, American, Midwest, and Pacific exchanges and NASDAQ over-the-counter issues.

It also can give you a report on a single day in history.

Suppose the question arose about how Goodyear Tires fared on November 1, 1985. To get that information, enter this command at the ENTER QUERY prompt: GT 11/1/85 (that is, the stock symbol for Goodyear, followed by a space and then the desired date). To that, the system replies:

```
DOW JONES HISTORICAL
STOCK QUOTE REPORTER SERVICE

STOCK GT

DATE          HIGH          LOW          CLOSE        VOL(100/s)
11/01/85      26 3/4        26 1/2       26 5/8          711
```

This is a composite quotation, based on the activity on major exchanges. Just as you did with //CQE, you can request //HQ to give you historical data from the individual exchanges, as we'll see shortly.

But first, probably more important than an individual day in history is an overview of the trends for a specific issue, in the form of, say, monthly reports.

To see how Goodyear fared each month in 1985, enter the stock symbol followed by a space and the year and then a space and the letter M for monthly. Put it all together and it spells: GT 85 M. Enter that and you should see:

```
DOW JONES HISTORICAL
STOCK QUOTE REPORTER SERVICE

STOCK GT

      1985 MONTHLY SUMMARY
   DATE          HIGH          LOW          CLOSE        VOL(100/S)
   01/85         29 1/8        25 5/8       28 3/4        72997
   02/85         29 1/8        27 5/8       28 3/8        99763
   03/85         28 1/2        26           26 7/8        66706
   04/85         28 1/8        25 3/4       25 7/8        68499
   05/85         30 1/8        25 1/2       29 5/8        88488
   06/85         30 1/4        28 1/8       29 1/2        56157
   07/85         30 1/4        27 5/8       28 7/8        88476
   08/85         29 5/8        27 5/8       27 7/8        57729
   09/85         28 5/8        26 7/8       27 3/8        58933
   10/85         27 5/8        25 1/8       26 5/8        62224
   11/85         29 1/4        26 1/4       28 3/4        67825
   12/85         31 1/4        28 1/4       31 1/4        74810

*COMPOSITE QUOTES BEGIN WITH OCTOBER 1981
```

Now, as someone once asked Alfie, what's it all about?

In this table the HIGH and LOW figures represent the highest and lowest quotes reported during each month. The CLOSE figure is the closing price reported by that security on *the last trading day* of the month. The VOL column shows the total number (volume) of shares traded during the month.

That's straightforward enough. What about quarterly reports? They're also easy to retrieve—just substitute a Q (for quarterly) for the M in the last command. Give it a workout with General Motors and look at 1984 rather than 1985. Enter GM 84 Q and you'll see:

```
DOW JONES HISTORICAL
STOCK QUOTE REPORTER SERVICE

STOCK GM

    1984 QUARTERLY SUMMARY
            HIGH        LOW         CLOSE       VOL (100/S)
FIRST       80 1/2      62 5/8      65          509862
SECOND      68 1/4      61          65 3/8      452050
THIRD       80 1/4      64 1/4      77 1/8      545387
FOURTH      82 3/4      73 3/8      78 3/8      409131

*COMPOSITE QUOTES BEGIN WITH THE 4TH QUARTER OF 1981
```

Beginning to see the power of this stuff? Well, it can get even better. In a later chapter we'll introduce you to some Dow Jones software that can pick up material from the //HQ database and do some financial wizardry with it offline, complete with graphs and charts. However, to use that software to its fullest, you should first learn to use the various databases manually, as we're doing here.

Suppose you needed to see how General Motors performed monthly, not in composite quotes but specifically on the New York Stock Exchange? No problem—the Historical Quotes database recognizes those same numeric codes //CQE used for the individual stock exchanges. Recall that 1 meant NYSE? Okay, try this—enter 1GM 85 M (telling //HQ "Check the NYSE for General Motors, monthly reports in 1985"), and the system displays:

```
DOW JONES HISTORICAL
STOCK QUOTE REPORTER SERVICE

STOCK 1GM

    1985 MONTHLY SUMMARY
DATE        HIGH       LOW           CLOSE        VOL(100/S)
01/85       85         75  1/4       83  3/8      146544
02/85       83  1/8    77            79  1/2      136835
03/85       80  5/8    72  1/2       72  7/8      116992
04/85       74  3/8    66  3/4       67  5/8      124896
05/85       72  5/8    66            71  5/8      123970
06/85       75         70  1/2       72  1/4      111627
07/85       73  7/8    67  3/8       70  3/4      116625
08/85       71  5/8    65  3/4       67  3/8       88392
09/85       69  5/8    65  7/8       67            92398
10/85       70  1/4    64  3/8       66  3/4      140144
11/85       72  1/8    66  3/8       70  1/8      142971
12/85       77  1/4    69  7/8       70  3/8      132060
```

Of course, if you wanted to look at the 1985 monthlies for GM on the Pacific Exchange, you'd enter 3GM 85 M, or on the Midwest Exchange, 4GM 85 M. Or you could examine quarterly reports instead by substituting Q for M in the commands.

Monthlies and quarterlies are powerful tools for getting a bird's-eye view of a company's activity over a year or so. Later on, when you're trying to decide whether to do business with these guys, the database can continue to help by giving a good look at the activity in the last dozen or so trading days. //HQ keeps records of the past 264 trading days online all the time, with composite quotes as well as quotes from the four major exchanges. The information is stored in 22 "pages," each containing quotes for 12 days.

Let's look at the first page of data (that is, the past 12 trading days) on Xerox.

Enter XRX P1 (meaning, "Check Xerox, page 1"). Note there is a space between the stock symbol and the P, but none between P and 1. The system displays something like this:

```
DOW JONES HISTORICAL
STOCK QUOTE REPORTER SERVICE

STOCK XRX

DATE          HIGH        LOW          CLOSE        VOL(100/S)
12/16/85      60          58  3/4      59  3/8      3317
12/17/85      60          59           59           4218
12/18/85      59  1/8     58  1/8      58  1/2      2436
12/19/85      58  5/8     57  3/4      58  3/8      2360
12/20/85      58  7/8     58  1/4      58  3/8      2543
12/23/85      58  5/8     57  1/8      57  3/8      1449
12/24/85      57  1/4     55  7/8      56  5/8      2454
12/26/85      57  1/2     56  5/8      57  1/2      1052
12/27/85      58  7/8     57  1/2      58  3/8      1444
12/30/85      59  7/8     58  3/4      59  7/8      2749
12/31/85      60          59  1/2      59  3/4      1843
01/02/86      59  7/8     59           59  1/4      2864
```

(These figures are composites. To see individual markets, again, use the codes: 1 for NYSE, 2 for Amex, 3 for Pacific, and 4 for Midwest.)

To see the *previous* 12 trading days, just press RETURN. Or you can "go" to a specific page. For instance, if you wanted to see what was happening on the 49th through the 60th trading days, you would enter P5. Figure the page numbers by dividing the highest target date by 12 (60 divided by 12 = P5)—or you can cheat and look at this handy table:

PAGE	COVERS TRADING DAYS
P1	1–12
P2	13–24
P3	25–36
P4	37–48
P5	49–60
P6	61–72
P7	73–84
P8	85–96
P9	97–108
P10	109–120

PAGE	COVERS TRADING DAYS
P11	121–132
P12	133–144
P13	145–156
P14	157–168
P15	169–180
P16	181–192
P17	193–204
P18	205–216
P19	217–228
P20	229–240
P21	241–252
P22	253–264

CHECKING THE DOW JONES AVERAGE

While we're thinking historically, we should look in on the Dow Jones Averages, the sophisticated tracking method Dow Jones provides to newspapers and broadcasters giving the market day's activity at a glance. As you'll come to expect, your electronic resource goes the print and broadcast sources one better—it offers history on demand.

To get to the database, enter //DJA to tell the system you're leaving //HQ for //DJA. Upon your arrival, the system reports:

```
DJ AVERAGES IS BEING ACCESSED

ENTER QUERY
```

The //DJA database is made up of daily summaries for the industrials, utilities, transportation, and 65 active stocks in the form of composite indexes. To use it, just remember these four codes:

IND for Industrials
TRN for Transportation
UTL for Utilities
65 for the 65 active stocks

Let's see what the industrial average was on November 1, 1985. To make the command, enter the code followed by a space and the date, like this: IND 11/1/85.

HISTORICAL DOW JONES AVERAGES

INDUSTRIALS

DATE	HIGH	LOW	CLOSE	VOL(100/S)
11/01/85	1393.58	1367.78	1390.25	139331

If you wanted the 65 active stocks for that date, the command would be 65 11/1/85; for transportation stocks, TRN 11/1/85, and so on.

Like the //HQ database, //DJA keeps 264 trading days' worth of averages online, similarly using 22 pages of information with each page containing a dozen days.

Try it again. Look up the transportation averages for the past 12 trading days by entering TRN P1. The system displays:

HISTORICAL DOW JONES AVERAGES

TRANSPORTATION

DATE	HIGH	LOW	CLOSE	VOL(100/S)
12/16/85	731.16	716.88	723.31	50332
12/17/85	728.82	713.01	719.57	57749
12/18/85	727.18	710.67	716.29	49121
12/19/85	724.49	704.00	713.37	62767
12/20/85	719.34	704.12	711.26	47450
12/23/85	712.31	697.57	702.25	34716
12/24/85	703.07	693.00	698.38	23643
12/26/85	704.59	695.34	701.78	26366
12/27/85	711.84	700.02	708.45	32915
12/30/85	714.15	700.74	709.52	33034
12/31/85	716.17	700.02	708.21	38300
01/02/86	714.03	698.24	706.55	32819

As with //HQ, you could press RETURN here to see the next page (the *previous* dozen trading days). Or, referring to the page chart you saw earlier, you could request a specific page. For example, entering P10 at the bottom of the page on your screen would give you averages for the 109th through 120th days.

At this point, you've seen four fundamental databases:

• //SYMBOL, which provides codes for companies you'll look up in the quotes databases.

• //CQE for today's latest stocks and news flashes.

• //HQ for historical quotes.

• //DJA for daily and historical Dow Jones Averages.

We'll have more to say about them when we get offline. However, why don't you take a moment now for another quick look at any or all of them. If you have a particular security you'd like to look up, revisit //SYMBOL and find its code, then return to either //CQE or //HQ and do a little quick research.

After you're finished, log off by entering DISC—remember, no slashes—and you should see the usual closing messages. Then break the phone connection, get your cup of coffee and meet us in the library.

FOLLOWING OPTIONS THROUGH CURRENT QUOTES

During the tour you saw most of what the Current Quotes feature does. In two ways, it's an ideal database—intelligent, and easy to get along with.

You also learned that certain codes can precede stock symbols to retrieve specific kinds of information. You saw how a plus sign (+) before a symbol told //CQE to look for mutual funds, a slash (/) meant corporate and foreign bonds, and a pound sign (#) signified U.S. Treasury bonds and notes.

Another code, the minus (−), tells the database you want information on stock options—*puts* (that is, options to sell) and *calls* (options to buy).

Now, we're not going to attempt to cover the ins and outs of options trading—that would take a book in itself—but generally speaking, options are purchased opportunities to buy or sell specified stocks (usually in blocks of 100 shares) at a particular price. Options come with an expiration date, assigned to one of three cycles: January-April-July-October, February-May-August-November, or March-June-September-December. Only three expiration months are available for trading in any one cycle at any one time.

Usually when an options trader is optimistic that a stock will rise in price, he or she purchases calls (options to buy that stock months in the future at current, lower prices). If the optimism was justified, the value of the call options will increase when the stock goes up. On the other hand, if the investor expects the price of a security to drop, he or she might elect to purchase puts (options to sell the security in several months at the current, higher prices). Either way, the investors buy a *premium* for the options, which is a fraction of the actual stock price.

To use //CQE to look up the costs of the premiums on puts and calls, you need to enter a minus sign, followed by the stock symbol, followed by a special code for the expiration month, followed by another code for the "striking price," or the anticipated value when the option expires.

That sounds complex but it's not if you have a couple of other charts to look at.

Here's the first one, a table of expiration month codes:

	CALL	PUT
January	A	M
February	B	N
March	C	O
April	D	P
May	E	Q
June	F	R
July	G	S
August	H	T
September	I	U
October	J	V
November	K	W
December	L	X

Now the striking price codes:

5	A	45	I	85	Q
10	B	50	J	90	R
15	C	55	K	95	S
20	D	60	L	100	T
25	E	65	M	7 1/2	U
30	F	70	N	12 1/2	V
35	G	75	O	17 1/2	W
40	H	80	P	22 1/2	X

(By the way, the letters U through Z also may stand for other nonstandard and fractionally adjusted strike prices.)

Fine, but how do you use this information?

Suppose you were interested in options on General Motors stock. Visiting the //CQE database, you first looked up today's price by simply entering the symbol GM at the ENTER QUERY prompt, and the system displayed:

```
STOCK  BID     ASKED
       CLOSE   OPEN    HIGH    LOW     LAST    VOL(100'S)
GM     71 5/8  71 1/2  71 5/8  71 1/4  71 3/8  2459
```

So, GM is selling for about $72 a share.

Now suppose it is January and you think that GM will rise to at least $75 a share by March. You might be interested in buying calls for that and you could check the cost of premiums by entering:

```
-GMCO
```

Consult our new tables as we break down that command's structure. First there's the minus sign (–) to signal options, GM as the symbol for General Motors, C as the code for calls expiring in March, and O as the code for a striking price of 75.

With that command, the system might respond (as it did for us):

STOCK	BID CLOSE	ASKED OPEN	HIGH	LOW	LAST	VOL(100'S)
GMCO	1 1/4	1 3/8	1 3/8	1 1/8	1 1/4	137

This is saying that the premiums on such options closed at $1.25 yesterday and that also was the most recent quote today (see the LAST column).

What if you thought GM might hit $80 a share by March? If you consult the two tables, you'll see how we've put together the appropriate command, which is –GMCP (P being the strike code for 80). And if you wanted to check the premiums on calls expiring in June with a strike of 80, the command would be –GMFP.

Checking premiums on puts works the same way, except you have to take care to use the right-hand column in the month code chart.

For example, let's pretend it's January and you think GM stock will fall from its present $71 or $72 a share to at least $65 by March, so you're considering put options. You could check the premiums on puts with a March expiration and a strike of 65 with the command:

-GMOM

(Again, the minus sign for options followed by the GM stock symbol, then O, meaning puts expiring in March, followed by M, meaning a strike price of 65).

When we did that in January, the system displayed this premium report:

STOCK	BID CLOSE	ASKED OPEN	HIGH	LOW	LAST	VOL(100'S)
GMOM	9/16	1/2	5/8	1/2	5/8	19

Incidentally, if you enter a command sequence for options that aren't available, perhaps because the month you've specified is outside that company's cycle or the striking price is outside its range, the system will respond with "Stock symbol in error," meaning no such options are available.

Options usually are available with expirations in three-months intervals, following the cycles we cited above, so if you find an option with an expiration of March, the next one available for that stock should have an expiration of June, and so forth.

REFINEMENTS TO //CQ: REAL-TIME QUOTES

As we mentioned, the quotes you receive with //CQE (and the older //CQ) are delayed by 20 minutes, as required by the stock exchanges themselves. For most applications, that's as "instant" as you may need them. However, some businesspeople need instant to mean, well, **INSTANT,** by golly. For them, Dow Jones has //RTQ, providing nondelayed market trading prices (or Real-Time Quotes) for stocks traded on the four major exchanges and 2,000 over-the-counter issues.

The commands used in //RTQ are the same ones you learned with //CQE.

//RTQ is a premium service; at this writing, the monthly surcharge was $18.50. Dow Jones passes the surcharge on to the exchanges, incidentally. If you think you might be interested in subscribing to Real-Time Quotes, you should call the customer service department at 800-257-5114 (in New Jersey, 609-452-1511.)

FROM THERE TO THE //FUTURES

There's been quite a change in the investing community in the last three decades. In the 1950s, commodities trading, which generally meant pork bellies, soybeans, and wheat, attracted fewer than 5 million contracts a year. However, these days commodity exchanges, dealing in contracts as diverse as foreign currencies and precious metals, attract an annual trading volume pushing 150 million contracts.

The experts tell us that one of the reasons for the growing interest has been the rapid improvements in communications, not the least of which is the worldwide link of computer communications.

In the first quarter of 1985 DJN/R, attempting to serve this rapidly growing community, introduced //FUTURES, a database of quotes and contracts from the nation's commodity exchanges.

It was no small task. "This was almost as big as building our stock quotes system," according to DJN/R's deputy editorial director Peter Schuyten. "We have made a considerable investment from a programming and hardware standpoint in creating a responsive system."

To get there, you enter //FUTURES, and the system will display something like this:

```
          DOW JONES FUTURES QUOTES
             COPYRIGHT (C) 1986
          DOW JONES & COMPANY, INC.

TO OBTAIN A QUOTE YOU CAN:

ENTER SP (RETURN)
FOR    CURRENT S&P 500 CONTRACTS

ENTER SP 12/30/85 (RETURN)
FOR    HISTORICAL S&P 500 CONTRACTS
       ON A SPECIFIC TRADING DAY
-----------------------------------------------------------
ENTER REQUEST, OR PRESS <RETURN> FOR INSTRUCTIONS AND
FUTURES INFORMATION
```

//FUTURES, being newer, is slightly different from the databases we've seen so far. Like //CQE, //HQ, and //DJA, it's ready to receive a query from you written in its own special codes. However, it also has a few extras online, such as its own bulletin board.

As the introductory message says, we can press RETURN for more information. If you do that, DJN/R shows you a menu, something like this:

```
          DOW JONES FUTURES QUOTES
        INSTRUCTIONS AND INFORMATION

PRESS  FOR

1 A Directory of Symbols
2 How to Access Quotes
3 Contract Sizes and Unit Prices
4 Historical Quotes Starting Dates
5 Understanding the Displays
```

```
6 How to Read Price Quotes
7 A Guide to the Exchanges
8 Futures Calendar
-----------------------------------------------------
ENTER SELECTION OR PRESS Q (RETURN)
TO ACCESS FUTURES QUOTES
```

Entering Q will take you back to the database's ENTER QUERY mode, or you can enter a number to read one of these background articles. Option 8, for instance, is the bulletin board, listing important upcoming dates in the community exchanges. Selecting that will show you something like this:

```
FUTURES                                    P133 ENDS AT 134

                    FUTURES CALENDAR
Dec. 30-Last Trading Day: December Bank CD's (IMM)

Dec. 31-Last Trading Day: December Grains (WPG);
        January Sugars-World (CSCE); January NY No. 2
        Heating Oil and NY Gasolines, Unleaded and
        Leaded (NYM)

Jan. 2 -First Notice Day: January Orange Juice (CTN);
        January Metals (NYM); January Platinum (MCE)

Jan. 15-Last Trading Day: January Soybean Meal
        (MCC); January Lumber (CME)

Jan. 17-Last Trading Day: January Stock Indices
        (CBT); January National OTC Index (PBT)
-----------------------------------------------------
Enter M (Return) for the help menu or Q (Return) for
a futures quote.
```

This particular calendar is two pages long. You can tell that by the message in the upper right hand corner: "P133 ENDS AT 134," meaning the current page is 133 and the document ends on page 134. (This is another kind of "page format" popular on Dow Jones.)

At this point you could press RETURN to see the next page of the calendar, Q to go to the ENTER QUERY stage, or M to return to this menu:

```
             DOW JONES FUTURES QUOTES
           INSTRUCTIONS AND INFORMATION

    PRESS   FOR

    1 A Directory of Symbols
    2 How to Access Quotes
    3 Contract Sizes and Unit Prices
    4 Historical Quotes Starting Dates
    5 Understanding the Displays
    6 How to Read Price Quotes
    7 A Guide to the Exchanges
    8 Futures Calendar
    ---------------------------------------------------
    ENTER SELECTION OR PRESS Q (RETURN) TO ACCESS FUTURES
    QUOTES
```

Option 1 gives you a list of the special symbols used by //FUTURES to identify the material you're interested in. At this writing there were about 70 different kinds of futures contracts documented in the database, each with its own unique code. We've listed the codes in the back of the book in the Online Survival Kit. However, if you become a regular user of //FUTURES, you'll want to check back periodically with the help menu to keep abreast of newly added codes.

Other menu options give you a rundown on how to retrieve the information and how to interpret it.

Before we talk about retrieving quotes, take a minute to find the list of //FUTURES codes in the back of the book, beginning on page 326.

Got it? OK, if you were online at this moment, you could enter Q to get back to the business end of this database. The system would show you:

```
FUTURES QUOTES BEING ACCESSED

ENTER REQUEST
```

Referring to the list in the Online Survival Kit, look up "corn" among the commodity symbols. You should find two symbols—C for corn traded on the Chicago Board of Trade (CBT) and XC for corn traded on New York's Mid-American Commodities Exchange (MCE).

Suppose you wanted to find out about all open contracts on corn on the Chicago Board of Trade. You'd need to enter only the symbol C at the prompt, and the system would display something like this:

```
CORN (CBT) 5,000 BU.; CENTS PER BU.; DATE: 1/3/86

        OPEN   HIGH   LOW    SETTLE   CHANGE      LIFETIME
                                                HIGH   LOW
MAR     2466   2472   2464   2464     -10        2970   2244
MAY     2512   2514   2504   2504     -12        2916   2310
JULY    2520   2520   2500   2502     -22        2860   2330
SEPT    2354   2354   2332   2334     -24        2700   2230
DEC     2256   2256   2226   2230     -30        2352   2202
MAR87   2330   2330   2306   2310     -20        2424   2306
MAY     2354   2354   2354   2354     -34        2420   2354
```

The top line of the display lists the commodity (corn), the market (Chicago Board of Trade), the size of a single contract (5,000 bushels), and the way the prices are quoted (cents per bushel).

You also could access data for a specific trading date by entering a space and the date after the symbol. For instance, if you wanted to see the activity on January 3, 1986, you would enter C 01/03/86. The system's response would be:

```
Corn (CBT) 5,000 BU.; CENTS PER BU.; DATE: 1/3/86
        OPEN   HIGH   LOW    SETTLE  CHANGE    LIFETIME        OPEN
                                              HIGH  LOW     INTEREST
MAR     2474   2476   2470   2474    - 6       2970  2244    322685
MAY     2514   2520   2512   2516    - 4       2916  2310    123160
JULY    2522   2526   2520   2524    - 4       2860  2330     83725
SEPT    2374   2374   2354   2360    -16       2700  2230     10750
DEC     2280   2280   2254   2260    -20       2352  2202     77485
MAR87   2350   2350   2330   2330    -22       2424  2314      4455
MAY     ....   ....   ....   2390    -10       2420  2390        30

VOLUME 79,645; Volume 12/31/85 59,485
OPEN INTEREST 622,290; CHANGE +210
```

Again, there's the summary material at the top of the screen.

About those other columns—OPEN, HIGH, and LOW mean the same as they do in stock quotes—the opening price of the day, the highest price of the day, and the lowest.

SETTLE (that is, "settlement") is a concept unique here. In commodity markets, the "close" includes a brief period (about two minutes) during which transactions may continue. The closing figure actually is a range of prices including the high and low prices during the closing period. CHANGE represents the difference between the latest settlement price and the one for the last trading day. LIFETIME HIGH and LOW are the highest and lowest prices at which each contract month has traded.

Finally, the OPEN INTEREST column is an indicator of the buying and selling; it shows the number of contracts outstanding (the higher the number, the more likely the buyer will want to meet sellers and sellers will want to meet buyers).

But how do you read these figures? In the first column, that "2474" of what?

For help with that, check the Online Survival Kit (page 329) for a list called Understanding //FUTURES' Price Quotes, which interprets the figures for each type of commodity. Using that list, you'll see that the example for corn says that "2734" would be read as "273½ cents per bushel." That means that the first column in our example begins with the price $2.735 a bushel." To figure the actual cost of the contract, multiply the price by the quantity—in this case, 5,000 bushels, or $13,675 a contract.

Finally, //FUTURES also can look up a specific contract month, if you use the month codes which also are listed in the Online Survival Kit (page 326). Suppose you wanted to look for the January 2, 1986, activity for corn contracts for December. Since Z is the code on the list for December, you would enter the commodity code (C for corn on the Chicago exchange), followed by the year (86), followed by the month code (Z), then a space and the date, or: C86Z 01/02/86. The system would display:

```
CORN (CBT) 5,000 BU.; CENTS PER BU.; DATE: 1/2/86

      OPEN HIGH LOW  SETTLE CHANGE   LIFETIME OPEN
                                     HIGH LOW  INTEREST
DEC   2280 2280 2254 2260    -20     2352 2202 77485
```

SUMMING UP

In this chapter we had our first hands-on experience with the all-important //SYMBOLS database. We'll be coming back to that one from time to time to get the addresses of major companies for use in other features.

In the main part of the chapter we took a close-up look at DJN/R's resources for gathering all kinds of raw data. With Current Quotes, we saw how to get information on prices of common stocks, as well as specialized data on stock options, mutual funds, and so on. In Historical Quotes and Dow Jones Averages, we learned how to access backlogs of information for specific dates or a range of trading days. Offline we talked about one of Dow Jones's newer databases, the specialized //FUTURES feature for tracking commodities.

Also along the way we learned a little more about how information is stored in pages on this system and how to navigate back and forward between them, and we gathered some important tables and charts for future reference.

Chapter 6

THE BEST OF THE LOT: FINANCIAL ANALYSIS TOOLS

For most of America the name Dow Jones means investments. At the heart of Dow Jones News/Retrieval are its investment tools, reservoirs of stock market data and analyses that can help you make informed decisions.

For some time now the big investment houses have been using powerful systems to help make their daily decisions. On more than one occasion these well-tempered computers, processing millions of pieces of information in seconds to issue their recommendations, have themselves caused the market to rise and fall, while human operators seemed merely to "look on," as the newspaper caption writers say.

The gurus of the industry are debating whether these sophisticated systems are any better than the average investor at spotting market trends. However, none disputes the value of the information itself. In the world of modern investing, if you don't have the latest and best information, you're out of the game.

As a Dow Jones subscriber, you have at your disposal much of the same data and thoughtful analyses as the big machines, and that's the subject of this chapter and the next.

We'll be going online again, this time to visit some databases that provide both the raw and compiled data that every investor needs: We'll:

• Go first to Media General Financial Services, Inc., where you can retrieve five pages of vital information on nearly 4,300 companies and 170 industry groups.

• Stop by Investext, which provides the latest opinions of top analysts about thousands of companies. This is the kind of information you used to have to depend on a broker to forward to you.

• Look in on a database provided by one of the best-known names in the business of business, Standard & Poor's.

• Make a quick trip to the Corporate Earnings Estimator. A simple database that's powerful in its scope, it produces figures that give a consensus of opinion from analysts about how a stock is expected to perform in the months ahead.

• Wrap up in DISCLOSURE ONLINE, a famous electronic service that contains many of the summaries of documents public companies file with the Securities and Exchange Commission. Instead of waiting days or weeks for them to come in the mail from the SEC, you have instant access to information that can affect your portfolio.

DISCLAIMING AGAIN . . .

Before we begin, indulge us as we once again state our disclaimer:

Remember that many of the displays you see in the book will not match what you see on the screen. Most of these databases change daily—some by the minute—as new information pours in. The good news is that, although the data change, the structure does not. The logical and standard presentation in these databases gives you the opportunity to become familiar with the content of each as well as the order in which the material is presented. You won't find a hodgepodge of data here; the manner in which data are presented will in time become as familiar to you as the way stories and columns are presented in your favorite newspaper.

So that everyone will be together, we'll use International Business Machines as the company to scrutinize on this tour, but of course in subsequent visits you can substitute the symbols of the companies you're researching.

READY, SET . . .

When you're ready to start Tour 3, log on to the system as you usually do.

At the first ENTER QUERY prompt, enter //MG (or //mg; remember, DJN/R isn't persnickety about uppercase or lowercase). This will take us to the Media General database.

(Incidentally, if you're a long-time Dow Jones subscriber, you may be used to entering //MEDGEN to reach this service. In early 1986 Media General revised its features under the new //MG command. At this writing, entering either //MEDGEN or //MG would reach Media General, but in a slightly different format. More about that in the next chapter.)

The first screen of the //MG database is an introductory page that looks something like this:

```
      MEDIA GENERAL FINANCIAL SERVICES, INC.
               COPYRIGHT (C) 1986
               ALL RIGHTS RESERVED

ENTER STOCK SYMBOL FOR A COMPANY REPORT
AND RELATED INDUSTRY INFORMATION.

OR ENTER AN INDUSTRY CODE FOUND IN
//SYMBOL.
-----------------------------------------------------
PRESS <RETURN> FOR LEGAL DISCLAIMERS.
```

You could get right down to business at this point by entering a stock symbol—any stock code found in the //SYMBOL database—to set Media General to work. However, perhaps we should show you that we're not the *only* ones making disclaimers today. Press RETURN to see the first page of Media General's disclaimers:

```
         STATEMENTS OF LEGAL DISCLAIMER

    DOW JONES PUBLISHES ELECTRONICALLY NEWS AND
INFORMATION THAT MAY INCLUDE VIEWS, OPINIONS AND
RECOMMENDATIONS OF INDIVIDUALS AND ORGANIZATIONS
```

```
WHOSE THOUGHTS ARE DEEMED OF INTEREST. DOW JONES DOES
NOT ITSELF ENDORSE THE VIEWS OF ANY OF THE
ORGANIZATIONS, GIVE INVESTMENT ADVICE OR ADVOCATE THE
PURCHASE OR SALE OF ANY SECURITY OR INVESTMENT.
                        -MORE-
```

Press RETURN again to see:

```
   THE INFORMATION HEREIN INCLUDES MARKET AND
FUNDAMENTAL DATA ON COMMON STOCKS AND RELATED SUMMARY
MATERIAL ON INDUSTRY GROUPS. IT WAS OBTAINED FROM
SOURCES WHICH MEDIA GENERAL BELIEVES RELIABLE. MEDIA
GENERAL ENDEAVORS TO ASSURE THAT ALL SUCH
INFORMATION IS COMPLETE, ACCURATE AND TIMELY BUT DOES
NOT GUARANTEE ITS ACCURACY, COMPLETENESS OR
TIMELINESS.

ENTER QUERY
```

Here's a place where you can enter the symbol of the company you're researching.

To try it out, recall from our previous tour that "IBM" is the symbol for IBM, so enter that and the system should display something like this:

```
MEDIA GENERAL                                        PAGE 1 OF 5

02/07/86          INTERNATL BUSINESS MACH    COMPUTERS,SYS.,PERIPH.
PRICE CHANGE

   LAST TRADING WEEK                 2.8%                    3.2%
   LAST 4 WEEKS                      4.9%                    6.9%
   LAST 13 WEEKS                    17.5%                   19.1%
   LAST 52 WEEKS                    13.5%                    7.9%
   YEAR TO DATE                      0.2%                    2.7%

CHANGE VS. S&P 500

   LAST TRADING WEEK                 101%                    102%
   LAST 4 WEEKS                      101%                    103%
   LAST 13 WEEKS                     106%                    108%
   LAST 52 WEEKS                      96%                     92%
   YEAR TO DATE                       99%                    102%

PRESS <RETURN> FOR MORE, OR ENTER NEW STOCK SYMBOL OR INDUSTRY CODE
```

If your computer screen has a width of fewer than 80 columns, the display you see might not look exactly like our example. Long lines probably will "wrap around" to a new line. That's because the pages of Media General and a few other services on Dow Jones are formatted for a display wider than the usual Dow Jones News/Retrieval display of 32 columns. If your display is narrower than 80 columns, you should still be able to read the data easily with practice. If you can't, stay tuned; we may have an answer for you in the next chapter.

For now, notice that this is page 1 of five pages of information about IBM. Notice too that //MG has given you *more* than you asked for; the second column contains information about the industry group to which IBM belongs, Computers, Subsystems and Peripherals. No matter what stock you call for, //MG also provides relevant data for that company's industry group. Not bad—that gives you a chance to see how that company performed in comparison with its group as a whole.

This first page of information gives you price change data for the company and its industry group and also tells you how they performed when compared with the Standard & Poor's 500 stock list.

To see the next page of information, press RETURN.

```
MEDIA GENERAL                                   PAGE 2 OF 5


02/07/86           INTERNATL BUSINESS MACH    COMPUTERS,SYS.,PERIPH.


PRICE RANGE

   LAST CLOSE (IN $)              155.75              48.48
   52-WEEK HIGH (IN $)            158.75              52.80
   52-WEEK LOW (IN $)             117.38              34.33
   5-YEAR HIGH (IN $)             158.75              55.76
   5-YEAR LOW (IN $)               48.38              15.94


RELATIVE PRICE

   P/E RATIO, CURRENT              14.6                22.4
   P/E RATIO, 5-YEAR AVG. HIGH    13.3                 8.0
   P/E RATIO, 5-YEAR AVG. LOW      9.2                 7.4
   PRICE TO COMMON EQUITY         360%                276%
   PRICE TO REVENUE PER SHARE     191%                142%
   RELATIVE PRICE INDEX           128%                158%


PRESS <RETURN> FOR MORE, OR ENTER NEW STOCK SYMBOL OR INDUSTRY CODE
```

Page 2 provides information about price range and relative price data for IBM and its associated industry group.

To see the third page, press RETURN again.

```
MEDIA GENERAL                                            PAGE 3 OF 5

02/07/86          INTERNATL BUSINESS MACH      COMPUTERS,SYS.,PERIPH.

   PRICE ACTION
     BETA, UP MARKET                  1.11                      1.05
     BETA, DOWN MARKET                0.66                      0.93


   VOLUME
     SHARES TRADED THIS WEEK     7,343,000                90,403,000
     DOLLAR VOL THIS WEEK ($)  1,137,199,000            3,460,120,000
     % OF SHARES OUTSTANDING         1.19%                     2.67%
     LIQUIDITY RATIO            47,899,000                   370,000
     ON-BALANCE INDEX                 154                        82


   REVENUE
     LAST 12 MONTHS (IN $)      50,056 MIL               115,941 MIL
     LAST FISCAL YEAR (IN $)    45,937 MIL               113,372 MIL
     % CHANGE LAST QUARTER           18.3%                     -4.1%
     % CHANGE YEAR TO DATE            9.0%                      8.0%

PRESS <RETURN> FOR MORE, OR ENTER NEW STOCK SYMBOL OR INDUSTRY CODE
```

This //MG page is where you come to find price action, volume, and revenue data for the company and its industry group.

After you've looked this over, go on to page 4 by pressing RETURN and see:

```
MEDIA GENERAL                                            PAGE 4 OF 5

02/07/86          INTERNATL BUSINESS MACH      COMPUTERS,SYS.,PERIPH.

   EARNINGS 12 MONTHS ($)      6,555.0F MIL              7,254.4 MIL
   EARNINGS PER SHARE
     LAST 12 MONTHS (IN $)          10.67                      2.17
     LAST FISCAL YEAR (IN $)        10.67                      2.93
     % CHANGE LAST QUARTER          22.8%                     -6.5%
     % CHANGE FY TO DATE            -0.9%                    -18.2%
     % CHANGE LAST 12 MONTHS        -0.9%                    -27.3%
   5-YEAR GROWTH RATE               14.0%                      5.0%
```

```
DIVIDENDS
   CURRENT RATE (IN $)            4.40                  0.99
   CURRENT RATE YIELD             2.8%                  2.1%
   5-YEAR GROWTH RATE             5.0%                  5.7%
   PAYOUT LAST FISCAL YEAR         41%                   -9%
   PAYOUT LAST 5 YEARS             43%                    4%
   LAST X-DIVIDEND DATE       11-06-85                   N/A
```

PRESS <RETURN> FOR MORE, OR ENTER NEW STOCK SYMBOL OR INDUSTRY CODE

These statistics enable you to compare IBM with its peers in terms of earnings and dividends.

Page 5 (press RETURN) shows profit, assets, debt figures, and some statistics on stockholders:

```
MEDIA GENERAL                                    PAGE 5 OF 5

02/07/86          INTERNATL BUSINESS MACH   COMPUTERS,SYS.,PERIPH.


RATIOS
   PROFIT MARGIN                  13.1%                  6.3%
   RETURN OF COMMON EQUITY        24.8%                 12.3%
   RETURN ON TOTAL ASSETS         15.3%                  6.7%
   REVENUE TO ASSETS              117%                   108%
   DEBT TO EQUITY                  12%                    21%
   INTEREST COVERAGE              29.4                    8.4
   CURRENT RATIO                   2.1                    2.3

SHAREHOLDINGS
   MARKET VALUE (IN $)        95,761 MIL           164,216 MIL
   LATEST SHARES OUTSTANDING 614,837,000         3,387,503,000
   INSIDER NET TRADING            4,000             1,580,000
   SHORT INTEREST RATIO        2.0 DAYS              0.4 DAYS
   FISCAL YEAR ENDS              12 MOS                   N/A
```

As you can see, Media General packs a wealth of information into a small space and makes it easy to compare companies with their sectors of the economy.

There are many other ways to use //MG, including fast ways to look up individual industry groups. That's why we'll have much more to say about it in our offline discussion in the next chapter.

ON TO INVESTEXT

For now, we're moving on to a different investment resource, Investext, a service of Business Research Corp. This feature gives you the insights on scores of investment analysts with one stop.

At the bottom of the page on your screen take the express lane to Investext by entering //INVEST. You'll see:

```
                    INVESTEXT

               COPYRIGHT (C) 1986
          BUSINESS RESEARCH CORPORATION

           COMPANY AND INDUSTRY REPORTS
        FROM TOP BROKERS, INVESTMENT BANKERS
                AND OTHER ANALYSTS

Enter stock symbol for reports on one of more than
3,000 companies.

Or type INDUSTRY for reports on one of 50 industries.
----------------------------------------------------
PRESS <RETURN> FOR INSTRUCTIONS, RESEARCH PROVIDERS
AND LEGAL DISCLAIMERS.
```

(Time out for a bulletin from the New Business/Old Business Department: In early 1986 Dow Jones News/Retrieval officials indicated that the name of Investext might change soon. It was expected that even if a new name were chosen, the command //INVEST still would get you to this point. However, if you encounter difficulties, consult the //INTRO newsletter we showed you in Chapter 3. If that doesn't give you the information, remember that Dow Jones Customer Service stands ready to answer any questions.)

Just as with the Media General database, you could enter a company symbol at this point to get a collection of the latest research reports. (As the screen notes, reports on more than 3,000 companies are available.) But let's take a look at an overview by following the screen's advice and pressing RETURN.

```
PRESS  FOR
1 Legal Disclaimers
2 List of Research Providers
3 How to Use Investext
```

This menu tells you that option 1 provides legal disclaimers about Investext material, option 2 gives information about who provided this research, and option 3 gives a short course in using Investext.

To add Investext's disclaimer to our collection, enter 1.

Once you finish reading the material in the submenu, you can go back to the main menu simply by pressing RETURN.

```
                     INVESTEXT
              COPYRIGHT (C) 1986
          BUSINESS RESEARCH CORPORATION

            COMPANY AND INDUSTRY REPORTS
       FROM TOP BROKERS, INVESTMENT BANKERS
                AND OTHER ANALYSTS

Enter stock symbol for reports on one of more than
3,000 companies.

Or type INDUSTRY for reports on one of 50 industries.
-------------------------------------------------
PRESS <RETURN> FOR INSTRUCTIONS, RESEARCH PROVIDERS
AND LEGAL DISCLAIMERS.
```

Now let's get started. Enter IBM to see what Investext can tell us about Big Blue.

```
INVESTEXT                                              PAGE 1 OF 7

                    COMPANY REPORTS

PRESS FOR
  1    24 JAN 86    International Business Machines - Company Report
                    BEAR STEARNS & COMPANY
            BY      Mcmanus, J. 14 PAGES

  2    23 JAN 86    International Business Machines - Company Report
                    SMITH BARNEY, HARRIS UPHAM & CO., INC.
            BY      Haback, H.D., et al 11 PAGES

  3    21 JAN 86    International Business Machines - Company Report
                    DREXEL BURNHAM LAMBERT INCORPORATED
            BY      Labe, P. 14 PAGES

  4     6 JAN 86    International Business Machines - Company Report
                    PERSHING
            BY      Menear, J.F. 8 PAGES

  5     2 JAN 86    International Business Machines - Company Report
                    DONALDSON, LUFKIN & JENRETTE, INC.
            BY      Rooney, T.T. 83 PAGES
```

As you can see, this is a list of recent analysis reports by major observers. Research reports are added to Investext about four to eight weeks after they are released on paper to the clients of investment companies. They remain on Investext about one year. The latest reports always are at the top of the list options. Some lists will be shorter than the seven pages of reports we found here for IBM in February 1986.

Choose report number 1 on your list and we'll choose number 1 on ours. Notice that with the next screen, the report starts with a menu like this one:

```
INVESTEXT 01/24/86                               PAGE 1 OF 1

International Business Machines Corp. - Company Report
BEAR STEARNS & COMPANY

PRESS FOR
  1   ENTIRE REPORT
  2   Stock Price Data and Recommendation 1984-86
  3   Summary and Investment Conclusion
  4   Fourth-Quarter Results
  5   Table I - Fourth-Quarter and Full-Year Results 1984-85
  6   1986/87 Outlook
  7   Table II - Income Statement 1984-86
  8   Table III - Quarterly Earnings Per Share 1984-86
```

Option 1 on nearly every company report in this database lets you scroll through the entire report, pausing at the bottom of each screen page. And most, like this one, are subdivided to give you quick access to pertinent sections if you don't want to read the whole thing. For instance, in our example, if we wanted to see only Bear Stearns & Company's 1986/87 outlook for IBM, we would enter 6.

Let's assume we wanted to see the entire report; enter 1. (Don't worry. You're not going to have to wade through pages of a report you may not be interested in. We'll show you the escape hatch.)

```
INVESTEXT 1/24/86    IBM                    PAGE 1 OF 1


International Business Machines Corp. - Company Report
BEAR STEARNS & COMPANY
Mcmanus, J.


International Business Machines Corp. (IBM - 144)


Continuing Buy Recommendation


1984 EPS:                                        $10.77
1985 EPS:                                        $10.67
1986 EPS Est.:                                   $12.75
P/E 1985:                                         13.5x
P/E 1986 Est.:                                    11.3x
Dividend:                                         $4.40
Yield:                                             3.1%
1985/86 Price Range:                            159-117
Common Shares Out.:                         614,100,000


(Graphic Material Omitted: Stock Chart)
```

From here on out you can examine as many pages of the report as you'd like by pressing RETURN at the bottom of each screen.

Or you can return to the opening Investext menu by using a "local" navigation command (that is, a command available here but not in the system as a whole). The command, which can be used from nearly anywhere in Investext, is one slash and a T. Note that the usual *top* command on DJN/R is simply T; in Investext it is preceded by a slash.

So enter /T and we'll be whisked back to the top menu:

```
                      INVESTEXT
                 COPYRIGHT (C) 1986
           BUSINESS RESEARCH CORPORATION

             COMPANY AND INDUSTRY REPORTS
         FROM TOP BROKERS, INVESTMENT BANKERS
                 AND OTHER ANALYSTS

Enter stock symbol for reports on one of more than
3,000 companies.

Or type INDUSTRY for reports on one of 50 industries.
-----------------------------------------------------
PRESS RETURN FOR INSTRUCTIONS, RESEARCH PROVIDERS AND
LEGAL DISCLAIMERS.
```

We brought you back here for a reason. As this opening page points out, you also can retrieve analyses for an entire group of companies by entering the command INDUSTRY. (Investext has 50 industry groups analyzed.)

Try that. Enter INDUSTRY at the bottom of the opening page. That produces:

```
INVESTEXT                              PAGE 1 OF 5
                  INDUSTRY REPORTS

PRESS  FOR
  1    AEROSPACE
  2    AGRICULTURE
  3    AIR TRANSPORTATION
  4    APPAREL
  5    AUTOMOTIVE
  6    BANKING
  7    BEVERAGES
  8    BROADCASTING/CABLE TV
  9    BUILDING MATERIALS
 10    CHEMICALS
 11    COMPUTERS & OFFICE EQUIPMENT
 12    CONTAINERS & PACKAGING
```

There are five pages of options for industry groups, this being the first. We're interested in the Computers and Office Equipment, number 11 in our example, so enter the number of that option. That should prompt the system to show you:

```
INVESTEXT                                      PAGE 1 OF 22
                    COMPUTERS & OFFICE EQUIPMENT

PRESS  FOR

1  22 JAN 86 Computer-Integrated Manufacturing - Earnings Preview
            PRUDENTIAL BACHE SECURITIES INC.
       BY   Conigliaro, L., et al. 14 PAGES

2  21 JAN 86 Computer-Aided Engineering Industry
            DREXEL BURNHAM LAMBERT INCORPORATED
       BY   Heymann, P.E. 6 PAGES

3  17 JAN 86 High Tech Notes - Industry Report
            PRUDENTIAL BACHE SECURITIES INC.
       BY   Weisberg, M.R., et al. 73 PAGES

4  17 JAN 86 Computer Industry Report
            OPPENHEIMER & CO., INC.
       BY   Elling, G.D., et al. 66 PAGES

5  16 JAN 86 Computer Services - Industry Report
            ALEX. BROWN & SONS
       BY   Berkeley, A.R., et al. 98 PAGES
```

Well now, the computer industry certainly has the attention of the investment analysts; we found 22 pages of reports. Enter 1 to see the latest one. When we did that, we were shown:

```
INVESTEXT 01/22/86                             PAGE 1 OF 1

Computer-Integrated Manufacturing - Earnings Preview
PRUDENTIAL BACHE SECURITIES INC.

PRESS  FOR
  1  ENTIRE REPORT
  2  EPS & Ratings 1984-85: AITX; ATTC; CMZ; CVN; CTCO; DAZY; XLD
  3  Opinion Legend
  4  EPS & Ratings 1984-85: INGR; KMT; MNS; MENT; PDAS; TEK; VLID
  5  Key to the Earnings Surprise Model
  6  Opinion Legend
  7  Disclosure
```

Good—it's the same kind of menu structure you saw when you accessed a report for an individual company. That means you can enter 1 to see the entire report or another option to see just as much as you need. Suppose you wanted to see what the report has to say about Key to the Earnings Surprise Model. Entering that option (number 5 in our example), you'll see something like:

```
INVESTEXT 1/22/86                                    PAGE 1 OF 1

Key to the Earnings Surprise Model:

 • Consensus earnings-per-share estimate is developed by
Prudential-Bache. It comprises two parts: the I/B/E/S consensus
median (for which we thank Lynch, Jones and Ryan) and a trend-line
forecast based on historical earnings.

 • Percentile ranking, by comparing our analyst's forecast with the
consensus, is a barometer of positive or negative earnings surprises.
The numbers around 50 indicate "no surprise." The closer the number
gets to 99, the larger the positive surprise; the closer to 1, the
larger the negative surprise.

PRESS <RETURN> FOR NEXT MENU SELECTION
```

At the end of each section of a report, you have the opportunity to press RETURN to see the next section. If, for example, we wanted to go on to Section 6, we would press RETURN. If we wanted to get back to the top menu, we'd type /T.

And here's another of Investext's "local" commands: if we wanted to get back to the previous menu, that is, the menu for this complete report, we could type /M (the same as Dow Jones News/Retrieval's usual command, except that it's preceded by a slash).

Feel free to explore the report a little further. When you're ready to move on, continue reading.

"THE WORD" FROM STANDARD & POOR'S

If you were to go to a broker and ask for a report on an unfamiliar stock, it's likely one of the first things he or she would do is check to see what Standard & Poor's says about it.

The name Standard & Poor's is magic in the world of securities, and you can get the latest word from the company on more than 4,600 stocks on DJN/R. To get to the Standard & Poor's Online area, enter //SP to see the following top page.

```
(S&P) 3/07/86                               PAGE 1 OF 1
S&P Online Top Menu
            S&P Online Copyright (C) 1986
            Standard & Poor's Corporation
                All Rights Reserved

Enter Stock Symbol for Company Profiles
                      -or-
Press  For:
 1 Understanding S&P Online
 2 S&P Footnote Explanations
------------------------------------------------------
If you have not used S&P Online in the last month,
press return to see the current disclaimers. Any
other entry assumes you are aware of disclaimers.
```

At the bottom of this page you could enter the IBM symbol to see the menu of information about the company. However, if you need to find a symbol, Standard & Poor's has a nifty function which allows you to search for the symbol of a company without leaving S&P and going to the //SYMBOL database. To see how it works, enter /C at the prompt to see:

```
                ENTER COMPANY NAME
```

Just as in the //SYMBOL area, the more of the name you can enter the better. Enter INTERNATIONAL BUSINESS MACHINES at this prompt and you'll see:

```
PRESS FOR

1 *INTERNATIONAL BUSINESS MACHINES CORP.
-----------------------------------------------------
OR ENTER ANOTHER NAME OR /T FOR TOP
```

Had you entered less of the IBM name such as simply "International," you might have received more menu options. In this case, though, you probably received one option as we did. Choose 1 to see the top menu of IBM data.

```
(S&P) 3/07/86  (IBM)                    PAGE 1 OF 1

Int'l Business Machines

PRESS FOR

  1 SUMMARY
  2 OUTLOOK
  3 LINE-OF-BUSINESS RESULTS
  4 EARNINGS PER SHARE
  5 DIVIDENDS PER SHARE
  6 MARKET ACTION
  7 FINANCIAL OVERVIEW
```

The information for nearly all company reports in S&P is divided into the topics you see above. As with many other databases on Dow Jones, you can choose any of these numbers to see a specific piece of information, or you can choose 1 and keep pressing RETURN at the bottom of every page to scroll through all the sections. Let's do that. Enter 1 to see the summary.

```
(S&P) 2/28/86  (IBM)                    PAGE 1 OF 1

Int'l Business Machines: SUMMARY

World's largest maker of computers and info.
processing equipment . . . Holds 19% of Intel Corp.,
semiconductor manufacturer . . . Co. likely to become
increasingly aggressive in scientific/technical
```

```
markets . . . '86 earnings to recover sharply,
reflecting first full year of shipments of new
high-end mainframe & strong demand for personal
computers.
```

Since S&P information is constantly being updated, the information on your screen will probably look different. Notice too that the date the information was posted in the database appears on the top line of every page.

Now to go on to the next section, Outlook, it's not necessary to return to the IBM menu. Simply press RETURN.

```
(S&P) 2/28/86  (IBM)                    PAGE 1 OF 1
Int'l Business Machines

Outlook: '86 EPS seen at $12.50 vs. '85's $10.67
. . . Quarterly dividend of $1.10 minimum expected.
```

Most of the reports from S&P are quite short, making a trip to this database less time-consuming than others. To see the IBM product lines, press RETURN again.

```
(S&P) 2/28/86  (IBM)                    PAGE 1 OF 1
Int'l Business Machines: LINES

 Gross Revenues                          1984   1983
Processors and peripherals ...........    51%    54%
Programs/maintenance/other ...........    24%    23%
Office products ......................    21%    20%
Federal systems ......................     4%     3%

 Tel. #914-765-1900
```

Press RETURN again to see earnings-per-share information.

```
(S&P) 3/07/86   (IBM)                      PAGE 1 OF 1
           Int'l Business Machines

       --------- EARNINGS PER SHARE ---------

                                           . . . . .
       ...Prev. Yr.                        . . . . .
       Last 12 Mos                         10.67
       P/E                                 13.7
       5 Yr. Growth %                      +16
```

It's possible that you might see some disconnected lowercase letters in one or more of these displays. At first glance, it might appear as if they are typographical errors. They aren't. They are footnotes. To see what these footnotes mean, enter the footnote letter that's listed in parentheses at the bottom of the page. Then to return to the display, press RETURN again.

You can see an explanation of the footnotes by choosing number 2 from the opening S&P menu. Better yet, a list of the footnotes and their explanations can be found on page 339 of the Online Survival Kit.

Right now press RETURN again to see information about IBM dividends.

```
(S&P) 3/07/86   (IBM)                      PAGE 1 OF 1
Int'l Business Machines

       --------- DIVIDENDS PER SHARE ---------

       Rate                                4.40
       Yield                               3.0%
       Last Div. Q                         1.100
       Ex-Date                             02/07
       PayDate                          03/10/86
```

By the way, if you're unfamiliar with any of the terms you see in S&P, or the way S&P uses the terms, you can read their definitions in the Online Survival Kit on page 337. Now on to the next page of information. Press RETURN.

```
(S&P)  3/07/86  (IBM)                          PAGE  1  OF  2
Int'l Business Machines

         ----------- MARKET ACTION ------------

      1986 Range
       High                               161.00
       Low                                143.00
       Average Daily Volume              1860900
       Beta                                   .8
       Institutional Holdings              50%
       Primary Exchange                   NYSE
```

Here's where you're likely to find two pages of information. Press RE-TURN to see the second page.

```
(S&P)  3/07/86  (IBM)                          PAGE  2  OF  2
Int'l Business Machines

           ----------- MARKET ACTION ------------
           -------- CALENDAR YEAR HISTORY --------

Yr          High        Low     PE    Range      Div
85        158.75     117.38    14.9    11.0      4.40
84        128.50      99.00    11.9     9.2      4.10
83        134.25      92.25    14.9    10.2      3.71
82         98.00      55.62    13.3     7.5      3.44
```

Now, for the final section on IBM, press RETURN.

```
(S&P) 3/07/86  (IBM)                    PAGE 1 OF 2
Int'l Business Machines

          --------- FINANCIAL OVERVIEW ---------
          --------- FISCAL YEAR HISTORY --------

                                         Book
Fiscal                                   Value
Year                              Net     Per
Dec           EPS  Revenue Income       Share
85          10.67  50056.06555.0        51.96
84          10.77  45937.06582.0        43.22
83           9.04  40180.05485.0        38.01
82           7.39  34364.04409.0        33.13

     (Revenue and net income in millions)
-----------------------------------------------------
```

To get to page 2—you got it—press RETURN.

```
(S&P) 3/07/86  (IBM)                    PAGE 2 OF 2
Int'l Business Machines

          --------- FINANCIAL OVERVIEW ---------
          ----------- BALANCE SHEET -----------

          Current Ratio          2.28
          Long Term Debt      3955.00
          Shares               615.41
          Report of         12/31/85

     (Long term debt and Shares in millions)
```

We're at the final page of information about IBM, but press RETURN one more time to see some instructions.

```
FINAL PAGE IN THIS SECTION

PRESS   FOR
 /T      TOP MENU OF //SP
 /M      PREVIOUS MENU OF //SP

THEN PRESS <RETURN>
```

If you entered /T at this point, you'd go back to the S&P "front door," where you could request information about another stock. If you wanted to go back to the top of the IBM menu to look at your choices again, a /M would do it.

If you wanted to go to another database from here, you could do that too. And that's what we're going to do.

CORPORATE EARNINGS ESTIMATOR

Successful investors look both ways before they commit their money to a security. They look back in time, at how the company has performed (using resources like the //HQ Historical Quotes database from the last chapter), and into the future, by way of estimates of those who've made names for themselves predicting such things.

On DJN/R, Zacks Investment Research Inc. offers predictions through a service called the Corporate Earnings Estimator. To get there, enter //EARN and that should bring you to a menu like this one:

```
          CORPORATE EARNINGS ESTIMATOR
          ZACKS INVESTMENT RESEARCH INC.
               CHICAGO, ILL.

THIS WEEKLY DATABASE PROVIDES CONSENSUS FORECASTS
OF EARNINGS PER SHARE FOR 3,000 COMPANIES BASED ON
ESTIMATES PROVIDED BY 1,000 RESEARCH ANALYSTS AT
MORE THAN 60 MAJOR BROKERAGE FIRMS. FOR CONSISTENCY,
```

```
ESTIMATES ARE CONVERTED TO PRIMARY EARNINGS BEFORE
EXTRAORDINARY ITEMS.
```

```
PLEASE ENTER DESIRED STOCK SYMBOL AND PRESS <RETURN>
```

Well done, Mr. Zacks. This is a concise description of what the service offers: the consensus of a thousand researchers at some 60 brokerage houses, thinking about 3,000 different companies.

Once again, the stock symbols used here can be obtained in the //SYMBOL database. Suppose we've just visited there again and returned with the surprising news that "IBM" is the symbol for IBM. Enter IBM and see the first page of //EARN's report:

```
-FISCAL YEAR ENDS 12/86

EARNINGS PER SHARE ESTIMATE
-MEAN   12.65
-HIGH   13.50
-LOW    11.75
NUMBER OF ANALYSTS 33
P/E RATIO (ESTIMATED EPS) 12.25

PAST EARN PR SH ESTIMATES (MEAN)
  WEEK AGO   12.66
  13 WEEKS AGO   12.80
  26 WEEKS AGO   12.92
- - - - - - - - - - - - - - - - - - - - - - - - - - - - - - - - - -
PRESS <RETURN> FOR NEXT PAGE
```

Your screen is different, of course, but the information is presented in the same order as in our example, where we find that the predictions of 33 analysts were averaged to produce the mean earnings-per-share estimate for fiscal year 1986, which ends December 31. In addition, you see the highest EPS estimate among the 33 thinkers as well as the lowest.

It also provides a little historical perspective of its own—the analysts' mean estimate of a week ago, 13 weeks ago, and a half year ago.

Press RETURN to see the next page.

```
-FISCAL YEAR ENDS 12/87

EARNINGS PER SHARE ESTIMATES
-MEAN   14.87
-HIGH   15.50
-LOW    14.40
NUMBER OF ANALYSTS 4
P/E RATIO (ESTIMATED EPS) 10.42


PAST EARN PR SH ESTIMATES (MEAN)
-WEEK AGO   14.97
-13 WEEKS AGO   14.50
-26 WEEKS AGO   N/A
PLEASE ENTER DESIRED STOCK SYMBOL AND PRESS <RETURN>
```

Page 2 contains a summary of what the analysts have to say about the next fiscal year, in this case 1987. Notice in our example that only four analysts made predictions about 1987. Also notice that 26 weeks before we got our example, no analysts were making any predictions that far in advance.

The bottom of the page says to enter the desired stock symbol and press RETURN. If we wanted to check another stock, we could do that and retrieve a similar concise report on each company.

If you have other companies you want to check on, do it now. We'll wait. If you've forgotten their stock codes, enter //SYMBOL to make a quick check of that database, then //EARN to return here.

When you're ready to press on, we'll wrap up the tour with our first look at the powerful DISCLOSURE ONLINE database.

NEWS FROM THE SEC

Remember back in Chapter 4 when we took time out for some scenarios of how some people use all these databases in concert with each other? We pointed out it was often useful to see the information that public companies file about themselves.

Of course, the clearinghouse for such reports is the Securities and Exchange Commission, which collects all kinds of documents about publicly traded firms, from annual reports to messages from other stockholders to information about future projects. An investor planning a major financial commitment to a company often needs to know what the SEC knows about it.

Online, you can search through SEC filings with DISCLOSURE ONLINE. To get there, enter //DSCLO and see this introduction.

```
              DISCLOSURE ONLINE
              COPYRIGHT (C) 1986
              DISCLOSURE INC.

FINANCIAL, MANAGEMENT AND DETAILED OWNERSHIP INFORMATION
ON PUBLIC CORPORATIONS

NOTE: THERE IS A $6 PRIME-TIME ACCESS CHARGE FOR EACH COM-
PANY REPORT; $2 IN NON-PRIME TIME. THERE ARE ADDITIONAL
ACCESS CHARGES FOR DETAILED OWNERSHIP INFORMATION.
```

```
TO CONTINUE, ENTER COMPANY STOCK SYMBOL AND PRESS <RETURN>
```

By now you know the company and the symbol. Enter IBM to put //DSCLO to work. It displays something like this:

```
DISCLOSURE                    INTERNATIONAL BUSINESS MACHINES CORP

PRESS  FOR                    PRESS  FOR
  1 CORPORATE PROFILE          12 OWNERSHIP SUMMARY AND SUBSIDIARIES
  2 5-YEAR SUMMARY DATA        13 DETAILED OWNERSHIP INFORMATION:
  3 LINE OF BUSINESS DATA         INSTITUTIONAL, INSIDER AND 5%
  4 BALANCE SHEETS FOR 2 YEARS 14 OTHER CORPORATE EVENTS
  5 QUARTERLY BALANCE SHEETS   15 MANAGMENT DISCUSSION
  6 INCOME STATEMENTS FOR 3 YEARS 16 PRESIDENT'S LETTER
  7 QUARTERLY INCOME STATEMENTS 17 FULL CORPORATE RECORD (1-16 EXCEPT
  8 SOURCES AND USES OF FUNDS     DETAILED OWNERSHIP INFORMATION)
  9 FINANCIAL RATIOS           18 2-YR LIST OF REPORTS ON FILE
 10 WEEKLY PRICE-EARNINGS DATA    WITH THE SEC AND EXHIBITS
 11 OFFICERS AND DIRECTORS     99 ORDERING FULL TEXTS OF REPORTS
```

Lots of possibilities here. Let's pay particular attention to how this menu is organized. Option 1 gives pertinent information about this company in the form of a profile. Options 2 through 16 contain information gleaned from other public filings with the SEC. Option 17 will give you everything—the full corporate record—except for Option 13, which is a detailed report on institutions and insiders who own five percent or more of the company's stock. Option 18 gives you a two-year list of reports on file with the SEC as well as company exhibits. If you entered 99, you would get information on how to obtain the full printed text of SEC reports from the providers of DISCLOSURE ONLINE.

Option 1 should give us a taste of what //DSCLO has to offer. Enter 1 for the first page of a company profile of IBM.

```
DISCLOSURE                         INTERNATIONAL BUSINESS
MACHINES CORP
DISCLOSURE CO NO: 1510600000
COMPANY NAME: INTERNATIONAL BUSINESS MACHINES CORP
CROSS REFERENCE: NA
ADDRESS: NA
ARMONK
NY
10504
TELEPHONE: 914-765-1900
INCORPORATION: NY
EXCHANGE: NYS
TICKER SYMBOL: IBM
FORTUNE NUMBER: 0006
FORBES NUMBER: SA006 AS017 PR001 MV001
CUSIP NUMBER: 0004592002
D-U-N-S NO: 00-136-8083
SIC CODES: 3573 3572 3579 3679 3861 7379
PRIMARY SIC CODE: 3573
DESCRIPTION OF BUSINESS:
MANUFACTURES DATA PROCESSING EQUIPMENT AND SYSTEMS IN
THE INFORMATION-HANDLING FIELD, ENCOMPASSING
INFORMATION-HANDLING SYSTEMS, EQUIPMENT AND SERVICES
TO SOLVE THE INCREASINGLY COMPLEX PROBLEMS OF
```

There's much more; press RETURN to see additional pages, if you'd like. After that, to back up a page, use the R command you've already met.

Or if you wanted to see other pertinent documents about IBM, enter their menu number, such as 2 for the 5-Year Summary, or 4 for the Balance Sheets for 2 years, and so forth.

A note about the costs of using DISCLOSURE ONLINE: As of this writing, a subscriber was charged an access fee *each time* he or she entered a company symbol. That means that if you become a regular //DSCLO user, it's a good idea to keep a main menu handy for selecting options rather than entering a company stock symbol just to view the menu online again. Here's a rerun of that main menu:

```
DISCLOSURE                         INTERNATIONAL BUSINESS MACHINES CORP

PRESS  FOR                         PRESS  FOR
  1 CORPORATE PROFILE               12 OWNERSHIP SUMMARY AND SUBSIDIARIES
  2 5-YEAR SUMMARY DATA             13 DETAILED OWNERSHIP INFORMATION:
  3 LINE OF BUSINESS DATA              INSTITUTIONAL, INSIDER AND 5%
  4 BALANCE SHEETS FOR 2 YEARS      14 OTHER CORPORATE EVENTS
  5 QUARTERLY BALANCE SHEETS        15 MANAGEMENT DISCUSSION
  6 INCOME STATEMENTS FOR 3 YEARS   16 PRESIDENT'S LETTER
  7 QUARTERLY INCOME STATEMENTS     17 FULL CORPORATE RECORD (1-16 EXCEPT
  8 SOURCES AND USES OF FUNDS          DETAILED OWNERSHIP INFORMATION)
  9 FINANCIAL RATIOS                18 2-YR LIST OF REPORTS ON FILE
 10 WEEKLY PRICE-EARNINGS DATA         WITH THE SEC AND EXHIBITS
 11 OFFICERS AND DIRECTORS          99 ORDERING FULL TEXTS OF REPORTS
```

At this point, all the reports you access from //DSCLO deal with IBM. To switch to another security, simply enter a new stock code at the bottom of any page. For example, if you now wanted to look up the SEC documents filed by Gannett Co., Inc., you would first enter the stock symbol GCI at the bottom of any page to get to the Gannett Menu.

But note this about symbols. Remember when we used //SYMBOL in the last chapter, you learned that occasionally you can find listings with a D. prefix? We told you that the D. identified symbols used in DISCLOSURE ONLINE. In other words, DISCLOSURE ONLINE has a few unique symbols, so it would be a good idea to get into the habit of checking //SYMBOL *before* looking up a new company in //DSCLO.

When you're finished, end the tour by entering DISC.

SUMMING UP

In this chapter we were exposed to some strong analysis features, including some big names in the business, such as Standard & Poor's and the Securities and Exchange Commission.

We also learned a variation on the system navigation commands. Some features, notably Investext and Standard & Poor's, use /T and /M for "top" and "previous menu." That's because T and M standing alone could be interpreted in those databases as stock symbols, so the database is programmed to recognize the slash sign (/) as a prefix for a navigation command.

In the next chapter we'll go into a little more depth about what we've seen in this tour. We'll be discussing a couple of other services that investors can use to make their decisions.

Chapter 7

MORE ABOUT INVESTMENT TOOLS

The last chapter was a whirlwind tour designed to give you an overview of several of the most important investment databases on the Dow Jones system.

This time around we'll stay offline to go into greater depth about them as well as to introduce you to a few new utilities that can help you ride the bulls and bait the bears on Wall Street.

We'll:

• Learn some ways to use Media General's database for more specific information, along with some shortcuts.

• Put //EARN and //INVEST in perspective.

• Pick up some more details on the DISCLOSURE ONLINE system.

• Meet a feature designed to help you plan your strategies in the money market.

• And even find a handy online dictionary of financial terms.

MEDIA GENERAL'S INDUSTRY GROUPS

When we toured Media General Financial Services last time, we observed that //MG actually gave us more information than we asked for. You'll recall that when we entered the symbol for IBM, the database provided the statistics for that company *along with* figures for the computer industry group as a whole. That made for easy comparison.

However, there are times when you might want a summary of only an industry group rather than a specific company. That's an easy chore for //MG. All you have to do is enter a three-digit industry group code for the sector you're interested in. For example, the //MG code for the Computers, Systems and Peripherals industry happens to be the number 170. On the tour, had we entered 170 rather than IBM at //MG's ENTER QUERY prompt, Media General would have provided only the statistics for the entire group.

Media General has summaries for hundreds of industries, each accessible with its own three-digit code. When you're online, you can search for the Media General codes you need by using an option in the //SYMBOL database.

This idea of industry groups—summarizing an entire sector of related companies—is not a new one to you. You saw the same concept at work when you explored Investext and used its INDUSTRY command. That allowed you to gather analyses on any of 50 different business groups. In later chapters we'll see some examples of how Dow Jones News/Retrieval allows you to take a broad view of an entire industry. For instance, when we begin learning about DJN/R's business news features, you'll use the system to keep tabs on what's hot in specific industries and even specific departments of the government by using codes that are different in appearance but work the same way.

//MG VS. //MEDGEN

Speaking of Media General, remember that we said there are actually *two* versions of the database online? The one we visited with the //MG command is the newer version, which we recommend for general use because it provides that nifty automatic comparison with industry group statistics.

However, some subscribers still prefer the older version, which you can reach by entering //MEDGEN. The original version is particularly popular with subscribers whose computer screens are fewer than 80 characters wide. That's because //MEDGEN, unlike //MG, presents the information in pages of lines no longer than 32 characters, which can be displayed easily on most computers.

While the actual data provided by //MG and //MEDGEN are the same, there are some other differences in presentation. For instance, in //MEDGEN:

• The information can be displayed for a company or for an industry group but not on the same screen, side by side.

• The information is organized in a slightly different order on the pages.

• Stock symbols or industry codes must be followed by one slash and the letter F for "fundamental information" or the letter P for "price and volume information."

This last item is the most striking difference. For example, let's say we had accessed Media General by entering the //MEDGEN command to look up information on IBM. At the bottom of the introductory page we would have entered IBM/F to get what Media General considers the "fundamental" information about IBM. Here's what we might have seen:

```
INTERNATL BUSINESS MACH
-FUNDMNTL DATA- 02/14/86 (170)
REVENUE          (1)
-LAST 12 MOS $50,056 MIL
-LAST FISCAL YEAR $45,937 MIL
-PCT CHANGE LAST QTR 18.3%
-PCT CHANGE YR TO DATE 9.0%
EARNGS 12MOS $6,555.OF MIL
EARNINGS PER SHARE
-LAST 12 MONTHS $10.67
-LAST FISCAL YEAR $10.67
-PCT CHANGE LAST QTR 22.8%
-PCT CHANGE FY TO DATE -0.9%
-PCT CHANGE LAST 12MOS -0.9%
-FIVE YR GROWTH RATE 14.0%
```

The report is for IBM only, not for the computer industry group. Note, however, that the industry group code, 170, is included in parentheses at the top of the page as a reference point in case you wished to pursue the industry research.

If you pressed RETURN, you'd see the second page of fundamental data about IBM.

```
DIVIDENDS         (2)
-CURRENT RATE $4.40
-CURRENT RATE YIELD 2.8%
-5 YR GROWTH RATE 5.0%
-PAYOUT LAST FY 41%
-PAYOUT LAST 5 YEARS 43%
-LAST X-DVD DATE 02-07-86
RATIOS
-PROFIT MARGIN 13.1%
-RETURN ON COMMON EQUITY 24.8%
-RETURN ON TOTAL ASSETS 15.3%
-REVENUE TO ASSETS 117%
-DEBT TO EQUITY 12%
-INTEREST COVERAGE 29.4
-CURRENT RATIO 2.1
```

Pressing another RETURN results in display of the final page:

```
SHAREHOLDINGS     (3)
-MARKET VALUE $96,068 MIL
-LTST SHR OUTSTND 614,837,000
-INSIDER NET TRADING -2,000
-SHORT INTEREST RATIO 2.0 DYS
-FISCAL YEAR ENDS 12 MOS
```

At the end of this page, or of any page in the database, you can retrieve IBM price and volume information by typing IBM/P. You would see something like this:

```
INTERNATL BUSINESS MACH
-PRICE & VOLUME- 02/14/86 (170)

PRICE CHANGE(1)
-LAST TRDNG WK 0.3%
-LAST 4 WKS 3.6%
-LAST 13 WKS 14.3%
-LAST 52 WKS 18.9%
-YR TO DATE 0.5%
CHANGE VS. S & P 500
-LAST TRDNG WK 98%
-LAST 4 WKS 98%
-LAST 13 WKS 103%
-LAST 52 WKS 98%
-YR TO DATE 97%
```

You'd press RETURN to see the second page.

```
PRICE RANGE      (2)
-LAST CLOSE $156.25
-52 WEEK HIGH $158.75
-52 WEEK LOW $117.38
-5 YEAR HIGH $158.75
-5 YEAR LOW $48.38
RELATIVE PRICE
-P/E RATIO CURRENT 14.6
-P/E RATIO 5 YR AVG HI 13.3
-P/E RATIO 5 YR AVG LOW 9.2
-PRICE TO COMMON EQUITY 361%
-PRICE TO REV PER SHARE 192%
-RELATIVE PRICE INDEX 126%
```

A third RETURN displays the final page:

```
PRICE ACTION     (3)
-BETAS UP 1.09
-BETAS DOWN 0.66
VOLUME
-THIS WK SHRS 7,583,000
-THIS WK DOLLAR $1,184,069,000
-THIS WK % SHRS OUTSTND 1.23%
-LIQUIDITY RATIO 47,899,000
-ON BALANCE INDEX 144
```

In //MEDGEN you also can use the /F and /P commands after an industry code to get the same material about an entire business sector. Since we already know that the computer industry is group 170, we could pick up fundamental data for that sector by entering 170/F at the bottom of any page in Media General to see something like this:

```
COMPUTER,SYS.,PERIPH.
-FUNDMNTL DATA- 02/14/86
REVENUE         (1)
-LAST 12 MOS $115,938 MIL
-LAST FISCAL YEAR $113,458 MIL
-PCT CHANGE LAST QTR -3.0%
-PCT CHANGE YR TO DATE 8.0%
EARNINGS 12MOS $7,375.6 MIL
EARNINGS PER SHARE
-LAST 12 MONTHS $2.25
-LAST FISCAL YEAR $2.83
-PCT CHANGE LAST QTR 14.5%
-PCT CHANGE FY TO DATE -12.7%
-PCT CHANGE LAST 12MOS -20.2%
-FIVE YR GROWTH RATE 6.0%
```

And so on. To find the price and volume information for 170, enter 170/P:

```
COMPUTERS,SYS.,PERIPH.
-PRICE & VOLUME- 02/14/86

PRICE CHANGE        (1)
-LAST TRDNG WK 1.1%
-LAST 4 WKS 4.4%
-LAST 13 WKS 17.0%
-LAST 52 WKS 14.3%
-YR TO DATE 3.7%
CHANGE VS. S & P 500
-LAST TRDNG WK 99%
-LAST 4 WKS 99%
-LAST 13 WKS 106%
-LAST 52 WKS 94%
-YR TO DATE 100%
```

The bottom line is this: //MG and //MEDGEN provide the same information. //MG makes a few assumptions for you: it automatically provides comparable industry group figures if you look up an individual company, and it automatically provides fundamental and pricing information in its five-page report. On the other hand, //MEDGEN can be useful if you have a narrow screen display on your computer or you want to zero in quickly on very specific information such as pricing in a particular industry group.

WHAT DOES IT MEAN AND HOW DO YOU USE IT?

Some of the statistics you'll see in the Media General database (whether you use //MG or //MEDGEN) are easy to understand, particularly in the area of fundamental data. However, other data are "extracted information," derived from using complex ratios and formulas. You'll find an explanation of terms used in Media General in the Online Survival Kit, beginning on page 332.

As far as using the information is concerned, there are many applications because the system is designed to help serious individual investors and the professional investment managers with decision making. For example:

• If you are looking for a steady source of income from stock dividends, you might access Media General to look at such things as the current dividend rate on a stock (in the Current Rate entries), the yield, calculated according to that rate (Current Yield), the percentage of earnings paid as dividends in the most recent fiscal year (Payout Last FY), the percentage of earnings paid out as dividends over the last five fiscal years (Payout Last 5 Years), and the most recent deadline for purchasing shares in order to be eligible to collect the next quarterly dividend (Last X-Dvd Date).

• On the other hand, if you're more interested in capital gains, you might look for stocks with low price earnings or price/revenue ratios or a high five-year growth rate.

Of course, no database on the system is a miracle worker. "If there were any guarantees in the stock market, who wouldn't be a millionaire?" Michael Buettner, an assistant to the editor of the *Media General Financial Weekly* wrote in a recent issue of *Dowline* magazine. "However, by performing a little fundamental analysis, we've done a great deal to reduce our risk and enhance our potential profit," he added, "and one thing is for certain. It's better than throwing darts at a newspaper."

//INVEST-ING ON DOW JONES NEWS/RETRIEVAL

Smart investing, like smart business in general, means not taking all your advice from a single source. That's why on the tour we followed Media General with a sample of the resources of Investext, and you undoubtedly saw what a gold mine it can be for the investor. Unless you deal with 25 or 30 brokerage houses with research services, there's no way you can get the information that's available from a single foray into Investext.

The Business Research Corp. of Boston gathers some 13,000 full-text analyst reports from a variety of Wall Street firms, regional firms, and foreign firms for its online investment service.

But here's a secret—there's more available in //INVEST than simply investment information. In fact, it's also a great place to go for "business intelligence," that is, keeping track of what the competition is doing and how the analysts say the competition will be doing in the future.

For instance, included in Investext's troves are hundreds of reports about many of the 12,000 stocks traded over-the-counter in the United States. If you've ever tried to find analyst reports on these OTC stocks, you know how frustrating it can be.

The Unlisted Market Service obtains financial statements and annual reports from a company with OTC stock, then supplements that information with management interviews. Analysts distill the data and present them in reports which include:

- A description of the company's business.

- Stock price data for the previous 12 months.

- A detailed three-year income statement.

- A comprehensive two-year balance sheet.

- Data on the company's last underwriting and long-term debt situation.

- Current officers.

- Names and phone numbers of the company's market makers.

Some of the best stock buys in recent years have been in the OTC market, and with Investext you have the opportunity to investigate the possibilities in this fertile area.

WHAT'S SO HOT ABOUT //EARN?

A share of stock, like most other tradable instruments, is worth only what traders say it's worth. When it comes to securities, though, the opinions of some traders are more important than the opinions of others.

According to Leonard Zacks, founder of Zacks Investment Research Service, which has provided the Corporate Earnings Estimator online since 1981, the average analyst at a brokerage firm probably is responsible for following 20 or 25 companies. "His whole job revolves around understanding everything about those firms," Zacks says. "He meets with management on a regular basis. He talks to suppliers, he talks to customers, he goes on plant tours, he reads everything printed by the company. Analysts are the most knowledgeable people in the United States about their twenty assigned companies."

It's little wonder, then, that when an analyst talks about a company, everyone listens. And when those people take the analyst's advice, the price of a stock is affected, sometimes dramatically. Institutional investors listen intently to analysts and these institutional investors have a profound effect on the market. Stock prices are determined by investor expectations, particularly the expectations of the big investors.

It's little wonder, then, that the Corporate Earnings Estimator can be an important tool in making decisions about stock purchases. It makes available to the general public information that previously was available only to the big investors. //EARN takes the opinions of many analysts, arrives at an "average opinion," and presents it in an easy-to-read and quickly accessible form.

In fact, even when the analysts are wrong, the Corporate Earnings Estimator can be important. If the stock performs differently during a quarter from what the analysts have predicted, the result is the so-called "quarterly surprise," which can have a dramatic and immediate effect on the price of the stock, Zacks notes.

Thus, using the estimator in conjunction with other investment programs such as Media General can round out your investment strategy.

DISCLOSURE ONLINE: WHERE'S THAT FILING?

It's October 2 and a company you've had your eye on for six months ended its fiscal year on September 30.

You enter the DISCLOSURE ONLINE database on Dow Jones to get a look at the company's management and financial position at year's end. After all, it's supposed to file a 10-K report with the Securities and Exchange Commission at the end of its fiscal year, and DISCLOSURE ONLINE gets its information from SEC filings.

Then why is there no year-end information online yet?

According to Susan Wilner, a documentation editor at Disclosure, Inc., the owners of DISCLOSURE ONLINE, there could be several reasons.

As soon as a company filing is made at the SEC, that document is delivered to Disclosure, Inc., usually within 24 to 48 hours. A list of these documents from which Disclosure gets its information for the database can be found in the Online Survival Kit.

However, the SEC allows companies a maximum of 90 days after the end of the fiscal year to file the 10-K report. Thus, the company could wait until December 30 before filing the report and still be within the time limit.

Ms. Wilner reports that it can take up to six weeks for Disclosure to extract information and post it on the database. However, within five to ten days after the document is received, news of its availability is posted online in section 17 of the company's menu under the heading, 2 YR LIST OF REPORTS ON FILE WITH THE SEC.

If you're in a hurry to see the year-end information, you can order it directly from Disclosure, Inc., on paper as soon as it's available.

If you're not sure whether Disclosure has received a company's 10-K report or any other report, or if you want to check to see if a company's full online record has been updated, you can call Disclosure at 800-638-8076.

If you want to get the full text of documents from the Disclosure Demand Center, call toll-free 800-638-8241 and tell them you are a Dow Jones News/ Retrieval subscriber. Option 99 from the report menu in DISCLOSURE ONLINE will give you more information about ordering full-text reports.

MMS: MONEY IDEAS GALORE

Since money is the fuel that powers all our businesses, forecasts about money—its availability and its current value—get a top priority in the investment community. Money Market Services, Inc., offers a weekly economic and foreign exchange survey which you can reach by entering //MMS.

The MMS database is simple to use. It always contains five sections.

Section 1 provides an analysis of the U.S. economy and money matters. Each week between 40 and 50 dealers at leading financial institutions are questioned about such things as money supply, the unemployment rate, the federal funds rate, the consumer price index, the producer price index, and retail sales.

The second section includes median forecasts of monetary and economic indicators and compares the current survey's results with the previous week's actual figure on the same indicators after they have been released by the government.

In Section 3 are charts showing the distribution of the forecasts by those queried. It shows the number of participants in the survey, the median range, and related information.

Section 4 is a text presentation of foreign exchange forecasts and analysis. Each week about 35 foreign exchange dealers are surveyed, with two major topics being covered on alternate weeks. For example, one week the dealers will analyze the Eurodeposit market and the next week they'll concentrate on the two-week and three-month estimates of exchange rates.

The last section contains charts showing the forecasts of foreign exchange rates similar to Section 3's charts of U.S. forecasts.

Incidentally, if you intend to read the bar charts in Sections 3 and 5, it's best to have a screen that displays 80 columns or a printer that can print 80 columns.

DEFINING THE WORDS OF WALL STREET

It's easy to get lost in the language of Wall Street. It's likely that from time to time you'll run into terms online that you simply don't understand. When that happens, it's time to //DEFINE.

That's the way you get to a special DJN/R service that offers definitions of more than 2,000 business and financial terms.

If you enter //DEFINE from the bottom of almost any page in the system, you'll be taken to a menu like this:

```
              WORDS OF WALL STREET
        A DICTIONARY OF INVESTMENT TERMS
        COPYRIGHT (C) 1986 DOW JONES-IRWIN

ENTER THE WORD, PHRASE OR ACRONYM FOR WHICH YOU ARE
SEEKING A DEFINITION. FOR EXAMPLE, YOU CAN:

ENTER     CHICAGO MERCANTILE
   OR     MERC
   OR     CME

TO FIND CHICAGO MERCANTILE EXCHANGE

ENTER REQUEST
```

You can then enter the word or phrase for a definition. It's not necessary to enter the entire word or phrase. Enter only as much of it as you know. If there's more than one term beginning with the same letters or words, a menu will appear. You press the number of the definition you want.

At the bottom of the definition you've requested, you can enter another word or phrase to be defined.

LOOKING AHEAD

This chapter and the previous two have given you the lowdown on Dow Jones News/Retrieval's wealth of resources for raw financial information and told you where to turn for analysis of those data. If you were an investor, you could use these tools before a visit to your broker. In fact, since late 1985 Dow Jones subscribers have not even had to leave their keyboards to visit a broker. In the next chapter you will see how you can use the system to order and sell stocks online.

Looking ahead, after that we'll change course and learn about a different kind of vital business information—using Dow Jones to track the daily news.

Chapter 8

BUYING STOCKS (AND MORE) ONLINE

Now that you've seen the power and potential of Dow Jones News/Retrieval for getting what you need to compete in the business world, it's time to show you the service's "ace in the hole."

It would be ironic if you could learn so much about stocks and not be able to convert your decisions into action with the same electronic medium.

That used to be the case, but no more. These days, using a relatively new DJN/R feature, you can actually buy and sell securities right from your keyboard. The service is provided by Fidelity Brokerage Services, Inc., a Boston firm that in 1979 became the first major financial organization to offer discount brokerage services.

Once you establish an account with Fidelity, you can use News/Retrieval to buy and sell stocks the same way you would with any other broker—except that you can communicate with your electronic broker nearly any time of the day or night. If, for example, you have a vision at 2:00 A.M. to buy a certain stock, there's no need to wait until daybreak to place an order. You can do it when the spirit moves you (except between the hours of 4:00 and 6:00 A.M., Eastern Time, when Dow Jones News/Retrieval is taken offline for routine maintenance).

And if the market isn't open when you place your order? No problem—the order will be there for Fidelity to receive and execute as soon as the market opens.

Regular per-minute Dow Jones charges do not apply to Fidelity Investor's EXPRESS. Fidelity rates are generally lower. A one-time signup fee is charged, $49.95 at this writing.

REACHING THE BROKER

The command for locating Fidelity on Dow Jones is //FIDELITY. Even if you don't have an account with Fidelity, the host firm invites you to "come in" and look around.

The opening page of the Fidelity service looks like this:

```
                    WELCOME TO
              FIDELITY INVESTMENTS

           INVESTOR'S EXPRESS SERVICE

           ONLINE INVESTMENT SERVICES

          Personal Portfolio Accounting
          Order Entry for Stocks and Options

           SPECIAL INFORMATION SERVICES

          Brokerage and Mutual Fund Services
          Best Selling and New Mutual Funds
                IRA and Keogh Services

          Enter your Master Account Number
            or Press <RETURN> to Continue
```

If you are already a Fidelity subscriber, here is where you would enter the "master account number" the brokerage has provided you, after which you'd be admitted to a special area for Fidelity customers. It's in that area that you can buy and sell stocks, maintain one or more portfolios, and exchange electronic mail with Fidelity Investment employees in service centers throughout the United States.

If you don't have a master account number with Fidelity, you still have the option of reviewing the services. As the message at the bottom of the example indicates, all you need do is press RETURN. That would show you a menu something like this:

```
            FIDELITY PRODUCTS & SERVICES
                   MAIN MENU


SELECTIONS:

1.  Investors EXPRESS - Buy and Sell stocks on your
    Personal Computer.
2.  Fidelity Mutual Funds - offering a wide range of
    investment alternatives.
3.  Fidelity Special Products and Services - Discount
    Brokerage, Asset Management, Retirement Accounts,
    Variable Annuity.
4.  Fidelity Local Investor Centers to help serve you.
5.  Fidelity Investments - who we are.
6.  End Product Review

ENTER SELECTION
```

If you wanted to learn about EXPRESS, Fidelity's name for its online stock transaction system, you could enter 1 and see:

```
            FIDELITY PRODUCTS & SERVICES
             Fidelity Investor's Express


Fidelity Investor's Express with Dow Jones News/
Retrieval. Now you can trade on-line twenty-two hours
a day. You can take advantage of one of the world's
largest sources of financial information and trade
stocks through your personal computer. With your PC,
a modem and a local phone call you can access DJN/R
and place orders in minutes twenty-two hours a day
and as a Fidelity
```

```
ENTER (I)nformation to be Mailed
        (P)revious Menu
        (M)ain Menu of Product Review
        (C)ontinue
```

Note that the text has ended in the middle of a sentence and the last four lines of the screen are used for tips on what commands are available at this point. Entering C (for Continue) would let you view the remainder of the information.

```
        FIDELITY PRODUCTS & SERVICES
          Fidelity Investor's Express

customer, you can save up to 75% ($30 minimum
commission) on commissions compared to full cost
brokerage rates and enjoy all the benefits offered by
one of the nation's largest independent money
managers.

ENTER (I)nformation to be Mailed
        (P)revious Menu
        (M)ain Menu of Product Review
```

This is the end of the article about EXPRESS. If you wanted additional information mailed to you, you could enter I at this point and reply to subsequent queries about your name and address.

If you entered M, you'd be taken back to the main menu:

```
        FIDELITY PRODUCTS & SERVICES
                MAIN MENU

SELECTIONS:

1. Investors EXPRESS - Buy and Sell stocks on your
   Personal Computer.
2. Fidelity Mutual Funds - offering a wide range of
   investment alternatives.
```

```
3. Fidelity Special Products and Services - Discount
   Brokerage, Asset Management, Retirement Accounts,
   Variable Annuity.
4. Fidelity Local Investor Centers to help serve you.
5. Fidelity Investments - who we are.
6. End Product Review

ENTER SELECTION
```

Note that there are six selections on this menu, each dealing with a different aspect of Fidelity and its financial services. You can read about each by choosing the corresponding number. At the end of each page you have the opportunity to return to this main menu by entering M.

To leave this product review area, you would enter 6 and be prompted to enter your master account number if you're already a customer or to press RETURN if you're not, to go back to the main DJN/R query prompt.

BUYING AND SELLING ONLINE: WHAT'S IT LIKE?

You may find the idea of stock trading online intriguing, but you have to wonder just how fail-safe the system is and how easy it is to use. For instance, is it so "easy" that a slip of the digit on a keyboard causes you to wind up buying a hundred blocks of Aunt Emma's Buggy Whips, Inc.? Or is it so difficult that you waste connect time trying to figure how to get the electronic broker's attention?

Well, Fidelity has considered these concerns and provides you with some extra assistance if you decide to subscribe.

For starters, as a Fidelity EXPRESS subscriber, you receive a user's manual with about 200 pages of instructions. That might make the feature sound overwhelming, but it isn't. All of Fidelity EXPRESS is menu-driven. As we've seen on our tours, that means at each step in the process your main options are outlined in a list presented on the screen.

Let's suppose for a moment that you are a Fidelity subscriber. You'll recall we said that the first step to entering the Fidelity customer area is to enter your master account number. But that isn't all. After you enter your number, you are then asked for your master EXPRESS word. It's a special password to give you extra security.

After entering your account's password, here's the first menu you'll see:

```
            FIDELITY INVESTOR'S EXPRESS
                   Main Menu

SELECTIONS
  1. Customer Mailbox
  2. Account Management
  3. Trading
  4. Portfolio Management
  5. Quotes
  6. Fidelity Products and Services
  7. End EXPRESS

ENTER SELECTION
```

Selection 1 gives you access to an area where you may send mail to a Fidelity representative or receive mail from Fidelity. This is the place where you'll be notified when a stock trade you have requested has been completed. You also can use the online mail to keep in contact with Fidelity officials, who say they answer their electronic mail in at least 48 hours from the time you send it.

Selection 2 allows you to manage your account, or accounts. You may open more than one trading account with Fidelity just as you might do with a broker in your own town. Each account has its own number and password. Incidentally, you can change your master password or individual account passwords from this area as well.

In addition to multiple accounts, you can maintain multiple portfolios online. Selection 4 enables you to keep records of those portfolios. When you trade online, the portfolio automatically is updated by Fidelity. In addition, you can add and delete stocks not traded through Fidelity using this option.

Selection 5 gives you direct access to delayed stock quotes and options. This is similar to the Current Quotes feature you've already seen, except that these quotes are provided by Fidelity. Selection 6 tells you more about Fidelity's other products and services, and Selection 7 is used to exit the service.

GETTING DOWN TO BUSINESS

We've saved the best for last. It's Selection 3—Trading—where most of the action takes place.

When you select 3 from the main menu, you'll see yet another list of options:

```
        FIDELITY INVESTOR'S EXPRESS
             Trading Menu

SELECTIONS
  1. Place a New STOCK Order
  2. Place a New Option Order
  3. Cancel & Replace an Order
  4. Cancel an Order
  5. Review Current Orders
  6. Lookup Company/Stock Symbols
  7. Access Another Account
  8. Return to Previous Menu

ENTER SELECTION
```

(If you have used an **EXPRESS** account number prior to entering the Trading Menu, you'll first be asked for an account number and account password.)

Let's say you want to buy 100 shares of IBM. You'd begin by entering 1, "Place a New STOCK Order." That would whisk you away to the New STOCK order menu, which looks like this:

```
        FIDELITY INVESTOR'S EXPRESS
          Place a New STOCK Order

SELECTIONS
  1. Buy Stock
  2. Sell Stock
  3. Return to Previous Menu

ENTER SELECTION
```

Since you want to buy IBM stock, you'd enter 1 at this menu and see:

```
                    TRADING
                   Buy Stock

EXPRESS Account: 123456789

Stock Symbol:
```

Entering the IBM symbol, you'll see the latest quote for IBM, such as:

```
            INT'L BUSINESS MACH
Delayed Price: 123 1/2              Time: 12:01 PM
```

Next you'll be asked to provide answers about your stock trade. As each query is presented, you must enter a suitable answer before the next question is asked. These are the queries:

```
Number of Shares . . . .
(M)arket, (L)imit, (S)top .
Your price limit. . . . .
(G)tc, (D)ay Order. . . . .
(C)ash, (M)argin Account. .
Update Portfolio (Y) (N). .
Portfolio Name. . . . . .
```

Let's say you've asked Fidelity to purchase 100 shares for you with a limit of 123⅝. You've asked the order to remain good until you cancel it. (The Fidelity manual provides a code for this and other shorthand; in this case the code, GTC, means "Good Till Canceled.") You want to purchase the stock with a margin account and you want the stock to be added automatically to a portfolio you previously have named MYPORTFOLIO, which will be updated.

After you've answered all the queries, you have a chance to review your order when the system displays:

```
              FIDELITY INVESTOR'S EXPRESS
              Place a New Option Order

SELECTIONS
  1. Buy Put to Open
  2. Buy Put to Close
  3. Buy Call to Open
  4. Buy Call to Close
  5. Sell Put to Open
  6. Sell Put to Close
  7. Sell Call to Open
  8. Sell Call to Close
  9. Return to Previous Menu

ENTER SELECTION
```

Suppose your research has led you to believe that "smart money" is buying calls on IBM stock and you want to take options on ten contracts. You would choose number 3, Buy Call to Open, and the system would display:

```
                    TRADING
              Buy Call to Open

         EXPRESS Account: 123456789

           Option Symbol:
```

At this point you would enter the option symbol for IBM to see the delayed price and a series of queries:

```
              INTL'S BUSINESS MACH IBM JUL 125
Delayed Price: 5 3/4                    Time: 12:01 PM

    Number of Contracts. . . .
    (M)arket, (L)imit . . . . .
    Your Price Limit. . . . . .
    (G)tc, (D)ay Order. . . . .
    (C)ash, (M)argin Account. .
    Update Portfolio (Y)(N) . .
    Portfolio Name. . . . . . .
```

Finally, the fail-safe page where you get to check your order to make sure it's correct.

```
                        TRADING
                   Buy Call to Open

              EXPRESS Account: 123456789

              INT'L BUSINESS MACH IBM JUL 125
Delayed Price: 5 3/4                    Time: 12:01 PM

    Quantity . . . . . . .10
    Order Type . . . . . .Limit
    Your Price Limit . . .5 7/8
    Time in Force. . . . .GTC
    Account. . . . . . . .Margin
    Portfolio Name . . . .MYPORTFOLIO

        **** PLEASE REVIEW THE ABOVE ORDER ****

ENTER 1. PLACE the Order
      2. CHANGE the Order
      3. DELETE the Order Request
```

When you are satisfied with your order, you select 1 and see this message:

```
DATE: 01/15/86                              TIME: 12:02 PM
       A GTC order to BUY 10 contracts of IBM
 JUL 125 CALLS to Open at 5 7/8 has been submitted.

For future reference,
your Order Number is 157N5534.

Press <RETURN> to Continue
```

As with stock orders, this means Fidelity will post a note in your electronic mailbox and give you full details in the Review Current Orders section of the Trading menu.

TRADING IN THE FAST LANE

Once you become familiar with the way Fidelity operates, you can take express routes with EXPRESS to get to the menu option you want. Each menu item has a "shortcut" number associated with it; these numbers are provided in the EXPRESS manual. Instead of moving slowly through the menu, you type a > and the associated shortcut number to take you directly to the menu item you want. Doing this saves online time and money but shouldn't be used until you understand completely how EXPRESS operates.

HELP FROM FIDELITY

Fidelity maintains its own customer service signup and hot lines. You can ask for EXPRESS signup information while online, as you saw earlier in this chapter. If you'd rather begin the signup procedure on the telephone, though, you may call Fidelity at 800-544-6666. In Massachusetts, Alaska, and Hawaii dial 617-523-1919.

If you have problems navigating the EXPRESS service once you are a subscriber, you can get help by calling customer assistance at 800-225-5531.

SUMMING UP

Obviously, this chapter wasn't designed to take the place of Fidelity's own user's manual, but rather to give you a taste of what it's like to trade online.

Keep in mind that there are other options available, not only to buy and sell securities but also to manage portfolios and keep tabs on various records for tax purposes. Among them are options to check the net worth and current market value of all portfolios; review account balances, positions, and trading limits; maintain tax records outlining short- and long-term gains and losses; display estimates of annual dividends and income from stocks and bonds; and review regular investments, IRAs, and Keogh portfolios.

## Chapter 9

SCOOPS:
HOT NEWS THROUGH
DOW JONES

One of the things that makes Dow Jones News/Retrieval unique among electronic information services is that it puts a higher priority on the quality of its information—its accuracy and timeliness—than on niftiness of its software and hardware. Dow Jones & Co. is a *news* organization, not a computer company.

Back in 1977 Richard Levine stepped down as a chief correspondent for *The Wall Street Journal* to become editorial director of the newly formed Dow Jones News/Retrieval. He brought with him the *Journal's* philosophy that accuracy is paramount. After all, the *Journal* has more than a hundred years invested in its reputation as the authority on business news, and Levine expects News/Retrieval to live up to that reputation.

He put together an electronic newsroom of more than 50 staffers who today still compile, verify, and package the news for you every business day. We've already seen two examples of this team's fine work. In Chapter 3 we looked at how the //NEWS feature can keep you abreast of national and international news through reports prepared by Levine's staff using dispatches from the Associated Press. Then when we toured the Current Quotes database (//CQE) back in Chapter 5, we noted that Dow Jones News/Retrieval actually reviews the stock quotes as they arrive and, when it comes upon one that seems questionable, a staffer calls sources to verify it before passing it along to you.

No other dial-up information service goes so far to make sure its information is correct.

In this chapter and the next two we'll concentrate on how you can get the most out of the primary news resources of DJN/R. Shortly we'll be going online to see how to:

• Use the Dow Jones News (//DJNEWS) database for up-to-the-minute information about a specific company or an entire industry group. The resource is a famous one in business, sometimes called the Dow Jones "Broadtape."

• Stay on top of late-breaking sports news through //SPORTS.

• Have the system itself capture news of interest to you through a relatively new feature called //TRACK. With it, you can have DJN/R gather information around the clock on companies and industry groups you've specified, filing them away in electronic file folders.

• Keep up with important Japanese economic news through a database called //KYODO.

Then in the next chapter we'll begin a close look at the Text Search Services (//TEXT), with which you can delve into literally years' worth of *Wall Street Journals* and *Washington Posts* in seconds and come up with precisely the stories you're interested in.

GETTING STARTED

Let's hit the news beat, then.

Have a scratch pad and a pencil handy—we'll have a few notes to jot down along the way—and log on to Dow Jones News/Retrieval.

As usual, the system starts right out with news, through an opening bulletin that you've seen on your earlier tours. It changes regularly, often several times during a day, and usually looks something like this:

```
          DOW JONES NEWS/RETRIEVAL
             COPYRIGHT (C) 1986
          DOW JONES & COMPANY, INC.
             ALL RIGHTS RESERVED

NEW TESTIMONY IN SHUTTLE PROBE
SEE //NEWS FOR DETAILS
SEE .G/CFT 01 OR .I/CMD 01 FOR
NEWS ON COMMODITIES, SEE
//FUTURES FOR QUOTES.

ENTER QUERY
```

As we've mentioned, this is called the *copyright page* and it contains tips about retrieving important breaking news as well as information on News/Retrieval developments and special offers. You receive it automatically every time you log on. In addition, you can take another look at this "front page" from anywhere in the system by entering //COPYRT.

By the way, speaking of bulletins, when the stock markets are experiencing unusually heavy trading, the Current Quotes database sometimes is delayed in reporting. Recently, in response to customers' requests, Dow Jones decided to use the //COPYRT statement to notify subscribers of delays.

GOING FOR THE BUSINESS NEWS

Our main news resources in this chapter will be //DJNEWS, where you have instant access to stories about thousands of companies and industries that were reported any time from today back to 90 days ago.

To begin our research, we visit //SYMBOL because //DJNEWS, like so many of Dow Jones's databases, uses codes to facilitate the searching.

Enter //SYMBOL and see this familiar fellow:

```
              DIRECTORY OF SYMBOLS
              COPYRIGHT (C) 1986
            DOW JONES & COMPANY, INC.

PRESS  FOR
   1   STOCK SYMBOLS
   2   COMPANY NAMES USING STOCK SYMBOLS
   3   STOCK OPTIONS
   4   MUTUAL FUNDS
   5   U.S. CORPORATE BONDS
   6   FOREIGN BONDS
   7   U.S. TREASURY NOTES & BONDS
   8   NEWS/RETRIEVAL CATEGORY CODES
   9   MEDIA GENERAL INDUSTRY GROUP CODES
  10   RECENT SYMBOL CHANGES

OR, PRESS <RETURN> FOR INSTRUCTIONS
```

Select option 1, STOCK SYMBOLS, to reach the ENTER QUERY prompt.

One of the companies we want to read about this time is MGM, so enter that at the prompt and the system should display:

```
SYMBOL    STOCKS                          PAGE 1 OF 1

GRH   *MGM GRAND HOTELS INC. - NY
GRHP  MGM GRAND HOTELS INC. $.44 CUM.
        REDEEM. PFD. SERIES A - NY
MGM   *MGM/UA ENTERTAINMENT CO. - NY
MGM%  MGM/UA ENTERTAINMENT CO. WT - NY
-------------------------------------------------------
ENTER QUERY
OR PRESS <RETURN> FOR MAIN MENU
```

There's more than one MGM; there's MGM Grand Hotels, Inc. and there's MGM/United Artists. Let's take the second one; the symbol is easier to remember. On your notepad make a heading called Companies, and under it write MGM.

Now, remember what we said about those asterisks (*)? //SYMBOL uses an asterisk to denote a symbol that works with //DJNEWS, so whenever you have a choice of symbols and you're heading for //DJNEWS, just pick the one that's marked with an asterisk.

While we're here, let's get symbols for three other companies—Procter and Gamble, Dow Chemical, and U.S. Steel. If you think you need the practice with //SYMBOL, look them up for yourself. If not, take our word for it—the symbols are, respectively, PG, DOW, and X. Jot those three down under the Companies heading.

Before we move on to //DJNEWS, let's get a couple of more codes. Go back to the main menu of the database by entering //SYMBOL at the prompt to see this again:

```
              DIRECTORY OF SYMBOLS
              COPYRIGHT (C) 1986
            DOW JONES & COMPANY, INC.

PRESS  FOR
   1   STOCK SYMBOLS
   2   COMPANY NAMES USING STOCK SYMBOLS
   3   STOCK OPTIONS
   4   MUTUAL FUNDS
   5   U.S. CORPORATE BONDS
   6   FOREIGN BONDS
   7   U.S. TREASURY NOTES & BONDS
   8   NEWS/RETRIEVAL CATEGORY CODES
   9   MEDIA GENERAL INDUSTRY GROUP CODES
  10   RECENT SYMBOL CHANGES

OR, PRESS <RETURN> FOR INSTRUCTIONS
```

Notice option 8. It promises "category codes" for use in //DJNEWS. Enter 8 and see:

```
PRESS  FOR
   1   INDUSTRIES
   2   STOCK MARKET NEWS
   3   ECONOMIC NEWS
   4   U.S. GOVERNMENT NEWS
```

```
5   FEDERAL REGULATORY AGENCIES
6   GENERAL NEWS
7   FOREIGN NEWS BY AREA
8   ALPHABETICAL DIRECTORY OF NEWS CATEGORIES
```

Earlier we talked about DJN/R's penchant for collecting information about industry groups. In //DJNEWS it works this way: In addition to compiling mountains of material on individual companies, the News/Retrieval editors cross-reference the major stories into industry and government categories. That means that with a single command, you can see the recent top stories of an entire industry, anything from accounting to utilities. So, a big story about IBM will show up in the online file of IBM stories; in addition, if it's significant enough, the story also will appear in the "computer industry" category.

These categories have their own codes. Select option 1 (for industry category codes), and the system will display something like this:

```
SYMBOL   INDUSTRIES                        PAGE 1 OF 5

    I/FIN   ACCOUNTING
    I/TNM   ACQUISITIONS
    I/MKT   ADVERTISING
    I/ARO   AEROSPACE
    I/AIR   AIRLINES
    I/TEX   APPAREL
    I/ELE   APPLIANCES
    I/AUT   AUTOS, AUTO PARTS
    I/BCY   BANKRUPTCIES
    I/BNK   BANKS
    I/TEL   BROADCASTING
    I/CNO   CASINOS AND GAMBLING
    I/CHM   CHEMICALS
    I/EDP   COMPUTERS
```

It's a long list (this is page 1 of five) and there's no need to look through them all right now; the whole list of industry codes, government codes, and so forth, is contained in the Online Survival Kit in the back of the book.

Just note the codes for the computer industry and the auto industry, both of which are shown in this example. On your notepad, make a new heading of Category Codes, and under it write down I/EDP and I/AUT. (Note that these symbols are different from the run-of-the-mill stock symbols; each is preceded by I/ and then a code, usually three letters. Incidentally, if you were to look up government category codes here, you'd find them preceded by G/.)

ON TO //DJNEWS

Okay, we're ready for some searching. Enter //DJNEWS and the system will display a brief welcoming message:

```
            DOW JONES NEWS

ENTER A PERIOD (.) FOLLOWED BY A STOCK
SYMBOL OR NEWS/RETRIEVAL CATEGORY

CODE FOUND IN //SYMBOL.

   ENTER .AAPL 01

   FOR   THE FIRST PAGE OF COMPANY
         HEADLINES ABOUT APPLE

ENTER REQUEST OR SEE //DJNEWS HELP.
```

Those instructions are fairly clear—and they already may sound a little familiar. Think back to Chapter 5, when we toured the Current Quotes databases (//CQE) and mentioned that when you looked for a stock quote, the system automatically checked //DJNEWS for breaking news about the company. We said that if you were tipped off about a news story, you could read it by simply entering a period (.) followed by the stock symbol.

As it turns out, the period is a powerful command on Dow Jones; from here (and from virtually *anywhere* in the system) entering a period followed by a symbol will whisk you away to //DJNEWS.

Try it out. Type this:

```
.MGM<RETURN>
```

Note there's no space between the period and the symbol, MGM.

In a moment the system will show you the latest story it has on file on MGM/United Artists (*not* MGM Grand Hotels, Inc.—that would have been a different symbol, .GRH, right?)

Of course the story you receive on your screen will be different from the one we have here, but it should look something like:

```
N MGM   01/03 BB 1/5
            /GW   MGM   TRSP WCI /FLX   /
         01/03 DESPITE HOLIDAY RECORD,
         (WJ) MOVIE INDUSTRY HAD TOUGH 1985
   THANKS TO A BANNER CROP OF CHRISTMAS RELEASES, THE
MOVIE INDUSTRY IS BREAKING RECORDS BOTH AT THE BOX
OFFICE AND IN THE VIDEOCASSETTE MARKET FOR THE 1985
HOLIDAY SEASON THAT WRAPS UP THIS WEEKEND.
   BARRY REARDON, PRESIDENT OF DISTRIBUTION FOR WARNER
BROS., PREDICTS THAT WHEN THIS WEEKEND'S RESULTS ARE
TABULATED, THE CRUCIAL THANKSGIVING-TO-NEW YEAR'S
MOVIE SEASON "COULD BE 20% TO 30% BETTER THAN LAST
YEAR."
   BUT BOX-OFFICE REVENUES FOR ALL OF 1985 MAY HAVE
REACHED ONLY $3.75 BILLION, COMPARED WITH $4 BILLION
IN 1984, PREDICTS A.D. MURPHY, A FILM PROFESSOR AT
THE UNIVERSITY OF SOUTHERN CALIFORNIA WHO TRACKS BOX
OFFICE PERFORMANCE.
```

Take a minute to compare our printed example with the story now on your screen and you should see similarities.

For one thing, it appears that both displays begin with two lines of gobbledygook, followed by a couple of lines for the headline and then, finally, the actual text of the story. A closer examination of the gobbledygook shows that, while most of the codes are for DJN/R's internal use and of no importance to us, the lines also contain some useful information. For instance:

• In the first line we see the stock symbol (MGM), followed by the date that the story was filed (01/03 or January 3). The date is important because //DJNEWS keeps a backlog of 90 days' worth of stories. When you enter a period and a symbol, you always receive the *latest* story available, whether it's one that was filed today or two months ago. So watch the dates.

• After that, the BB code is a story identifier. (Hold that thought—we'll be seeing BB again.)

• The last code on that line tells us how long the story is. In our example, 1/5 means that this is the first of five pages (or screens) of text. The story on your screen probably is of a different length, but the code always is in the same place.

• On the second line most of the codes are not really important to us, except for the last one—/FLX in this case. That's the story's industry category. As you learned in //SYMBOL a few minutes ago, DJN/R assigns major business stories to industry groups. You've collected two so far—I/EDP (computers) and I/AUT (automobiles). Now add this one to your list. Under the Category Codes heading write "I/FLX" (films).

• The next couple of lines of the display contain the story's headline and a repeat of the filing date. The lines also contain (in parentheses) an important code that tells you the source of the story you're reading. In our example, notice the code (WJ). That tells us that DJN/R's editors compiled this story from a report in *The Wall Street Journal*. You may have a different code in the story on your screen. Consult this list:

WJ — The Wall Street Journal
BN — Barron's
DJ — The Dow Jones News Service (the Broadtape)
DW — The Dow Jones News Service and The Wall Street Journal
NR — Dow Jones News/Retrieval

To read the next page of the MGM story, you'd simply press RETURN. In our example, since it is comprised of five pages, you'd press RETURN at the bottom of this and the next three screens to read the whole thing.

Or you could abandon this story and retrieve the latest story on another company. Entering .DOW would give you the first page of the most recent story on Dow Chemical; .X would retrieve the latest on U.S. Steel and soon. In other words, you don't have to return to the top of //DJNEWS just to look up another story.

GETTING THE LONG VIEW

Retrieving the latest new stories on individual companies is great, particularly if you plan to check the wires every day. Still, there will be times when you want to see a list of all the stories Dow Jones News/Retrieval has on hand about a specific firm. //DJNEWS makes that easy. Simply add a space and 01 to the command you've already used.

Try this. Enter .MGM 01 (that is, period, followed by MGM, followed by a space and then zero-one) and watch the system produce a list of MGM-related stories:

```
N MGM   01/04
BB 01/03 DESPITE HOLIDAY RECORD,
 (WJ) MOVIE INDUSTRY HAD TOUGH 1985
BA 01/03 MGM/UA POSTPONES SHAREHOLDERS
 (WJ) MEETING FOR ACQUISITIONS VOTE
AZ 12/24 TURNER BROADCASTING TO ISSUE
 (WJ) ADDED $125 MILLION OF DEBT
AY 12/18 TURNER TO FILE MGM FINANCING
 (DW) PLAN DESPITE VIACOM TALKS
AX 12/10 MGM-UA HOLDERS SUBSCRIBE FOR
 (DW) 7 MILLION SHRS OF UTD ARTISTS
AW 12/05 UNITED ARTISTS CORP. NAMES
 (WJ) CARSON A SENIOR VICE PRESIDENT
AV 12/04 MGM/UA ENTERTAINMENT AGREES
 (DJ) TO BUY KAY LABORATORIES LTD.
AU 12/04 ROBERT LAWRENCE NAMED
 (WJ) UNITED ARTISTS EXECUTIVE V.P.
At 12/03 VIACOM PLANS TO BID FOR
 (DW) CBS'S ST. LOUIS TV STATION
AS 11/27 ROSENFELT NAMED V.P., SPECIAL
 (WJ) ASSISTANT TO JERRY WEINTRAUB
AR 11/25 TRACINDA EXTENDS DEADLINE
 (DW) TO BUY UNITED ARTISTS STOCK
```

Wait a minute. Hold the phone. What's the 01 business all about?

//DJNEWS keeps its backlog of stories in pages of information. When you append 01 to your command, you're saying, in effect, "Give me the first page of the backlog." In a minute you'll see how to use these unique page numbers as a kind of navigation command, but first let's see what .MGM 01 hath wrought.

At first blush the display seems similar to the story we retrieved with simply .MGM, except this is obviously a kind of menu. The top of the display contains the stock symbol (MGM) followed (in our example) by the code 01/04. This is *not* a date—it's a page indicator. It's telling us that this is the 01st page of the collection which is 04 pages long.

Below that line begins the list of headlines of the stories on file, starting with the latest (the one you just read when you entered the .MGM command). Each headline is preceded by a unique two-letter code, the first one in the example being BB. To retrieve any story on this list, just enter its two-letter code—BB to get the first story here, BA the next one, AZ for the one after that, and so on.

After the code is each story's filing date, followed by the first line of its headline. Notice that the second line of each headline is preceded by a source code (in parentheses)—WJ for *The Wall Street Journal*, DJ for the Dow Jones News Service, DW for the News Service *and* the *Journal*, and so on.

Now for a little exercise. From the list displayed on your screen, select two stories and jot down their two-letter identification codes. (For instance, in our example, if we wanted to read the second story and the fifth story, we'd write down BA and AX.)

Okay, now enter the first two-letter code and you should be shown a story in a format like this:

```
N MGM   01/03 BA 1/2
   /MGM TBS    /FLX /
   01/03 MGM/UA POSTPONES SHAREHOLDERS
 (WJ) MEETING FOR ACQUISITIONS VOTE
   CULVER CITY, CALIF.  MGM/UA ENTERTAINMENT CO. SAID
IT WILL POSTPONE A JAN. 21 SPECIAL SHAREHOLDERS
MEETING TO VOTE ON ITS ACQUISITION BY TURNER
BROADCASTING SYSTEM INC. BECAUSE THE SECURITIES AND
EXCHANGE COMMISSION HASN'T FINISHED PROCESSING
DOCUMENTS RELATED TO THE MEETING.
   AN MGM/UA SPOKESMAN SAID THE DELAY DOESN'T
REPRESENT A THREAT TO THE TRANSACTION. THE STUDIO, IN
AN ANNOUNCEMENT LATE YESTERDAY, ATTRIBUTED THE DELAY
```

```
TO "HOLIDAY SEASON AND YEAR-END TRANSACTIONS" THAT
CREATED A LOGJAM AT THE SEC.
   MGM/UA'S PROXY MATERIALS WERE SUBMITTED LATE LAST
MONTH TO THE SEC AS PART OF A REGISTRATION STATEMENT,
UNDER WHICH TURNER BROADCASTING PROPOSED TO CHANGE
ITS FINANCING FOR THE $1.5
```

No surprises here—as far as format and codes are concerned, the story looks just like the first one we retrieved from //DJNEWS when we entered the simple .MGM command. To give yourself a good test, locate the important codes on the first few lines on your screen—the stock symbol, the date, the number of pages and so forth. If your story has more than one page, you can see the next screen by pressing RETURN.

Here's an important tip: when you're ready to see the second story you've chosen, you needn't go back to the menu if you already know the story's two-letter code. Try it—enter the second two-letter code you wrote down and you should be shown the first page of your second story.

But what if you *do* want to go back to the menu? No problem—just type in 01. Or if you want to go to the second page of the list of headlines—that's right—02, or 03 for the third page, and so forth. You may enter these numerical commands at the bottom of any screen to return to a specified page of stories.

The point of all this is that until you enter a period and a *new* stock symbol, //DJNEWS is going to assume that all the commands entered relate to its file of MGM-related stories.

Now, before we begin to look at how to use the industry category codes, continue your exercise for a few minutes by retrieving news on the other companies on your list.

• Get the *latest* story on file about U.S. Steel (by entering simply .X).

• Pick up a *list* of stories about Dow Chemical (with .DOW 01—remember, the 01 means "Get the first page of stories").

• Retrieve several stories from the Dow Chemical list by entering their two-letter identification codes.

• Finally, return to the Dow Chemical story list (by entering 01 for the first page or 02 for the second page, etc.) and move from page to page on the list. You don't have to read the list in sequence, either. If the list is 15 pages long, you could jump right to the end of the list (to oldest stories) by entering 15, and then back to the newest stories by entering 01.

When you're comfortable with this facet of //DJNEWS, meet us back here and we'll see how to use this database to gather the big news on entire industries.

GETTING THE BROAD VIEW

So far we've been using //DJNEWS for a microcosm—stories on specific companies. But the database's strength is that it can be used just as easily to get The Big Picture. Using the category codes we've been collecting along the way, we can have Dow Jones provide a list of 90 days' worth of major *related* stories, information with which you can take the pulse of an entire industry, government group, or market.

The most recent code you've added to your notepad was /FLX, the film industry code you took right off the top of the first MGM menu you read. Let's see what else is happening in the film industry.

Type this, but *don't* press RETURN yet:

```
.I/FLX 01
```

Note that most of this command is familiar: the preceding period tells DJN/R that you want to use //DJNEWS; the trailing 01 instructs the database to give you the first page of its historical backlog of stories. FLX is the symbol for the group you're researching (films). The new part of the command is the prefix I/, which tells //DJNEWS to look in its industry groups for the data. (We'll be seeing other prefixes in a minute.)

Now press RETURN and, after a second, the database should show you something like this:

```
N I/FLX   01/05
BS 01/13 MGM/UA, TURNER BROADCASTING
 (DW) IN TALKS TO RESTRUCTURE MERGER
BR 01/13 G&W'S PARAMOUNT AGREES
 (WJ) TO DISTRIBUTE RKO MOVIES
BQ 01/09 TWENTIETH CENTURY FOX AND
 (DW) COLUMBIA PICTURES SETTLE SUIT
BP 01/07 VESTRON TO PRODUCE MOVIES,
 (WJ) PURCHASE OTHERS FOR RELEASE
BO 01/06 TELEPICTURES, LORIMAR MERGER
 (DJ) FILINGS DECLARED EFFECTIVE
BN 01/03 DESPITE HOLIDAY RECORD,
 (WJ) MOVIE INDUSTRY HAD TOUGH 1985
BM 01/03 MGM/UA POSTPONES SHAREHOLDERS
 (WJ) MEETING FOR ACQUISITIONS VOTE
BL 12/31 DISNEY TO PREVIEW ITS FIRST
 (WJ) 'R' MOVIE IN 36 CITIES
BK 12/26 ASSOCIATES OF BASSES HOLD
 (DW) SHORT POSITION IN DISNEY STOCK
BJ 12/26 MURDOCH BORROWED $488 MILLION
 (WJ) FOR PURCHASE OF FOX FILM
BI 12/24 SOUTH KOREA AGREES TO BOOST
 (WJ) IMPORTS OF AMERICAN FILMS
```

This list of headlines, selected by News/Retrieval's editors as tops in the film industry these days, is formatted just like the lists you saw. Its code (FLX) and its number of pages (01/05) are listed in the first line. At this point you can carry on as you have with the other files you've retrieved; you can move on to another page of the list (by entering 02 or 03, etc.), retrieve a story from the list (by entering its unique two-letter code), or go on to an entirely different collection of stories by entering a period and a new symbol.

Many subscribers who use //DJNEWS for business research start by looking at an entire category and then focus on companies of interest. For instance, suppose you came across the list we have in our example and the Disney Studios story (story BL) caught your eye. After reading it, you might decide to follow up with a collection of other Disney stories. You wouldn't have to return to //SYMBOL to find the code for Disney. As you've already seen, a company's stock symbol always is listed in the first lines of the story. So, when you retrieved the Disney report here by entering BL, you would find the Disney code (which happens to be DIS). To follow up with a list of Disney-related stories, you'd simply enter .DIS 01.

So, the only difference between retrieving industry group stories and news about specific companies is the use of the I/prefix before the industry code.

Another important prefix is G/, which gives government-related news groups. With that, you can follow developments in government departments and regulatory agencies, from Agriculture to Treasury.

Take a moment now to look over the list of industry, government, and subject symbols in the Online Survival Kit, beginning on page 321.

The first thing you should notice is that, while most of the codes begin with either I/ or G/, not all of them do. Dow Jones News/Retrieval has added some special codes—.LABOR for labor news, .FORGN for foreign news, .GOVMT for a general government summary, .JAPAN for top news of that country, and so forth. Notice that what they all have in common is that they require only a period preceding them.

Of course also, as you've seen, it's often useful to end the command with a space and 01. For example, .LABOR will give you the latest single story in the labor file, while .LABOR 01 will compile a list for you.

It's important that you feel quite comfortable with //DJNEWS, so we propose that you practice a few more minutes, this time using category codes. You can start with the remaining two you jotted down—.I/AUT 01 will give you a collection of top stories from the automobile industry, and .I/EDP 01 is for the latest and greatest from the world of computers.

You don't have to stop there; feel free to look at the list of codes in the back of the book and pick out a few that strike your fancy. Try out a government code or two. .G/CNG 01 for news from Congress; .G/EXE 01 for reports from the executive branch.

While you're practicing, we'll point out a few special subject codes that many News/Retrieval subscribers seem to like:

.H/ stands for hot business news of the day.

.I/HOH means headlines of the hour.

.I/STK retrieves general stock market news.

.I/ACT is for the active stocks.

.I/DJA is for the latest Dow Jones Average.

.I/EMI is for a summary of the leading economic indicators.

.I/NDX is for the stock indexes.

.I/BCY is for reports of bankruptcies.

.I/INI is for news of initial stock offerings, what's new to the market.

.I/CEO gets news about chief executive officers around the country.

.MARKT is for a roundup of the financial markets.

By the way, while exploring //DJNEWS stories, you may occasionally notice the code QQ displayed in the top left corner of a story. The QQ informs you that the news item will appear only that day. At the end of the day it will be removed from the file and replaced by the next day's information. QQ usually appears on many of the items listed under .I/NDX (the stock index), for example.

When you feel you know your way around //DJNEWS, log off the system and meet us at the next heading. Then we'll show you how to automate Dow Jones News/Retrieval so that it will work for you even when you're not online.

USING //DJNEWS

Now that you've been around the block with //DJNEWS, you no doubt already are thinking about ways you can use this massive database for getting tips on investment opportunities, staying up-to-date on the trends in your own business, keeping an eye on your competitors, and the like.

There are many possibilities. If you'll recall our collection of scenarios in Chapter 4, almost all of our imaginary stars used //DJNEWS at one point or another in their research. That's because some of the //DJNEWS news categories are just right for supplementing your use of other databases.

Consider this: Back in Chapters 6 and 7 you met some of Dow Jones News/Retrievals' top-flight financial analysis services for tracking trends in business. Well, the information you find there can be enhanced with several //DJNEWS categories:

• .I/ECO, which contains commentaries, forecasts, and news of the general economic climate of the country.

• .I/EMI, which provides statistics, including economics and monetary indicators.

• .I/MON, which provides coverage on the money supply and the U.S. dollar domestically and internationally.

You've also already used the Corporate Earnings Estimator (//EARN), which offers a consensus forecast by Wall Street analysts for 3,000 widely followed companies. A fine companion to //EARN is .I/ERN, which provides current-day corporate earnings reports *the day before* they will appear in *The Wall Street Journal*.

MIXING AND MATCHING NEWS AND QUOTES: //TRACK

We've made a big deal out of the idea of using Dow Jones's databases in concert with each other. That was the whole point of Chapter 4's scenarios. In that chapter also we mentioned in passing that DJN/R itself is beginning to think in terms of coordinating databases.

That thinking is evidenced by one of the system's newest features, //TRACK, which brings together in a new way two databases that just naturally go together, Current Quotes (//CQE) and the news (//DJNEWS).

Using //TRACK you can create and store online "profiles"— kind of electronic file folders—each containing symbols for various companies. Then from virtually anyplace in the system you can call up the latest stock quotes *and* the latest news on all the companies in a profile by simple entering //TRACK followed by a space and the name of the profile you want to check.

In addition to giving you quick access to the stock quotes, //TRACK in essence lets you set your own industry group for //DJNEWS. The idea, of course, is to group similar companies in the same profile. For instance, you might have one profile for companies in which you already own stock (perhaps called STOX); another could contain symbols for companies you're watching as possible investments (maybe call that one PROSPECTS). Other profiles could follow the big players in your industry. For instance, we set up profiles called COMPUTERS to follow the largest and smallest companies, TELECOM to track telecommunications movers and shakers, and so on.

It costs a little extra to use //TRACK. At this writing, News/Retrieval charged $5 a month for the service. For the fee, you can establish up to five profiles, each containing up to 25 company symbols. We'll give you a good test run of //TRACK from the relative safety of your easy chair and then you can decide if the feature fits your game plan.

CREATING YOUR FIRST PROFILES

To create //TRACK profiles, you should start right where you are now—offline. Remember that each profile is like a file folder, so give some thought as to which companies belong in which folders. You also might want to think about the order in which the companies are listed; //TRACK will report the current stock quotes and then any news it finds for each company in the order you've specified.

Do your preliminary work with a pencil and paper, jotting down the names of each company to be listed in each profile. Then you're ready to go online.

Go first, not to //TRACK, but to //SYMBOL, where you can get the code for each company and write it next to its name on your list. After you have all the symbols you'll need for each profile, you can reach the tracking feature by simply entering //TRACK.

If it's your first visit to the feature, the system will display an introductory message that reminds you of the surcharge and then prompts you to make up a four-digit PIN (Personal Identification Number). This is a little extra security to keep nosy folks out of your profiles. On all subsequent visits to //TRACK, you'll be prompted for your PIN, so you'll need to store that in a secure place, perhaps with your password.

After that bit of housekeeping is done, you'll see this straightforward menu:

```
            Dow Jones Tracking Service
               Copyright (C) 1986
            Dow Jones & Company, Inc.

Press  To
  1  Create a Profile
  2  Review or Change the Companies In a Profile
  3  Delete a Profile
  4  Execute a Profile Search
  5  Learn More About The Dow Jones Tracking Service

See //MENU for a description of other Dow Jones
News/Retrieval services
```

When you choose option 1, the system will display a message summarizing the //TRACK features and then prompt you to give the profile a unique name. It can be up to 10 letters, but since you'll be using it a lot, shorter names are better. Certainly make it something easy to remember. For instance, WATCH would be a good name for companies you're tracking as potential investments.

After you've specified the name, the system will tell you to enter the symbols of the companies you wish to track, separating each with a space, such as:

```
MGM IBM RCA TNDM MLT . . . etc.
```

You can enter up to 25 symbols. Press RETURN when you're finished. If you accidentally press RETURN before you're finished, don't worry about it. The system is prepared for you—it will display a message like this:

```
YOU CURRENTLY HAVE ROOM FOR 20 COMPANIES IN YOUR
PROFILE. PLEASE ENTER STOCK SYMBOL(S) OR ENTER A
SINGLE SLASH (/)
```

At this point you may enter more symbols, or enter a slash to tell Dow Jones, "All done," and you'll be returned to the main menu.

USING //TRACK

You can track your stocks from virtually anywhere on the system by entering //TRACK and the profile name, such as //TRACK WATCH. If it's your first time into //TRACK during that online session, you'll be prompted for your four-digit PIN, and then the system will start at the beginning of your symbols list, first automatically checking //CQE and displaying something like this:

```
DOW JONES STOCK
QUOTE REPORTER SERVICE
STOCK QUOTES DELAYED
OVER 15 MINUTES
*=CLOSE ADJ. FOR EX-DIVIDEND

STOCK           MGM
BID/CLOSE       20
ASKED/OPEN      22 1/2
HIGH            22 3/4
LOW             22 1/8
LAST            22 1/2
VOLUME (100'S)3993
```

It will pause at the bottom of the screen. When you press RETURN, the
system then will check //DJNEWS for the latest on MGM and report something
like:

```
N MGM    01/03 BE 1/3
 /BRY MGM MZ  TWA /SCR TNM/
   01/16 SOME BUYOUTS ENCOUNTER WOES;
(WJ) MARKET MAY BE COOLING DOWN
   NEW YORK -- IN THE WAKE OF THE BIGGEST YEAR EVER
IN TAKEOVERS, SOME MAJOR DEALS ARE RUNNING INTO
TROUBLE.
   FOR EXAMPLE, AN R.H. MACY & CO.

                    etc.
```

Pausing at the bottom of each page, it will display the latest story it's found
about the first company, then move on to the //CQE and //DJNEWS report on
the next firm. If it finds no news of the day for a company, it'll say, "THERE IS
NO CURRENT NEWS ABOUT IBM."

All this is handy, but having to press RETURN at the bottom of each
screen can be nuisance if it's a long profile. That's why News/Retrieval has
added a command—NP (for No Pause)—which can be appended, such as:

//TRACK WATCH NP

Now the system will display the complete profile without stopping at the bottom of each screen. Of course, you still can freeze and unfreeze the display with Control S and Control Q. (The No Pause option is especially useful if you're sending the report directly to your printer.)

There are a couple of other special commands Dow Jones has added for using //TRACK in a hurry.

Suppose you want to check your WATCH folder but you don't have time to read every story on every company. The command HL will give you only the headlines of the daily reports, not the complete stories. It's appended just as in the example above—//TRACK WATCH HL.

If you use //TRACK several times a day, you'll like the NO command. It tells DJN/R, "Show me NO old news"—that is, display only today's news received since you last //TRACKed that profile.

In addition, you can mix and match the commands. For instance, when we're in a hurry, we use this command:

TRACK WATCH NP HL NO

That means, do it fast and low ("Don't stop, give me headlines only, and don't bother me with stuff I read in my //TRACKing session earlier today.")

To that, the system would respond with something like this:

```
DOW JONES STOCK
QUOTE REPORTER SERVICE
STOCK QUOTES DELAYED
OVER 15 MINUTES
*=CLOSE ADJ. FOR EX-DIVIDEND

STOCK          MGM
BID/CLOSE      20
ASKED/OPEN     22 1/2
HIGH           22 3/4
```

```
LOW              22 1/8
LAST             22 1/2
VOLUME (100's)4081

N MGM  01/03
BE 01/16 SOME BUYOUTS ENCOUNTER WOES;
 (WJ) MARKET MAY BE COOLING DOWN
BD 01/16 MGM-UA - TURNER BROADCASTING
 (DJ) -2-
BC 01/16 MGM/UA, TURNER BROADCASTING
 (DJ) TO RESTRUCTURE TAKEOVER TERMS

END OF NEWS ABOUT MGM
```

---

and go right on to //TRACKing IBM.

Of course, if any of those MGM story headlines strikes our fancy, it's a simple matter to access //DJNEWS directly, with .MGM 01, and pick up the complete text.

SOME FINAL THOUGHTS ABOUT //TRACK

Once you have a profile created, you can maintain it—add or delete companies for searching, delete the entire profile, and create additional profiles (up to five)—by returning to the main //TRACK menu. Just enter //TRACK anywhere in the system. As you've seen, the options for adding and deleting symbols from profiles are provided on the menu.

A few notes:

Once you've entered //TRACK and set up a PIN, you'll automatically be charged the $5 monthly storage fee, whether you have five profiles or none. Important—if you delete all your profiles and decide to stop using //TRACK, call the News/Retrieval customer service people and arrange to have your PIN deleted. Otherwise, you'll continue to be billed $5 a month.

Also call the customer service folks if you forget your PIN. They can look it up on their end and tell you over the phone.

It's not possible (at this writing) to use //TRACK to retrieve quotes without news stories. However, using the HL option will provide headlines only. If you absolutely, positively, don't want interruptions for news, don't use //TRACK, use //CQE directly.

Don't put //DJNEWS category codes, such as .I/EDP, in your //TRACK profiles. It will generate an error message when it tries to find the symbol in the Current Quotes database, since I/EDP is not a company.

As you saw, one of the options on the main //TRACK menu allows you to delete an entire profile. If you delete a profile by mistake, you can restore it if you move quickly. Just take the Create a Profile option and reenter the profile's original name. The system will reactivate the stock symbols you previously entered. However, this feature works only on the same day that you deleted it—hesitate and it's lost. If you want to delete a profile and reuse the name, it may be easier to delete the individual company symbols and leave the profile name intact.

Speaking of that main //TRACK menu, you probably noticed that one of the options (option 4) allows you to execute a profile search. Of course, if you're not at the main menu and want to //TRACK a profile, it's faster simply to enter //TRACK followed by the profile name. But if you're at the main menu, you can select option 4. And those nifty special commands—NP, HL, and NO—also are available at the menu. Simply enter 4 for the search option. You'll be prompted for the number of the profile you want to search. If it's number 2, you can then enter 2 NP HL.

HOT NEWS FROM JAPAN: //KYODO

The world's becoming a smaller place, and these days news halfway around the globe can affect business in your backyard. That's certainly the case with American and Japanese economics, and, through an accident of astronomy, Dow Jones News/Retrieval can give you news of Japan before many of the Japanese businesspeople see it.

That's because the close of the business day in Japan, when the writers for Kyodo News Service write and transmit their Japan Economic Daily, works out to be the beginning of the workday in the United States. So by entering //KYODO shortly after 9:00 A.M. any business day, you'll see business news from Japan before you can read it in a newspaper.

//KYODO, which has been available through DJN/R, since 1983, provides about 10,000 words a day on the top business stories, reports from the government and industry sectors, and a comprehensive wrap-up of the Japanese financial market activity. It also keeps a backlog of its four previous issues.

Once again, Dow Jones News/Retrieval's emphasis on the quality of information has been at work. When //KYODO first came online, it included a healthy amount of general news as well. Explaining the product's evolution into more of a business-oriented publication, one DJN/R editor commented that the subscribers "wanted business news from Japan, not news on train delays or political in-fighting."

YOUR ELECTRONIC SPORTS PAGE

Finally, not all news on News/Retrieval is designed strictly for the business world. For instance, when you're online, you're one command away from the sports pages.

Entering //SPORTS at any prompt will take you to the reports of athletic events, prepared by the DJN/R editors from Associated Press dispatches. The opening menu looks like this:

```
        DOW JONES NEWS/RETRIEVAL SPORTS REPORT
          FRONT PAGE AT 12:41 P.M. WEDNESDAY
                     FROM AP

PRESS  FOR
1   Caps Take Over 1st in Patrick; Resch, Tonelli,
       Duguay Traded
2   NCAA Tournament Opens Thurday * College Basketball
       Report *
3   NFL To Allow Officials To Use Limited Video
       Replays In 1986
4   Lakers Win Latest Battle Of L.A.; Kings' Theus
       Confounds Spurs
5   Wednesday's National Scoreboard
--------------------------------------------------------
PRESS N FOR MORE NEWS OR F FOR FULL SCORES, STATS
AND STANDINGS.
```

This should look familiar; it's very much like the top menu of the national and world summaries you've retrieved with //NEWS.

Note the message at the bottom of the example tells you about two "local" navigation commands—N to see more sports news and F for a rundown of scores, statistics, and standings. All the other navigations commands—T for top, M for previous menu, R to return to a page—work in //SPORTS as they do elsewhere in the system.

CONCLUSION

In this chapter we learned how to use //DJNEWS to:

• Retrieve the latest story on a specific company by entering a period followed by the company's stock symbol, such as .MGM.

• Gather a list of recent stories about a company by appending a space and a page number to that command, such as .MGM 01 or .MGM 05.

• Look at an entire category of related stories by entering .I/ and an industry code, such as .I/AUT for automotive news, or .G/ and a government code, such as .G/CNG for congressional news.

An important thing to remember about the Dow Jones company news is that it is not necessary to type //DJNEWS to get it. On the contrary, from virtually anywhere in the system you can enter a period and a symbol for a quick burst of the news.

We also saw how to use //TRACK to make personal use of //DJNEWS and Current Quotes (//CQE) and saw three special commands available there:

NP for "No Pause."
HL for headlines only.
NO for "No old news."

Chapter 10

FIRST-CLASS NEWS RETRIEVAL: //TEXT

When you were just beginning to think about bringing computers into your life and work, someone probably told you that they would be the key to enormous reservoirs of information. So far, you've seen some pretty impressive databases on Dow Jones News/Retrieval. However, when it comes to getting historical information from the news backlog, nothing beats //TEXT.

//TEXT, also called the Dow Jones Text-Search Services, is a database with few equals among the large electronic information services. With it you can launch sophisticated searches and in seconds cull literally tens of thousands of articles to pick up just the ones that meet your specific needs.

The sources of information are some of the most respected in the community. Some you've already met. During the last chapter's tour we told you that //DJNEWS keeps 90 days' worth of stories online from *The Wall Street Journal*, *Barron's*, the Dow Jones News Services' Broadtape, and other sources. //TEXT also has those resources available, but with a big difference—//TEXT's files go back to June 1979.

More important, the same commands you'll be learning in this chapter and the next will enable you to use //TEXT to search the full text of *every issue* of *The Wall Street Journal* and *The Washington Post* back to January 1984. Incidentally, Dow Jones News/Retrieval is the only online information service with which you can electronically search *The Wall Street Journal*.

Furthermore, News/Retrieval officials hint that even more news sources will be added to //TEXT as time goes on. The commands you learn here will prepare you to use them too.

//TEXT is quite sophisticated, and, unfortunately, that means it can be complicated—so much so, in fact, that some subscribers have bad initial experiences with the database and decide never to try it again. It doesn't have to be that way. Many times the bad first impressions come about because the subscribers, having heard about //TEXT's enormous potential, rush into it with no preparation.

In this chapter we'll stay offline, so get comfortable and we'll walk through a few sample sessions of //TEXT. As you'll see, the beauty of this database is that, because its commands are so logical, it's possible to plan entire search strategies offline with a pencil and paper. Then all you have to do is log on and follow the script you've written for yourself.

In these two chapters we'll approach //TEXT in three assaults:

• First, to get familiar with the principles involved, we'll start with some simple ways to use //TEXT.

• Then we'll move on to some useful shortcuts.

• Finally, we'll wrap up with some advanced commands that you can incorporate later on.

Important: What we've been preaching about News/Retrieval in general is especially important in connection with //TEXT—please don't try to memorize all the commands. Shoot for understanding the concepts. You can always come back to this chapter later to review the syntax of a specific command or function.

//TEXT, THE EASY WAY

Okay, let's pretend you're online now. To get to the Text-Search database, you enter //TEXT and the system displays a menu something like this:

```
            DOW JONES TEXT-SEARCH SERVICES
                  COPYRIGHT (C) 1986
               DOW JONES & COMPANY, INC.

PRESS  FOR
  1   THE WALL STREET JOURNAL: FULL TEXT FROM JANUARY
         1984

  2   DOW JONES NEWS: BROADTAPE, AND SELECTED STORIES
         FROM BARRON'S AND THE WALL STREET JOURNAL
         FROM JUNE 1979

  3   THE ELECTRONIC WASHINGTON POST: FULL TEXT FROM
         JANUARY 1984
```

In our example, there are *three* //TEXT databases—the full text of *The Wall Street Journal* (option 1), the Dow Jones News (the same resources as //DJNEWS), and the full text of *The Washington Post*. (By the time you visit //TEXT, there may be a fourth database called "The Business Library," an assembly of assorted business publications that was under development at the time of this writing.) They all work the same way. No matter which collection of news stories you choose to search, your next prompt will look like this:

```
DJ/NRS- SEARCH MODE - ENTER QUERY
    1__:
```

The prompt is telling us we're in search mode (there is another mode—print mode—for displaying what we found in our searches; we'll see that one in a few minutes). The system's waiting for us to begin our search strategy.

Now, these terms may be unfamiliar to you if you're not used to working with databases. To understand them, think of each of these three databases as containing the text of tens of thousands of articles, millions of words. With //TEXT, you can "query" about those words, a little like playing Twenty Questions.

For instance, at the first search prompt you might say, in effect, "Set aside all the articles that contain the phrase 'ice cream.' " The database would make a search and then report the number of "hits," that is, the number of articles it found that mentioned "ice cream," and then give you the second search prompt.

Then you might say, "Okay, now find articles that use the word 'production.' " That would lead //TEXT to make another search of its entire database and report back with the number.

Finally, you might say, "Now tell me how many of these articles that contain the phrase 'ice cream' *also* contain the word 'production' "—and so forth. With a few carefully planned questions, you soon could isolate a collection of articles about the business of making ice cream.

To put these ideas to work, let's suppose you are Bob, the imaginary character in Chapter 4 who was the public relations officer for a major pharmaceutical company. Your assignment today is to study the use of aspirin by children, particularly in light of concerns about Reye's Syndrome, and to see how the story has been covered, how long it's been in the news, and so forth.

Using //TEXT, you would select the database you want to search and perhaps enter as your first query:

```
            1__: ASPIRIN
```

After a moment, the system responds with like something like:

```
RESULT                                    102 DOCUMENTS
    2__:
```

So //TEXT found 102 articles that contain the word "aspirin." After reporting the result, /TEXT provides the prompt for your next query ("2__:")

Next, you might enter:

```
    2__: CHILDREN
```

---

and be shown

```
RESULT                                        862 DOCUMENTS
     3__:
```

The result of the second query means that 862 documents in the database contain the word "children" (and the system is ready for the next query, 3).

We don't know yet if *any* of the articles found by the first query also were found by the second—that is, we don't know how many documents contain *both* the words "aspirin" and "children." Let's find out:

```
                       3__:    1 AND 2

RESULT                                          8 DOCUMENTS
     4__:
```

This third query—"1 AND 2"—introduces a new idea. We're telling //TEXT to find documents that meet the conditions of both the first query (ASPIRIN) *and* the second (CHILDREN), and not to bother telling us about any articles that meet only one or the other of the conditions.

AND is one of several online tools called *operators,* and it can be used in different ways. For instance, //TEXT has now located eight documents that contain both "aspirin" and "children" and it would be useful to know how many also mention the word 'syndrome" as in Reye's Syndrome. We could enter:

```
     4__: 3 AND SYNDROME
```

Translation: "Find those documents that meet the conditions of query 3 *and* contain the word 'syndrome.' " You might then find:

```
RESULT                                          6 DOCUMENTS
     5__:
```

Finally, suppose your research required that you look only at those reports from the year 1985. //TEXT gives you an easy way to do that:

```
5__:  4 AND YR85

RESULT                                              3 DOCUMENTS
   6__:
```

That fifth query tells the database to keep the conditions from the fourth query and add the condition that the stories have to have been published during the year 1985.

So, as the RESULT shows, we've sorted through thousands of stories and come up with three that meet our specifications.

Now put a bookmark on this page; we'll be referring to this little exercise later in the chapter.

VIEWING STORIES IN //TEXT, THE EASY WAY

Finding the stories is half the job in //TEXT; the other half is displaying them, or, in the database jargon, PRINTing them.

The stories that a query finds are always available in reverse chronological order—that is, just as the stories in //DJNEWS were filed—with the most recent ones always on the top of the heap.

To view the stories found in your latest query is simply a matter of entering two periods and the letter P (..P). The "period-period" part of the command tells //TEXT that you're changing from search mode to print mode; the P tells it to print the first page of the most recent story found by the latest query. In our case, after we entered ..P, something like this appeared:

```
DOCUMENT=   1 OF  3                         PAGE  =  1 OF  2
AN    130124-0525.
HL  * WARNINGS - ASPIRIN USE -2-
DD    01/23/85
SO    DOW JONES NEWS WIRE (T)
CO    SGP GOVMT
IN    PHARMACEUTICALS, HOSPITAL SUPPLIES, MANAGEMENT (PHA)
```

```
TX     MEMPHIS -DJ- PLOUGH INC. A UNIT OF SCHERING-PLOUGH CORP.
  * SAID IT IS AMONG ASPIRIN MAKERS WHO HAVE AGREED TO ADD
    WARNINGS TO THE LABELS OF ASPIRIN-CONTAINING PRODUCTS.
    THE LABELS WILL WARN OF A POSSIBLE RELATIONSHIP BETWEEN
  * REYE'S SYNDROME AND THE USE OF ASPIRIN BY SOME ILL CHILDREN.
    BUT J. RICHARD BRISCOE A PLOUGH EXECUTIVE VICE PRESIDENT
  * SAID 'THE CAUSE OF REYE'S SYNDROME IS UNKNOWN AND ON THE BASIS
    OF OUR REVIEW OF THE SCIENCE WE CONTINUE TO BELIEVE THERE IS
  * NO CAUSAL RELATIONSHIP BETWEEN ASPIRIN AND THIS RARE DISEASE
  * IN CHILDREN AND TEENAGERS.'
```

Let's examine the various sections of this document.

Right off the bat, you probably see some similarities to stories you retrieved earlier with //DJNEWS. It's even in all-caps, just as the //DJNEWS stories were. That's because the database we used for this example was Dow Jones News, option 2 on the main menu. That database contains exactly the same stories as //DJNEWS, just more of them, all the way back to 1979, instead of just 90 days' worth. (The stories you'll find in //TEXT's *Wall Street Journal* and *Washington Post* databases, options 1 and 3, are displayed in more conventional upper-lowercase and generally are longer than the Dow Jones News reports.)

Now notice the codes along the left margin in our example. They illustrate the various parts of each document. Here's what they mean:

AN, the story's unique identification number.

HL, the headline of the story. (In *The Wall Street Journal* and *Washington Post* databases the HL section also includes the byline of the writer.)

DD, the date.

SO, the source of information used in the story.

CO, the Dow Jones company code, just like the ones you find in //SYMBOL.

IN, the industry group code, again the same as you could find in //SYMBOL.

TX, the actual text of the story.

In the next chapter we'll show you how to use these codes for more elaborate searching and printing.

Still looking at the document we've retrieved, notice the asterisks (*) down the left side. These mark the lines in which at least one of our queries appears—ASPIRIN, CHILDREN, and SYNDROME.

Finally, the line at the top tells us that this is the first of three documents it has waiting for us (remember, our last query found three stories published in 1985) and that this is the first of two pages in that document.

To see the next page of the document, we would need to press RETURN. That would show us the rest of the text, and then end with this message:

END OF DOCUMENT

Pressing RETURN again would show us the first page of the second document found in the latest query, and we could keep pressing RETURN at the bottom of each page until we'd gone through all three documents and would eventually be shown this message:

R0601 * END OF DOCUMENTS IN LIST - ENTER RETURN OR ANOTHER COMMAND

You also can go back a page, or several pages, within a document. You can enter P–1 (that is, "page minus one") to back up one page; P–2 to back up two pages, and so on. You can enter P+2 to jump forward two pages; P+3 to jump forward three pages, and so on. Or you can go to a specific page with P = and a number, such as P=4 to look at the fourth page of a story.

You don't have to read through all the documents just because you've located them. At the bottom of any screen you can:

• Return to search mode by entering two periods and the letter S (..S).

• Or leave //TEXT altogether by entering period-period-OFF (..OFF), which would cause you to exit //TEXT and return to the regular Dow Jones News/Retrieval.

Time out. //TEXT is one of the few services from which you cannot log off directly. In other words, you first must exit //TEXT with ..OFF *before* you can DISConnect from the system.

USING //TEXT WITH A LITTLE MORE FLAIR

We've just put //TEXT through it easiest, most basic operation, and it really wasn't very complicated. Let's sum up what we've learned so far:

• As of this writing, //TEXT has three databases, Dow Jones News Services, *The Wall Street Journal*, and *The Washington Post*, but they all work the same way.

• Upon entering any of the databases, you're prompted for your first query or question, entered in the form of a word or phrase.

• After you enter a query, //TEXT will search that particular database and report the number of "hits," that is, the number of documents it has available meeting the condition you've specified.

• You can make queries more specific by using operators, like AND.

• When you're ready to display what you've found, you can change to print mode by entering ..P; that will display the first page of the most recent story in the latest query.

• Later you can return to search mode by entering ..S or can leave the database by entering ..OFF.

One more point before we press on: //TEXT handles each query independently, and the order in which they're entered usually is not critical to your strategy. A complex search strategy might have 10 or 15 individual queries, with the latest queries linked to earlier ones by operators like AND. The queries don't have to be in sequence in order to be linked. For instance, query 10 in a strategy could be "2 AND 6," meaning "Meet the conditions of the second and sixth queries."

BETTER WAYS TO ENTER QUERIES

Defining queries is what makes a database perform, and //TEXT has a number of advanced features that make for easier querying.

Let's start with the way we enter the words that make up queries. In our

example, we used three words—ASPIRIN, CHILDREN, and SYNDROME—
all of which were specifically what we were looking for. However, there are
times when one word just doesn't do the trick.

If, for instance, we were looking up stories about computers, we'd want to
find those that mention "computer," "computers," computing," and other forms
of the word. It would be tiresome if we had to enter a separate query for each
variation of the word. Fortunately, //TEXT allows what's called *truncation*: you
can enter the first part of the word followed by a dollar sign ($), such as:

```
1__:  COMPUT$
```

That means, find documents that contain words that begin with "comput." You
even can use the dollar sign followed by a number to indicate a specific number
of letters in the word. Suppose, for instance, we wanted stories that mentioned
"computer," "computers," and "computing," but *not* "computations." We could
enter:

```
1__:  COMPUT$3
```

That would indicate you wanted documents containing words that began with
"comput" and had no more than three additional letters. It would bypass
"computation," "computations," and "computerists," because they're too long
to pass the test.

Truncation is particularly useful in dealing with plurals (AGENC$ would
find "agency" and "agencies") and with variations on nouns and verbs
(EXPLOR$ to find "explore," "exploration," "explorer(s)," "exploring,"
etc.).

Also there's no rule that says each query has be a single word. If the
subject you're looking for can best be summed up in a two-word phrase, then
enter it as a query:

```
1__:  OIL EMBARGO
```

That will find stories that mention the phrase "oil embargo" (as well as those that contain up to two words or characters between the search words. Therefore, this example also would retrieve a story with the phrase "oil product embargo.")

In fact, there are many ways to include more than one word in a query, and some of them can really save you searching time. Read on.

THE OPERATORS AT WORK

In the earlier test drive we used the word AND in queries 3 through 5 and called it an *operator*. //TEXT recognizes four operators—AND, OR, NOT, and XOR—and each has its own powers.

When we use AND in a query we mean that *both* conditions must be met. For instance:

```
1_:  IBM AND BURROUGHS
```

This example specifies that we want documents that contain both the word "IBM" and "Burroughs" and ignore all documents that contain only one or neither of them. With AND, the words don't have to appear side by side in the text or in that order so long as they both are somewhere in the story.

Also, as you've seen, we can use AND to connect entire strategies:

```
6_:  4 AND PROFIT$
```

That tells //TEXT to retrieve stories that meet the specifications of whatever query 4 was *and* contain at least one word beginning with "profit" ("profit," "profits," "profiting," etc.).

AND also can link a number of words and phrases in a single query. We said that our Reye's Syndrome example, which took five steps, could have been done in one:

1_: ASPIRIN AND CHILDREN AND SYNDROME AND YR85

Pretty slick. Compare that with the exercise you've bookmarked and you'll see that this line does it all.

But we must be careful in using AND (and all the other operators we're seeing here) because //TEXT takes us literally. In this example, to be flagged for our attention, a document must meet each one of those conditions.

Operators are confusing to some users, not because they're complicated but because they're not complicated enough. When we speak to other human beings, we use words like "and" rather loosely. You might say to your broker, "I want to buy some stocks and bonds."

As you've seen, if your broker were //TEXT, it would assume that you were interested only in deals that involved both stocks *and* bonds, when what you probably meant was "I want to buy something—maybe some stocks, maybe some bonds, maybe both." In other words:

1_: STOCKS OR BONDS

The OR operator retrieves stories that contain one word (or phrase) *or* another word (or phrase) in a query. It's okay if the document contains both; it *has* to contain at least one of them to pass the test.

Often OR is used when there are several words that mean the same thing, such as:

1: BUY OR ACQUIRE OR MERGE

Stories that contain at least one of those words will be retrieved.

Like AND, the operator OR also can be used to link with previous queries:

2__: 1 OR OIL PRODUCTION

That directs the database to find stories that meet whatever conditions were specified in query 1 *or* contain the phrase "oil production."

Generally speaking, queries using AND *ex*clude a lot of documents quickly, while those using OR *in*clude a lot.

The next operator is NOT. With it, //TEXT locates stories that contain the first search word *and not* the second one. We might say something like:

1__: NEWSPAPER$ NOT EARN$

That would give us stories that mention "newspaper" or "newspapers" but *not* those that also mention "earnings," "earned," "earns," and the like.

NOT can be useful for pruning a group of documents. Suppose in the first query you've grouped stories about transportation regulations and you want to make sure the search concentrates only on *ground* transportation. You might enter as your second query:

2__: 1 NOT AIR$6

---

to exclude those about "airplanes," "airlines," and so on.

The last major operator is XOR. It's one that confuses people, partly because it's not an English word like AND and NOT. Fortunately, it's also of limited usefulness—it will retrieve documents that mention one word or the other in a query, but not *both*. For instance:

1__: ICE XOR CREAM

That would give you stories that mention "ice" and stories that mention "cream" but not stories that mention "ice cream"—both words could not appear in the same story.

Similarly, DOW XOR JONES would retrieve any stories on hand about Dow Chemical and about Jones Spacelink Ltd., but *not* Dow Jones.

//TEXT'S TABOOS; STOP WORDS, SYNTAX

Certain words and characters *can't* be used as part of a search query, usually because //TEXT already is using them as commands, operators, and other tools. It makes sense that you can't use the word AND as part of your search phrase, since //TEXT uses AND as an operator. The same is true of the words OR and NOT.

These are referred to as *stop words*, that is, words reserved by //TEXT for its own use. Here is a complete list of stop words which you should avoid in defining search queries:

a	for	must
about	found	no
all	from	not
among	further	of
an	has	on
and	have	or
are	however	same
as	if	several
at	in	some
be	into	such
been	is	than
between	it	that
both	its	the
but	made	their
by	make	these
do	many	they
during	may	those
each	more	through
either	most	to

toward	was	will
upon	were	within
used	which	would
using	while	

Speaking of rules, //TEXT has its own way of looking at things. For instance:

Commas: //TEXT doesn't care for them. If you're searching for a company name that includes commas or other punctuation—such as Merrill Lynch, Pierce, Fenner & Smith—just leave out the commas, like this:

```
1_: MERRILL LYNCH PIERCE FENNER SMITH
```

Periods: If a company name begins with initials, such as "C. E. Bowen & Company," do it this way: drop the periods and the word "Company" and type in just the first initial and the rest of the name, like this:

```
1_: C BOWEN
```

When it comes to middle initials, like David *A*. Peyton, just leave them out, since you don't know if the stories will include the middle initial anyway. Do it as:

```
1_: DAVID PEYTON [or perhaps DAV$ PEYTON]
```

Hyphens: //TEXT will recognize them if you want to use them in a query, although they usually aren't necessary—either "TIMES-MIRROR" or "TIMES MIRROR."

Company names: In addition to typing in a company's name, you can search for a publicly traded firm by simply entering its symbol (as found in //SYMBOL), such as:

```
1_:  AAPL
```

to find stories about Apple Computer, Inc. That can save you a lot of time.

DEALING WITH TIME

Speaking of time, when you're dealing with databases as large as these, you need to have some fast ways to specify the time period you're interested in. //TEXT has many date-related commands.

To begin with, as you've already seen, //TEXT, like //DJNEWS, puts its material in reverse chronological order, so you know that the latest stories are always on top. That means that if you want to display the most recent story found in a query, you need only enter the ..P command.

Also we've already used another handy time command—YR85. We used it in query 5 in our first example (4 AND YR85). Similarly, you could use YR79, YR80, and so on.

//TEXT recognizes a similar "month" command, with "MN01" meaning January and "MN12" meaning December. The month commands can stand alone or can be used with a YR command. For instance, in our Reye's Syndrome example, if we had wanted stories from April 1985 in query 5, we could have entered:

```
5_:  4 AND YR85 MN04
```

That means, "Find stories that meet the specifications of query 4 and also were published in the fourth month of year 1985."

In addition, the month command doesn't *have* to be used with a year. Suppose you had built a search strategy to follow the interest in a particular soft drink and now you wanted to concentrate on the stories that were published during the hot summer months. You might enter:

```
1__: MN06 OR MN07 OR MN08
```

---

to locate stories published in June, July, or August regardless of the year.

What if you want a specific date from the database? A command recently added to //TEXT makes this a piece of cake; it's simply DATE followed by a numeric representation of the day in which you're interested. This is particularly useful with *The Wall Street Journal* and *The Washington Post* databases, since they contain entire issues. Since today's *Journal* is online electronically well before the beginning of the business day, it is easy to search it electronically for stories of interest. For example, if today were January 27, 1986, and you wanted to see stories that mentioned "computers," you could access //TEXT, specify *The Wall Street Journal* database, and then enter as your first query:

```
1__: DATE 1/27/86 AND COMPUT$
```

(Incidentally, the DATE command also will accept dates with hyphens rather than slashes, such as 1-27-86.)

Sometimes you may need to find documents that were published within a specified time frame. //TEXT has the ability to locate stories published:

- Before a certain date (which it thinks of as "Less Than").

- Since a certain date ("Greater Than").

- Between two dates ("Within the Limits of").

- And outside two dates ("Outside the Limits of").

The format for this operation, called ..LIMITing, admittedly is a little tricky, but it's easier to remember once you understand the principle. The ..LIMIT command tells //TEXT to limit a previous query to a date specification. In use, the command looks like this:

2__: ..LIMIT/1 DD GT 850801

Of course, as *anyone* can see, that means we're looking for stories that have been published since August 1, 1985.

Beg pardon?

Uh, you're right. It's not a model of clarity. Let's break it down.

The first part of the command—..LIMIT/1 DD—instructs the database to "limit query 1 to the following date—DD—specifications."

After that, GT means "greater than."

The remaining part, the number, is a crunched form of the date. The ..LIMIT command requires that all dates be entered as six-digit numbers in the form: yymmdd (year-month-day), so August 1, 1985, becomes 850801, while February 20, 1986, would be 860220, and so forth.

"Less Than" (that is, *before* a certain date) works the same way, except that it contains LT (for "less than") instead of GT ("greater than"). To limit, say, query 9 to stories *before* October 24, 1985, would be:

12__: ..LIMIT/9 DD LT 851024

To ..LIMIT a query to documents published between two dates requires a change of codes—WL ("within the limits")—and two dates, the earliest first, followed by a comma and a space, and then the latest date. Here's how you could limit query 6 to stories published between January 1, 1982, and January 1, 1984:

7__: ..LIMIT/6 DD WL 820101,840101

And "Outside the Limits" (OL) works just the same way:

7__: ..LIMIT/6 DD OL 820101,840101

This says you want all the documents specified by query 6 that were published anytime *other than* January 1, 1982, through January 1, 1984.

TIME FOR REFLECTION

Congratulations. You now have at your disposal the majority of the commands you need to find documents in the //TEXT repositories. Before moving onto the advanced commands, we'll take a break and let you mull over what you've seen in our first foray.

For instance, you've seen that, while //TEXT has many add-on commands that make it flexible, it's really rather simple:

• It has two modes of operation, *search mode* and *print mode*.

• To use it in its simplest form, you enter a few key words and phrases, like a game of Twenty Questions (except you're not limited to 20 queries), and then print out the articles you've found. To help you increase or decrease the number of "hits" (that is, located articles), //TEXT recognizes four *operators*—AND, OR, NOT, and XOR.

• The search words can be *truncated* using the dollar sign ($)—CHILD$ would find documents containing "child," "children," "childhood," and so on.

//TEXT also has a number of date-related commands:

YRxx (such as YR85, YR80, etc.) to specify documents filed in a particular calendar year.

MNxx (such as MN02 for February, MN11 for November) to locate stories from a particular month.

DATE (such as DATE 3/13/85) to find stories published on a specific date, particularly useful when searching *The Wall Street Journal* or *The Washington Post*.

..LIMIT, which can find stories published before a certain date (LT, less than), since a certain date (GT, greater than), between two dates (WL, within the limits of), and outside two dates (OL, outside the limits of).

In addition, you've seen a list of words, called *stop words*, that cannot be used in queries because //TEXT reserves them for commands.

You learned a special kind of navigation command unique to //TEXT—two periods together, which move you from one mode to the other. For instance, ..P takes you from search mode to print mode, and ..S takes you from print mode back to search. There are several ways to print (that is, display) documents in //TEXT, which we'll be seeing in the next chapter.

Before you move on to Chapter 11, give some thought about what you've seen, but please *resist* the temptation to log on and begin experimenting. The material we'll present in the next chapter will prepare you for that step.

Chapter 11

MORE ON USING TEXT-SEARCH

If you've taken time to weigh what you learned about the Text-Search Services in the last chapter, you now might have some questions.

For example, we've learned some high-flying ways to put together search queries, using operators like AND and OR, and time elements like the ..LIMIT command. However, when it comes to actually displaying the stories we find, so far we have only a rather pedestrian print command. We saw how to use ..P to display the first page of the latest document located, and how to view subsequent pages by pressing RETURN. But surely //TEXT offers faster ways to see the documents, right? It would be drudgery to have to page through 25 or 30 stories that way.

Fortunately, //TEXT does have a range of display commands which we'll learn in this chapter.

Also you may recall in Chapter 4 one of the scenarios mentioned that //TEXT could be used to look up specific features of *The Wall Street Journal*, such as "Heard on the Street" columns in back issues. We'll put that lesson on the agenda, as well as learn how to collect stories according to the subjects' "industry groups," just as you've done with //DJNEWS.

Finally, this chapter will give you an example of how you can plan your //TEXT searches offline with just a notepad, a pencil, and, as Hemingway once described it, "a clean, well-lighted place."

SEARCHING BY SECTIONS

In reviewing the previous material, you may have noticed that the DD code used in the ..LIMIT command—as in "..LIMIT/6 DD LT 851024"—looked a little familiar. You even may have backtracked a little and discovered that DD was one of the codes that appeared in the left-hand margin of a document we displayed in the first few pages of the last chapter. Take a minute and look at that document again. It's on page 176.

As we pointed out, each document in //TEXT has several coded sections. There's AN (its unique number), HL (the headline), DD (the date), SO (the source material), IN (the industry group code), perhaps GV (its government group code), and finally TX (the actual text).

As it turns out, you can manipulate, that is, search or print, specified sections of the document. In fact, that's precisely what the ..LIMIT command does; the DD portion of the command tells //TEXT to search only the DD (date) section of each document for some specified information.

In a similar way, you can search other sections of the documents in the database. Suppose you wanted to find stories about the film industry. We know from experience that the Dow Jones News/Retrieval's industry code for films is FLX. Using that information in a //TEXT query, the query would look like this:

```
1_: FLX.IN.
```

Note the syntax—the industry code first, then a period, the code IN, and another period, with no spaces in any part of the command. This directs the database to look only at the IN section of its documents to find those which Dow Jones's editors had assigned to the FLX industry group.

It works the same way with government groups. If you were to visit //SYMBOL and look up the Federal Reserve Bank in the list of government codes (or simply refer to our list of them in the Online Survival Kit), you'd find it is G/FED. To use that in a //TEXT search, the query would be:

```
1_: FED.GV.
```

Notice that the category prefixes—I/ for industries, G/ for government—are used in //DJNEWS only; when using category codes in //TEXT, drop the prefix, as in the example.

We told you at the end of the last chapter that you can search for public companies by entering their stock symbols as a query. (Remember? We used Apple Computer, AAPL, as the example.) However, you also can search by the CO portion of each document, as in:

1_: IBM.CO.

In other words, entering just IBM as a query tells //TEXT, in effect, to search the *entire* document, from headline and date to the bottom of the text, for IBM. On the other hand, entering IBM.CO. says to search only the CO section of the document for the *symbol* IBM. That makes this method a little faster and preferred by many //TEXT regulars. (By the way, at this writing, searching by the CO field worked only with the Dow Jones News and *Wall Street Journal* databases, not with *The Washington Post*.)

Searching just the SO (source) portion of documents can be useful if you're collecting material from a specific publication. In our example on page 176, the SO part of the story says, "Dow Jones News Wire (T)." The (T) means that the story comes from the "broadtape" of the Dow Jones News Service. The other source codes used in //TEXT are:

B for *Barron's*

J for *The Wall Street Journal*

N for the News/Retrieval Service

W for *The Wall Street Journal and* the Dow Jones News Service.

So, if you were looking specifically for stories from *Barron's*, you could enter a query of:

1_: B.SO.

Of all the section codes, HL—headlines—is the most useful. With it, you can search documents for keywords in the headlines. More important, //TEXT stores regular features with their titles and bylines in the HL section. That means that you can electronically stay up-to-date with your favorite columns in *The Wall Street Journal* and *The Washington Post*.

If you wanted to collect "Heard on the Street" columns from *The Wall Street Journal* database, you'd query:

```
1__: HEARD STREET.HL.
```

(Noting that "on" and "the" are stop words, we've dropped them out of our query.) Subsequent queries could then zero in on specific subjects or a range of dates, and so on.

Bylines also are part of the HL field. Dow Jones News generally doesn't provide bylines of its writers, but *The Wall Street Journal* and *The Washington Post* databases do. So, if you wanted documents by *Post* columnist Meg Greenfield, you would visit the *Post* database and enter:

```
1__: MEG GREENFIELD.HL.
```

Many //TEXT enthusiasts use the service to follow regular features in the *Journal* and *Post*, doing their searching with the HL and SO fields. To save you some time in finding the good stuff, we've provided a list in the Online Survival Kit, beginning on page 331.

Another handy use of the HL section is to look at two important tables, the Key Interest Rates and the Consumer Savings Rates. A while back DJN/R noticed that this information wasn't available in any concise form in the Dow Jones News database, so the programmers decided to add the tables under their own headlines. To view them, simply access the Dow Jones News database in //TEXT and design a query that includes the name of the table you wish to see, followed by .HL., such as:

```
            1_: KEY INTEREST RATES.HL.
```

or

```
            1_: CONSUMER SAVINGS RATES.HL.
```

DISPLAYING WHAT YOU FIND

All the nifty search functions in the world do precious little good if you don't have some flexibility in displaying them.

We've discussed the general command for printing—..P—which takes you from search mode to print mode and displays the first page of the latest document. But what if you wanted to print the latest documents from an *earlier* query? Suppose your most recent query was number 6, and you wanted to see the documents found by query 5? No problem:

```
            7_:  ..P  5
```

This command would take you to print mode and print the first page of the most recent story found by query 5. (The space between the P and 5 is mandatory, incidentally.)

The lesson here is that //TEXT always looks behind the P for the identifying number of the query to be displayed. If there is no number there, //TEXT assumes you're talking about the latest query.

Also you can use print mode to look at selected portions of your documents, and this feature can be very useful.

Suppose your best search strategy has come up with 25 documents, and you have neither the time nor inclination to look at every page of every one of them just to find the ones of interest.

There are several good ways to go about this. One is with the relatively new P* command. It works like this:

You begin displaying your document with the ..P command, which prints the first page of the latest story in the query. Then, at the bottom of the first page, enter P* (note there is no space between the P and the asterisk). That will cause //TEXT to jump to the first page that contains one of your search terms. (Remember when we were looking at the sample document on page 176, we noted that there were asterisks along the left-hand side? The P* command will search out those pages with at least one asterisk.) When it comes to the end of the references in a document, it will display the last page of that document, at which point you can press RETURN to see the first page of the next story in the queue and enter another P* if you'd like.

So when would you use a command like P*?

It's designed to let you determine quickly if a particular story meets your needs. If you had 25 stories in a query, you could use P* to scan them, making notes of the numbers of documents of interest. You then could specify the stories you wanted displayed in full, with something like this:

```
..P/DOC=2,5,7,10,12
```

And this brings us to a new command: /DOC=.

One of the things that seems to confuse new //TEXT users is how to print a selected story. Invariably, when they want to print document number 5, they type ..P 5. However, as you've already seen, //TEXT interprets ..P 5 to mean "Print Query 5."

If you get in the habit of calling the stories in these databases "documents," it'll be easier to remember the new syntax:

```
..P/DOC=5
```

Just remember that /DOC=5 will print Document Number 5.

GETTING THE HEADLINES

Another handy way to assess the value of a large number of stories in a query is by examining their headlines and dates of publication. That way you can make a note of the ones that look promising and then come back to retrieve the full text of the documents you've noted. Take a look at this command:

```
5_:  ..P HL,DD
```

It's saying, "Take me to print mode and display the headline section (HL) and the date section (DD) of the most recent story in my latest query." //TEXT will display the latest story's date and the HL section (which, in *The Wall Street Journal* and *The Washington Post* also includes the bylines, remember), and if you want to see the same material for the next story, press RETURN.

These commands can also mix and match. For example, if you wanted the same material on your third query rather than your most recent one, the command would be:

```
5_:  ..P 3 HL,DD
```

That would produce something like this:

```
        DOCUMENT=   1 OF              6 PAGE  =   1 OF   1
HL   WARNINGS - ASPIRIN USE -2-
DD   01/23/85
        END OF DOCUMENT
```

Note the document number at the top, followed by the headline and the date. To see the next headline in the query, press RETURN and see:

```
          DOCUMENT=  2 OF  6                          PAGE =  1 OF  1
HL    * MANUFACTURERS TO WARN ABOUT ASPIRIN USE BY ILL CHILDREN
DD      01/23/85

        END OF DOCUMENT
```

Press RETURN for the next one and so forth.

By the way, as we mentioned, *The Wall Street Journal* and *The Washington Post* put more information in their HL section than the Dow Jones News database, from which these two examples were taken. Therefore, when the same ..P 3 HL,DD command is issued in the *Journal* full-text databases, it produces a display something like this:

```
          DOCUMENT=  1 OF  12          PAGE  =  1 OF  1
HL    Auditors' Nemesis:
      Class-Action Lawyer
      Beats the CPA Firms
      At Their Own Game
      - - -
      Melvyn Weiss Uses Expertise
      In the Accounting Trade
      To Win Big Settlements
      - - -
      Two Aspirin Every Afternoon
      - - -
      By Lee Berton
      Staff Reporter of The Wall Street Journal
DD    12/04/85

        END OF DOCUMENT
```

After browsing the headlines, suppose you decided that document 5 was the one you wanted to see. All you have to do is enter ..P 3/DOC=5 and the system will print out the first page of the fifth document in the third query. You also could enter a range of documents to be printed with:

```
          . .P  3/DOC = 1 - 1 0
```

or

```
          . .P  3/DOC = 1 , 5 , 9
```

etc.

PRINT REVIEW

Stop the clock—time for a review. The information suddenly seems to be coming fast and furiously. Here are the essentials in what we've just learned about displaying documents:

• You can display stories found by earlier queries by simply adding a space and the query number to the ..P—as in ..P 5 to print the documents located by query 5.

• Printing can be limited to selected portions of the documents if you add the codes for those sections. For example, ..P 5 HL,SO,DD would print only the headlines (HL), sources (SO), and dates (DD) of the stories located by query 5.

• To print selected documents in a query, append the /DOC= command. In this command—..P 5/DOC=2—//TEXT would print the entire second document contained in the fifth query. Also you can print a sequence of documents, with /DOC=1–6 or /DOC=1,5,7 or DOC=2–7, and so on.

• Finally, the flexibility of //TEXT's print functions is in mixing and matching the commands. For instance, ..P 4 HL,DD/DOC=1–13 would provide a list of headlines and dates of publication for the first through the thirteenth documents in query 4.

CONTINUOUS PRINT—FASTER, FASTER

There will be times when you don't want to be bothered with having to press RETURN at the bottom of each screen of information. If you've already scanned some stories with the P* command or examined their headlines and dates with a ..P HL,DD combination, you may know for sure that you want the entire text of document 3. Why should you have to press RETURN eight or nine times just to get all of it?

Well, you don't.

//TEXT provides a Continuous Print (..CP) command just for these occasions, and it works with the same syntax as ..P. Therefore, if you knew you wanted to see all of document 5 in query 6, you might enter:

```
..CP 6/DOC=5
```

Continuous Print is even more useful for looking at a list of headlines. If you had 31 documents in query 7, you could see headlines and dates of all of them without ever having to press RETURN by entering:

```
..CP 7 HL,DD/DOC=1-31
```

---

or if you wanted to see headlines of just the latest ten in the query:

```
..CP 7 HL,DD/DOC=1-10
```

(Since you know the stories are in reverse chronological order, you know that documents 1 through 10 will be the latest.)

While the list is being displayed, remember that Control S and Control Q can stop and start the flow of information displayed.

..CP is a neat command, sort of like the NP—No Pause—command you saw in connection with //TRACK in Chapter 9.

However:

WARNING! WARNING! WARNING!

For All of Us Who Don't Like to Throw MONEY Away! (*That* probably got everyone's attention.)

You must use //TEXT's print commands, especially the Continuous Print command, with care. That's because once //TEXT begins processing a print request, *you can't interrupt it*. Even if you break the telephone connection, //TEXT will complete the task—and bill you for the time it took to do it.

With a regular print command, ..P, that's no problem, since //TEXT automatically pauses at the bottom of each page and you can discontinue the print sequence at any time by returning to search mode (with the ..S command you learned in the last chapter).

But because Continuous Print eliminates those pauses, there's no opportunity to break out of the sequence once it's begun, even by disconnecting your modem.

More than once a careless subscriber has ended up printing out the text of 25 documents when he really wanted only the *headlines* of those documents. You can see how that happens. What he meant to enter was:

```
..CP 5 HL,DD/DOC=1-25
```

However, what he typed was:

```
..CP 5/DOC=1-25
```

The first example says, "Continuously print, from query 5, the headline (HL) and date (DD) sections of documents 1 through 25." But the second example . . . well, you see the problem. Since the user left out the HL and DD codes, //TEXT took him at his word and assumed he wanted the full text of all 25.

Better still, condition yourself to use ..CP sparingly. When you type the command ..CP, a red flag should go up. Before you press RETURN at the end of the line, you should be asking yourself if you've specified the command correctly. If not, backspace—all the way to the beginning of the line, if necessary—and correct it.

When in doubt, use the safer, slower ..P, which will pause at the bottom of each screen.

CONNECTORS

For a moment, let's switch gears, leaving the print mode for the search mode so we can fill your //TEXT toolbox with some new commands.

In Chapter 10 you learned how to use the important operators AND, OR, NOT, and XOR. These search utilities have some first cousins, called *connectors*, that allow you to specify further the relationship of search words.

For instance, using ADJ in a search query will cause the database to look for documents in which the specified words are ADJacent to each other, as in:

```
1_:  CONTROL ADJ DATA
```

This tells //TEXT to fetch documents in which "control" and "data" are side by side, in that order. You can even use ADJ to specify the number of words that can be permitted between two words you're searching. ADJ1 says there may be one word or character between the words, ADJ2, two words or characters, and so on, up to ADJ7.

NEAR works like ADJ, except that the words can be in any order:

```
1_:  OPTIONS NEAR BUYING
```

would retrieve stories that contain "options buying" as well as "buying options." As with ADJ, you can specify a number of words between your keywords, with NEAR1, NEAR2, NEAR3, up to NEAR7.

Finally, SAME is a useful connection that specifies that two words must be in the same paragraph of the text, such as:

```
              1_:  OIL  SAME  PRODUCTION
```

That means you're interested in stories that contain those two words, not necessarily side by side or in that order, but in the same paragraph.

IN PRAISE OF PLANNING

You now have most of the commands and utilities you need in order to begin planning search and print strategies offline, even though you haven't actually seen //TEXT operating on your screen.

For the next few pages we'll show you how you might sketch out an online session, starting by identifying the problem and carrying it through a simulated online session.

Let's pretend you're an avid baseball fan. Realizing that //TEXT also can be used for applications outside the business world, you decide to see what //TEXT can tell you about how your team, the Mets, has fared against the Pittsburgh Pirates.

You've already decided to use *The Washington Post* database. (We all love the *Journal*, but it's out of its league when it comes to baseball, you know.)

Before you log on, you work out the search strategy with a pencil and paper.

For starters, you know from looking in the Online Survival Kit in the back of the book that you can search the individual sections of *The Washington Post*; the code for the sports section is SPORTS.SO. In the same query you can specify baseball. So, you write on your notepad:

NOTEPAD-> Query 1: SPORTS.SO. AND BASEBALL

That will cause //TEXT to search the thousands of stories the *Post* has published since 1984 to concentrate on those in the Sports Section that mention the word "baseball."

Your next consideration might be time. Since query 1 is likely to collect stories from several different years, it might be good to divide the stories into individual baseball seasons. We could use the ..LIMIT command—something like ..LIMIT/1 DD WL 840101,841231 to get all the stories published in 1984, then do another ..LIMIT for 1985, and so forth.

But, wait a minute—here's another idea. Since baseball seasons fall neatly within a calendar year, we can use the YR84 command. So . . .

NOTEPAD-> Query 2: 1 AND YR84
NOTEPAD-> Query 3: 1 AND YR85
NOTEPAD-> Query 4: 1 AND YR86

That's given you three pools of stories. Query 2 has the 1984 baseball reports, query 3 the 1985 stories, and query 4 has 1986 stories.

Now you're ready to target the Mets and the Pirates.

It stands to reason that any stories about the two teams playing each other would mention Mets and Pirates in the same paragraph somewhere in the story, right? So you can use that handy SAME command you just learned. You decide to start with the most recent season, noting:

NOTEPAD-> Query 5: 4 AND METS SAME PIRATES

In other words, query 5 tells the database to meet the criteria of query 4 (BASEBALL stories in the SPORTS.SO. section published in YR86) AND locate those that mention METS in the SAME paragraph as PIRATES.

At this point you decide to do some printing to scan what you've found. You choose to examine all the headlines and dates of the stories, with:

NOTEPAD-> ..P 5 HL,DD/DOC = 1-x

The x, of course, would be the number of stories we want to look at from the query 5 pool. Or you might decide on a Continuous Printing with:

NOTEPAD-> ..CP 5 HL,DD/DOC = 1-x

Either way, you plan to note the document number of each story that looks interesting, and on your notepad you write a reminder:

NOTEPAD-> ..P 5/DOC = x

or

> NOTEPAD-> ..CP 5/DOC = *x*

Again, *x* would equal the document number of an interesting looking story. Of course, if your headline list signaled more than one story of interest, you could make the command something like ..P 5/DOC = 3,5,8 or ..CP 5/DOC = 3,5,8.

After looking over those documents, you might want to return to search mode and take a similar reading on the 1985 season. So:

> NOTEPAD-> ..S

That, of course, means "Take me back to search mode." You would go right to where you left off. Your last query was number 5, so:

> NOTEPAD-> Query 6: 3 AND METS SAME PIRATES

Now notice how this works: query 3 has your pool of 1985 baseball stories, so query 6 says, "Take the query 3 stories and locate those with Mets and Pirates in the same paragraph." After //TEXT has found them, you can scan with the same print strategy you just used to look at headlines and dates. Then you can return to search mode, with ..S, and do the same kind of search on query 2 (3 AND METS SAME PIRATES) to examine the 1984 season.

At the bottom of the notepad you should remind yourself how to leave //TEXT:

> NOTEPAD-> ..OFF

Remember, you have to exit //TEXT *before* you log off DJN/R. Finally:

> NOTEPAD-> DISC

That logs off the system.

PUTTING THE PLAN INTO ACTION

With your homework in hand, it's just a matter of logging on to Dow Jones News/Retrieval, entering //TEXT to get to the text search service, selecting the database you want (in this case, *The Washington Post*) and following the script you've written for yourself.

If we're planning to get paper copies of the stories we retrieve, we find it's easier to turn on the printer as we enter //TEXT. For one thing, this saves time since we don't have to keep worrying about stopping and starting the printer. More important, it's often handy to have a printed copy of the various queries as they're defined.

Now a word about how we structured this make-believe search strategy. You may have noticed that we worked from the largest possible group (all BASEBALL stories in SPORTS.SO.) to the smallest groups. Doing this makes it easier if you decide to "ad lib" while online.

Suppose, for instance, after looking up the history of the Mets and Pirates in 1984 through 1986, you became curious about other baseball-related stories, such as the coverage of the 1986 playoffs. The way you've structured your strategy makes it easy to add queries. Query 4 already earmarks baseball stories in 1986, so it would be easy to define a new one as:

```
9__: 4 AND PLAYOFFS
```

Or suppose you were curious about how the *Post*'s sports staffers covered drug-related stories in baseball, regardless of the year. Query 1 already collects all the baseball stories in the sports section from 1984 to the present, so:

```
9__: 1 AND DRUG$
```

That would find "baseball" Sports Section stories that include words like "drug-related," "drugs," and so on.

We think you'll find it generally easier if you define one or two groups of documents that corral the general area of stories you want and then link them together in subsequent queries with the AND command.

For instance, every business day Charlie checks the latest *Wall Street Journal* for news about computers, and he usually does it with one query:

```
1_: DATE 1/29/86 AND COMPUTER$
```

Of course, he inserts today's date after the DATE command each morning. "COMPUTER$" also will pick up the word "computers."

That usually finds 15 or 20 stories. Then he scans them with ..CP HL,DD/ DOC = 1-x (with x being the total number found).

However, if he were going to look up today's WSJ reports on several subjects, he'd do it slightly differently. The first query would be simply:

```
1_: DATE 1/29/86
```

with today's date. That would create a pool of documents from today's *Journal*.

Then subsequent queries could be something like:

```
2_: 1 AND AUTOMO$
3_: 1 AND CHEMICAL$
4_: 1 AND RETAIL SALES
```

Query 1 corrals the main group of stories, today's issue of *The Wall Street Journal*, and each subsequent query works in concert.

The point is, keep it simple.

MISCELLANEOUS COMMANDS

Here are a few more //TEXT tools before you set out for your own exploration of this database. These are commands and techniques that are, frankly, a little esoteric, and we don't use them often ourselves. However, it's nice to know they're available if you need them.

Nesting: Sometimes, particularly when you're planning offline, you may want to tighten your strategy as much as possible by putting multiple queries on a line. You've already learned how to link some together with AND, such as our ASPIRIN AND CHILDREN AND SYNDROME AND YR85 example. Also you can tie together queries using parentheses ( ) to specify the order in which you want searches processed by //TEXT. This is called *nesting*.

Consider this example:

```
1__:  (REDS OR METS) AND PLAYOFFS
```

By putting REDS OR METS in parentheses (nesting them), you're telling //TEXT to first locate stories with one of those teams mentioned and then find those that also mention PLAYOFFS.

As a practical matter, most nested queries also can be performed in two steps. This one could be:

```
1__:  REDS OR METS
2__:  1 AND PLAYOFFS
```

Either style will work—whatever you feel comfortable with.

Stacking commands: A time-saver that some experienced //TEXT searchers use is to stack commands, that is, to link several together on a line, separated with a slash (/).

Suppose you planned to look up Apple Computer stories in //TEXT and then print the first page of the latest one found. You already know how to do it in two steps. Here's how to do it in one:

```
          1__:  AAPL.CO./..P
```

You're telling //TEXT to look in the CO section of its documents for the Apple company symbol (AAPL) and then proceed immediately to print mode and print the first page.

ROOT and SET commands: We've been lying to you all along. We've suggested that //TEXT searches the entire text of each document it has online each time you define a query. Actually, //TEXT stores every word in electronic alphabetic indexes along with the number of documents in which that word appears for quick referral.

Sometimes these indexes, which can be displayed with the ROOT command, may be useful to you if you want to know what the variations on a word are and which is the most commonly used form in that database.

Suppose you wanted to know variations on the usage of the word BOOK? You could enter ROOT BOOK and be shown something like this:

```
   00001 ROOT BOOK
 R1  BOOK$
 R2  BOOK                           2824 DOCUMENTS
 R3  BOOK-BINDING                      1 DOCUMENT
 R4  BOOK-CLUB                         1 DOCUMENT
 R5  BOOK-COOKING                      2 DOCUMENTS
 R6  BOOK-ENTRY                      123 DOCUMENTS
 R7  BOOK-EVALUATION                   1 DOCUMENT
```

Note the codes, R1 through R7, at the left side. These now can be used in your next query, such as:

```
          2__:  R4 AND COMPUTER$
```

There may be times, especially on complex search strategies, when you'd like a similar kind of report on all the queries you perform. You can have that by using the ..SET DETAIL command. Entering:

```
        1_: ..SET DETAIL=ON
```

and the system will respond with a message something like, "Set Command has been executed. RETURN to continue."

After pressing RETURN, you can enter your search words, such as:

```
     2_: ASPIRIN AND CHILDREN AND SYNDROME
```

Now //TEXT will report how many documents contain each of the words you've specified.

To turn it off again, enter ..SET DETAIL=OFF.

..DISPLAYing and PURGing: In a long session on //TEXT, moving back and forth between search and print modes, it's sometimes necessary to refresh your memory about your queries. That's why it's a good idea to have the printer turned on as you work. However, if you don't have access to the printer, then the ..DISPLAY command will come to the rescue.

With it, you can display the details of a single query:

```
        8_: ..DISPLAY 6
```

or several queries, with ..DISPLAY 1–6, or ..DISPLAY 1,3,6, or ..DISPLAY ALL.

In search mode you're allowed up to 99 queries per session. However, that's a misleading number, because at any time you can ..PURGE one or any of your queries, like cleaning the slate. You can:

```
        17_: ..PURGE ALL
```

or

```
20__:  ..PURGE 19
```

Some users feel it's less confusing if they PURGE old queries during a long session. Remember, though, that once a query has been ..PURGEd, it can't be retrieved.

Highlights, on and off: Finally, you have some control over the way the incoming material is displayed in print mode. Remember when we looked at documents found by the database, asterisks (*) showed up in the left margin beside lines in which search words appeared. Well, if you're getting paper copies of stories, you might want to turn off these asterisks (called *highlights*).

You can do that by entering the command ..SET HIGHLIGHT = OFF. To turn them back on, you guessed it—..SET HIGHLIGHT = ON.

IN CONCLUSION

In this chapter we filled in the gaps on how to use //TEXT.

For instance, we found out that individual sections of documents can be searched, with queries such as HEARD STREET.HL. to look for "Heard on the Street" as part of the headline (HL) section of documents. We learned, too, that industry codes, such as FLX for films, could be used in a query (as in FLX.IN.).

Also, we saw that //TEXT has some useful display commands, such as ..CP for Continuous Print, and that individual sections of documents could be printed, as in ..CP 5 HL,DD/DOC = 1–3, which would continuously print from query 5 the headline (HL) and date (DD) sections of documents 1 through 3.

We learned about *connectors*, which, like operators, can be used to increase or decrease the group of documents you're dealing with. Among them were:

• ADJ to find documents in which two words are adjacent to each other, as in CONTROL ADJ DATA.

• NEAR, which is similar to ADJ, except that the words can be in any order. CONTROL NEAR DATA would find documents containing either "control data" or "data control."

• SAME, which finds documents in which specified words are in the same paragraph.

Finally, we found out about a few commands for special occasions:

• ROOT, which can display all the variations of a search word on file.

• ..SET DETAIL = ON, which instructs //TEXT to report how many documents contain each word specified in a compound query.

• ..DISPLAY, which reports the details of an earlier query.

• ..PURGE, which removes earlier queries.

• ..SET HIGHLIGHTS = OFF, which turns off the asterisks displayed in the left-hand margin in retrieved documents.

Chapter 12

MCI MAIL:
THE DOW JONES
MAIL LINK

Since the dawn of computer communications, the idea of using the medium to transmit mail electronically has been a driving force behind the development of the technology. Being able to exchange written words instantly between computer users has obvious advantages to the business world, where the value of information so often depends on how fast you can get it.

Dow Jones News/Retrieval has chosen not to develop its own electronic mail system, but instead to contract with MCI Mail, which many analysts consider the best electronic mail system around.

MCI Mail allows instant electronic communications between MCI Mail subscribers, as well as with those who are *not* subscribers. In fact, you can use MCI Mail to correspond with people who do not even have a computer. In that case, your electronic message is routed to the MCI printing center closest to the recipient's location, printed in paper form by a letter-quality printer, and delivered in a bright orange envelope. From there, the last leg of the trip can be by courier in most major cities or by the U.S. Postal Service.

MCI Mail also is linked directly to the Telex system, so users can send Telex messages around the world.

THE BEAUTY OF MCI

All this may sound complicated, but it isn't. As with any good telecommunications system, you can operate MCI Mail on several levels, from novice to expert.

The beauty of MCI Mail is that at the novice level it's menu-driven, with options listed at every step to help you write your first MCI letter, whether it will wind up on some other subscriber's screen or in someone's U.S. Postal Service mailbox. From the earliest days of MCI Mail nearly every review of the system has said the same thing: because of those menus, the reviewer, entering the service the first time, was able, with little or no instruction, to mail a message.

This chapter will show you how easy it is to write and read letters with MCI Mail in novice mode. Then we're going to show you some of the advanced services you may find advantageous in streamlining MCI to meet your own needs.

We'll be doing all of this offline, so settle back and let us do the driving as we show you some of the menu screens you'll see as an MCI Mail user.

THE MCI-DOW JONES LINK

Signup for MCI Mail is not automatic for Dow Jones subscribers. Shortly after your News/Retrieval subscription is activated, you should receive a packet of MCI information. To subscribe, you must pay an annual fee. If you don't receive the packet, call MCI at 1-800-424-6677. (If you're in the Washington, D.C., area, call 1-202-833-8484.) Identify yourself as a DJN/R subscriber.

No monthly surcharge is levied in connection with your MCI Mail account, so if you choose not to use it, you won't be charged extra for the service. You're billed only for the letters you mail or the other MCI services you use, and those costs will be charged to your regular DJN/R bill.

LOGGING INTO MCI

Getting to MCI Mail is just like getting to any other database in the system: it starts with the // command. In this case, enter //MCI at nearly any ENTER QUERY prompt at the bottom of a screen page.

Once inside the MCI Mail area, you may enter EXIT at the main MCI Mail menu to return to the main News/Retrieval system. Your other usual navigation commands also will work; you can enter // and a database code to go from the main MCI Mail menu to a new service, or DISC to disconnect from MCI and News/Retrieval at the same time.

WRITING A NOTE ON MCI

As a new MCI subscriber, the first thing you'll probably do is write a note to someone. To give you an idea of how that works, let's see how Dave writes a note to Charlie.

From the ENTER QUERY prompt on the main system, Dave enters //MCI and is shown:

```
MCI IS ON LINE

Please enter your user name:
```

As we mentioned, the sign-up package you receive from MCI provides a special user name and a password. The user name (Dave's is DPEYTON) is important because it's the key to the front door of the online post office.

Dave enters the two pieces of information—the signup name and password—when the system prompts for them, and sees an introductory message which may contain some news headlines or system's announcements, something like this:

```
Welcome to MCI Mail!

Got something to say that will make a difference?
Send it in an envelope that has impact -- an MCI Mail
Letter.

Read //INTRO on Dow Jones -- FREE!

Today's Headlines at 3 pm EST:

--Israelis Intercept Libyan Plane In Effort To Find
  Guerrillas
--President To Seek Welfare Changes In State Of The
  Union Address

Type //NEWS on Dow Jones for Details.

MCI Mail Version 3.2

There are no messages waiting in your INBOX.

Press <RETURN> to continue
```

Note the message at the bottom of the screen. It always tells you how many messages are waiting for you in the INBOX, your MCI electronic mailbox in which the letters addressed to you by other MCI subscribers are stored until you read them. We'll see how to read messages shortly; for now, let's concentrate on writing.

Now Dave presses RETURN and sees the MCI main menu.

```
You may enter:

SCAN          for a summary of your mail
READ          to READ messages or LISTS
PRINT         to display messages nonstop
CREATE        to write an MCI Letter
CREATE LIST   to make a distribution list
DOWJONES      to Dow Jones News/Retrieval
ACCOUNT       to adjust terminal display
HELP          for assistance

Command (or MENU or EXIT):
```

This menu contains nearly every major command you need to know to make this service work:

SCAN gives you a summary of letters in your electronic mailbox, including the name of each writer and a description of his or her topic.

READ lets you display the contents of each message, with a pause at the bottom of each new screen.

PRINT also displays all waiting letters in their entirety, but *without* a pause. This is similar to the Continuous Print (..CP) command we saw in //TEXT and the NP (No Pause) command in //TRACK. MCI Mail's PRINT command is especially useful if you plan to route messages to a printer or disk for reading offline.

CREATE lets you write a letter either for delivery electronically to another MCI subscriber or for "paper delivery" from an MCI printing location via courier or the U.S. Postal Service.

ACCOUNT enables you to adjust how the MCI mail display is presented on your computer screen. You can adjust the length of each line as well as line feeds and carriage returns.

HELP is the word you use at any stopping place on MCI to get more information about a specific command.

As the prompt at the bottom of the display indicates, you can enter MENU at any point in the MCI feature to return to this main MCI menu. And, as we said, you can enter the word EXIT, which will take you out of the MCI service and back to the main DJN/R system.

Note: No doubt you noticed the command DOWJONES on this menu and may wonder why you wouldn't use it to return to the News/Retrieval instead of EXIT. If you were an MCI subscriber and *not* a Dow Jones subscriber, the command DOWJONES would be the one you would use to access DJN/R, and have the cost of using that service added to your MCI bill. But, as a News/Retrieval subscriber entering MCI through the Dow Jones service, you use EXIT to return to News/Retrieval.

FINDING ANOTHER SUBSCRIBER

In order to send an electronic letter to another MCI subscriber, you need to know the exact name the subscriber is using on MCI Mail or his or her user ID number. The way to find it is to use a command *not* on the main menu but easy enough to remember. It's FIND.

To locate information about Charlie's account on MCI Mail, Dave enters FIND at the end of the main menu to see:

```
You may enter:

NAME       for MCI Mail subscribers
SCRIPT     for scripts
LIST       for shared mailing lists
EMS        for electronic mail systems
BOARD      for bulletin boards
HELP       for assistance

Command (or MENU or EXIT):
```

This menu refers to some features we'll be discussing later. Note that MCI has private bulletin boards for groups of subscribers, as well as closed electronic mailing systems for organizations that use the MCI Mail system for their own private mailing purposes.

Dave will look for information about Charlie by his name, so he enters NAME at the colon prompt and sees:

```
                    Name:
```

When searching for another subscriber by name, it's often wise to enter the last name only. Unless the name is very common—friends of Smith, Jones, and Johnson, take note—the list shouldn't be too long.

Dave enters BOWEN at the colon prompt and sees a list something like this:

```
MCI Mail Subscriber Information

MCI ID    Name            Organization      Location
253-8554  Brad Bowen      Tele Masters      Dallas, TX
224-5135  Charles Bowen                     Huntington, WV
270-1428  Cindy Bowen     MCIT Mid-Atlant   Towson, MD
108-5725  Craig Bowen                       Arlington, VA
237-2901  Craig Bowen     MCIT              Arlington, VA
287-5660  George Bowen    Electric Utilit   Saddle River, NJ
221-0506  Jim Bowen       MCIT Pacific Re   Irvine, CA
256-2702  Jim Bowen       Jim Bowen Agenc   New Orleans, LA
280-4059  Jim Bowen       EI Du Pont de N   Toledo, OH
265-5031  Karen Bowen     MCIT              Washington, DC
226-4277  Karen K. Bowen  MCIT              Salt Lake City,
258-3091  Laura Bowen     MCI Southwest     Arlington, VA
100-7217  Nancy Bowen                       Alexandria, VA
225-5136  Pamela Bowen                      Huntington, WV
283-5954  Tom Bowen       Satellite Busin   McLean, VA
Press <RETURN> to continue
```

Note that each of these "Bowen" subscribers has a different MCI ID number and a location associated with the name. Some also include names of organizations with which they're affiliated. All of this is provided to help find the Bowen you're looking for.

If there were two Charles Bowens on this list, the address on the electronic "envelope" would have to include the MCI user account. But there's only one Charles Bowen of Huntington WV and that's all Dave needs to know to address a note to him. In other words, what's most important is how our Bowen has his name on the mailing list—"Charles Bowen," not "Charlie Bowen" or "Charles E. Bowen," or "C.E. Bowen."

Pressing RETURN, Dave returns to the main menu:

```
You may enter:

SCAN            for a summary of your mail
READ            to READ messages or LISTS
PRINT           to display messages nonstop
CREATE          to write an MCI Letter
CREATE LIST     to make a distribution list
DOWJONES        to Dow Jones News/Retrieval
```

```
ACCOUNT       to adjust terminal display
HELP          for assistance

Command (or MENU or EXIT):
```

Armed with Bowen's online address, Dave is ready to CREATE a letter. It's not important to MCI Mail at this point how he wants the letter delivered. Later he will have an opportunity to specify delivery electronically, as a Telex or by paper through the U.S. Postal Service or courier.

Dave enters CREATE and the system displays a TO: prompt, at which he enters Charlie's name—Charles Bowen—just as it appeared in the FIND list.

Now the system looks up Charlie's MCI ID number and his location and displays them like this:

```
224-5135                                        Huntington, WV

TO:
```

The second TO: prompt gives a chance for Dave to send the message to more than one subscriber. Here he could write the name of another subscriber, or of anyone with a postal address, and the message would be delivered. After he enters the last recipient, he simply presses RETURN at the TO: prompt and sees:

```
                             CC:
```

This is the standard business abbreviation for a "carbon copy." Recipients listed here would receive a message identified as a carbon copy of a letter sent to someone else. If there are no carbon copies to be sent, simply enter a RETURN here.

Next comes a SUBJECT: line. As the writer of the letter, you can enter several words describing the contents. Dave chooses to enter as the subject THE MCI CHAPTER, though he could choose to skip the SUBJECT option by just pressing RETURN.

After the SUBJECT option, MCI Mail gets down to business with this
message:

```
Text: (Enter text or transmit file. Type / on a line by itself to end.)
```

Here's where you write your text. If you're writing an electronic message
to another subscriber who'll be receiving it on a computer screen, you needn't
worry too much about formatting it, if it's just a simple message. The best idea is
to get into the habit of pressing RETURN at the end of each line as it appears
on your screen. You *must* enter a RETURN before the 255th character or space
occurs in the message.

If, however, you are writing a letter that will eventually wind up as a letter
printed on paper or a Telex, you should keep in mind that the length of lines
for printed matter sent via MCI is 69 characters and spaces. Thus, you have to
be a bit more careful about pressing the RETURN or ENTER key before that
69th space on a given line.

Here's the way Dave sends the electronic letter to Charlie:

```
Charlie: I'm currently writing the chapter on MCI <RETURN>
Mail. I thought I'd write a letter to you as an <RETURN>
example of how to send an instant letter to another <RETURN>
MCI Mail subscriber.<RETURN>
/<RETURN>
```

If you make an error while typing, simply backspace and correct it.

Notice that to tell the MCI system he is finished writing, Dave enters a
slash (/) as the first character on a new line and follows it immediately by
pressing RETURN.

That signals MCI Mail to display a new menu like this one:

```
You may enter:

READ         to review your letter
READ PAPER   to review your letter for paper
EDIT         to correct your letter
```

```
SEND            Postal delivery for paper; instant
                   electronic delivery
SEND ONITE  OVERNIGHT courier for paper; PRIORITY
                   electronic delivery
SEND 4HOUR  FOUR-HOUR courier for paper; PRIORITY
                   electronic delivery
HELP            for assistance

Command (or MENU or EXIT):
```

The command to send the message on its way electronically is **SEND**. Dave enters that and MCI Mail summarizes the transaction:

```
One moment please; your message is being posted.

Your message was posted: Tue Feb 04, 1986 10:51 pm EST.
There is a copy in your OUTBOX.

Press <RETURN> to continue
```

As the message says, a copy of what he just wrote is in his OUTBOX, a sort of personal text file storage area, and it will remain there for the next 24 hours. When he presses RETURN at this point again, Dave is returned to the main menu.

```
You may enter:

SCAN         for a summary of your mail
READ         to READ messages or LISTS
PRINT        to display messages nonstop
CREATE       to write an MCI Letter
CREATE LIST  to make a distribution list
DOWJONES     to Dow Jones News/Retrieval
ACCOUNT      to adjust terminal display
HELP         for assistance

Command (or MENU or EXIT):
```

PREPARING TO READ

On this menu, READ is a powerful command that can do more than simply read incoming messages. Entering READ at the main menu will produce this list of options:

```
You may enter:

INBOX    to READ your unread messages
OUTBOX   to READ messages you sent
DESK     to READ messages read before
DRAFT    to READ your draft message
ALL      to READ ALL your messages
LIST     to READ a LIST
HELP     for assistance

Command (or MENU or EXIT):
```

In other words, you can read unread messages you've received in your INBOX or those in your OUTBOX (messages you have sent within the previous 24 hours). You can read messages on your DESK—that is, all the messages you have received in the past 24 hours. If you have written a draft of a note and haven't sent it yet, you can read it by typing DRAFT at this READ menu.

If you enter ALL, you can read all messages in the previous categories. If you have created a special mailing list, you can see the addresses on the list by typing LIST.

Dave wants to see the message he sent to Charlie, so he enters OUTBOX. The message is displayed exactly as Charlie will see it in his INBOX the next time he checks into MCI mail:

```
Date:    Tue Feb 04, 1986 10:51 pm EST
From:    David A. Peyton / MCI ID: 162-9244

TO:      * Charles Bowen / MCI ID: 224-5135
Subject: The MCI Chapter
Message-Id: 13860205035131/0001629244N25EM
```

```
Charlie: I'm currently writing the chapter on MCI Mail.
I thought I'd write a letter to you as an example of
how to send an instant letter to another MCI Mail
subscriber.

Press <RETURN> to continue
```

When Dave presses RETURN again, he's shown yet another submenu.

```
You may enter:

READ       to READ this message again
ANS        to ANSWER the message sender
ANS EACH   to ANSWER the message sender and each recipient
NEXT       to go on to the NEXT message
HELP       for assistance

Command (or MENU or EXIT):
```

On this menu, READ would allow you to see the message again. If you were reading a message sent to you by another subscriber, entering ANS at this prompt would allow you to send an answer without having to address the message. (In other words, MCI "remembers" the address of the original message to which you're replying.) The next prompt you would get would be "Enter Your Text."

If you have received a message that was sent to several people on a list, you could enter ANS EACH and send your response to everyone on the list. If you were reading a list of messages, you could read the next one in the sequence by typing NEXT. Entering MENU now would take you back to the main menu.

READING MCI MAIL

Reading your MCI Mail is as easy as writing it because menus can guide you every step of the way. For instance, here's what Dave found when he logged into MCI Mail the day after he sent the message to Charlie. After the introductory material he saw the following:

```
                    MCI Mail Version 3.2

                 Your INBOX has 3 messages

                 Press <RETURN> to continue
```

If a message is in the INBOX, it means that it has not yet been read. A press of the RETURN key offers Dave the familiar list of options:

```
You may enter:

SCAN            for a summary of your mail
READ            to READ messages or LISTS
PRINT           to display messages nonstop
CREATE          to write an MCI Letter
CREATE LIST     to make a distribution list
DOWJONES        to Dow Jones News/Retrieval
ACCOUNT         to adjust terminal display
HELP            for assistance

Command (or MENU or EXIT): scan
```

Dave might jump right in to READ the letters, but first let's see how the SCAN option works. Dave enters SCAN and is shown another familiar submenu:

```
You may enter:

INBOX     to SCAN your unread messages
OUTBOX    to SCAN messages you sent
DESK      to SCAN messages read before
DRAFT     to SCAN your DRAFT message
ALL       to SCAN ALL your messages
LIST      to SCAN your LISTs
HELP      for assistance

Command (or MENU or EXIT):
```

Since all the messages to scan are new arrivals, he enters INBOX and sees something like this:

```
3 messages in INBOX

No.  Posted            From            Subject       Size
  1  Feb 09 15:12      Charles Bowen   GOT IT!         77
  2  Feb 09 15:22      Charles Bowen   HELP           172
  3  Feb 09 16:14      Charles Bowen   NEVER MIND      71

Press <RETURN> to continue
```

That tells him they're all from Charlie. According to the statistics in the Posted column, they were all sent within about an hour on the afternoon of February 9. The size refers to the number of characters in each message. It appears that all messages were short.

Now Dave presses RETURN to get more tips on his options.

```
You may enter:

READ    to READ the scanned messages
PRINT   to display messages nonstop
SCAN    to SCAN for other messages
HELP    for assistance

Command (or MENU or EXIT):
```

Dave decides to READ the scanned messages one at a time, so he enters SCAN and sees:

```
          Please enter scan numbers:
```

Note the prompt says "numbers," not "number." That means that if Dave wanted to read only one of them, he would enter only one number; if he wanted to read letters number 1 and 3, he could enter 1,3—that is, the two numbers separated by a comma.

However, Dave wants to read them all, so he enters 1-3 (separating the beginning and ending numbers with a hyphen) and the screen displays the first message.

```
Date:      Sun Feb 09, 1986 3:12 pm EST
From:      Charles Bowen /  MCI ID: 224-5135

TO:      * David A. Peyton / MCI ID: 162-9244
Subject:  GOT IT!

Got your message. You really know MCI Mail.
You ought to write a book!

You may enter:

READ       to READ this message again
ANS        to ANSWER the message sender
ANS EACH   to ANSWER the message sender and each
                    recipient
NEXT       to go on to the NEXT message
HELP       for assistance

Command (or MENU or EXIT):
```

Because Dave asked to read each message individually, he got a menu after the first message. Charlie's attempts at humor in the first note are short-lived. Dave has the last laugh in the second message.

Following the menu, Dave enters NEXT for the next message he's ordered up, and sees:

```
Date:      Sun Feb 09, 1986 3:22 pm EST
From:      Charles Bowen  / MCI ID: 224-5135

TO:      * David A. Peyton / MCI ID: 162-9244
Subject:  Help

Darcy, our cat, has been at work again. She ate
the copy of that mailing list we were
```

```
working on yesterday. Can you send me a
copy? I'll give you a cat in exchange for it.

You may enter:

READ        to READ this message again
ANS         to ANSWER the message sender
ANS EACH    to ANSWER the message sender and each
                       recipient
NEXT        to go on to the NEXT message
HELP        for assistance

Command (or MENU or EXIT):
```

After that second note Dave is anxious to see the final note in the batch, so again he enters NEXT:

```
Date:      Sun Feb 09, 1986 4:14 pm EST
From:      Charles Bowen  / MCI ID: 224-5135

TO:      * David A. Peyton / MCI ID: 162-9244
Subject:  Never Mind

I found a copy of the mailing list. The
offer for the cat still holds.

You may enter:

READ        to READ this message again
ANS         to ANSWER the message sender
ANS EACH    to ANSWER the message sender and each
                       recipient
NEXT        to go on to the NEXT message
HELP        for assistance

Command (or MENU or EXIT): menu
```

The messages have been read, but they remain in Dave's electronic "DESK" for 24 hours. That means that anytime he wants to reread them within the next day, he can go back to the main menu, enter READ, then enter DESK at the subsequent menu.

MORE THINGS TO KNOW ABOUT MCI

As you've seen, menus make MCI Mail easy for the first-time user in both reading and writing messages. If you get lost, usually all you need to do is enter MENU at the end of a page to get back to the main menu and start all over again.

But menus alone are not what have made MCI Mail so popular. It's also flexible—there are changes you can make to be more efficient with the time you spend in MCI Mail. Here are some of the extras.

CHANGING MCI'S APPEARANCE

You can modify the way MCI Mail is presented to you on your own computer screen by using the ACCOUNT command. For example, when you first log onto the system, it is set to display everything 80 characters wide and 24 lines deep. That's standard for IBM PCs and compatibles and many other personal computers.

The terminal type is preset to VIDEO, which means that the scrolling stops after displaying a set number of lines—in this case 24. The time zone is set to Eastern Time, which means that all mail you send will be time-stamped with the Eastern Time when you mailed it.

In addition, there are two other settings. They are "carriage return padding" and "line feed padding." These are preset to zero. That means there are no spaces placed at the beginning of a line to cause indented material.

By using the ACCOUNT command, you can alter any of these "default" settings. For instance, you can set display to PAPER instead of VIDEO, which means you can display data nonstop. This feature is particularly good if you have a terminal that makes paper prints rather than displaying on a video terminal.

You can adjust the number of characters that appear on a line of your terminal by resetting LINE. You can set the LINE command to between 39 and 132.

By adjusting PAGE in the ACCOUNT command submenu, you can adjust the number of lines that fit top-to-bottom on your screen before pausing. That number must be between 16 and 100.

You can adjust TIME using the standard abbreviations for time zones—CST for Central Standard Time, PST for Pacific Standard Time, EDT for Eastern Daylight Time, and so on. (By the way, when the country moves from standard time to daylight time and back again, it's your responsibility to reset the TIME using ACCOUNT.)

If you want to indent the MCI presentation on your screen or printing terminal, you may use either CR (carriage return) or LF (line feed) on the ACCOUNT menu to indent from one to seven spaces.

USING CONTROL ON MCI MAIL

You can use the CONTROL key and another key on your keyboard together while on MCI Mail to perform certain tasks that you may not be able to do with your terminal program. To use control keys, press the key labeled CTRL or CNTL or Control, and hold it down while you press one of the following:

H to erase one letter (backspace).

W to erase the word your cursor is on.

X to erase the line your cursor is on.

R to redisplay a line of text.

When reading or printing messages from your mailbox, you can stop the display by entering CONTROL S. To start the scrolling again, enter CONTROL Q.

When you're creating paper mail, you can force a page break anywhere by entering a CONTROL L.

STEPPING UP TO ADVANCED SERVICE

If you become a frequent user of MCI Mail and you want to save even more time, you might want to consider MCI Mail's advanced service. For an additional monthly surcharge, you're given extra services, including:

• The use of commands instead of menus to gain direct access to services quickly. For example, instead of going through menus, you could "chain" commands, such as SCAN INBOX SUBJECT "SALES REPORT" on 6-MAR-86.

• The capability for forwarding messages you receive to one or more people. These forwarded messages can include your own cover letter.

• Memo-style messages sent on paper, similar to the memo-style messages sent electronically.

• Registration of up to 15 signatures and letterheads for different purposes, formal or casual, when paper mail is sent.

• Up to 250 kilobytes of storage (which is more than 50 pages). In addition, messages and drafts are stored up to five days instead of 24 hours.

If you think you might be interested in MCI's advanced service, call Customer Support at the same number mentioned earlier in this chapter on page 214.

CREATING MAILING LISTS

As a user of the basic MCI Mail service, you can create mailing lists that make it easy to send the same letter to a number of people. For many businesses this option alone makes MCI Mail a popular service.

To make a mailing list, you need to use the CREATE LIST command displayed on the main menu.

After that, you'll be prompted to enter the name of the list, from 1 to 20 letters or numbers, and then, at the TO: prompts that follow, to enter the list of addresses. They may be addresses of MCI Mail subscribers or people to whom paper mail or Telexes should be sent.

Once a list is created, you can send a message to everyone on the list by simply entering the name of the mailing list at the first TO: prompt after using the CREATE option.

To change an existing mailing list, use the EDIT command at the main menu and follow the menu prompts. To DELETE the list, first enter SCAN at the main MENU prompt, then enter LIST at the next menu, then DELETE at the next menu. At the LIST prompt, enter the list name.

By the way, if you become an advanced service user, you'll have the ability to create and share mailing lists with others. This is a good service for those who want to share mailing lists with others in their organization.

A LETTER TO CONGRESS

MCI maintains a few mailing lists of its own.

For instance, you can address a message to all members of the U.S. Congress, or to just the members of one house or one political party, by using lists available to all MCI Mail users. Your message will be printed on paper with your registered letterhead and signature, if you have them on file, and sent in those bright orange MCI Mail envelopes.

If you post your message by 8:00 P.M. Eastern Time, it will be delivered the next day at the regular MCI Letter price. At the time of this writing, the price was $2 per copy for up to three pages.

To use one of these congressional lists, enter one of the following at the first TO: prompt after using the CREATE command:

US Senate   for all Senate members
US Senate D   for all Senate Democrats
US Senate R   for all Senate Republicans
US House   for all House members
US House R   for all House Republicans
US House D   for all House Democrats

SENDING A MAIL ALERT

Another unique feature of MCI Mail is the "alert" for important messages. With ALERT, you can post a message to another MCI Mail subscriber and have an MCI operator make a phone call to the recipient with word that there is an electronic message waiting for him or her on the service.

When you post an ALERT message, a copy of the address is sent at the same time to an operator—just the address and not the message itself. The operator will call the recipient and also notify you. The operator will tell your recipient that the mail has been delivered, then post a message in your MCI mailbox telling you when the recipient was reached.

In order to request ALERT, you must enter the word ALERT in parentheses after the name. Also include in the parentheses the recipient's phone number and the time the recipient should be called. For example:

```
TO: Joe Smith (ALERT) 202-555-3206 @ 9:00 a.m.)
```

The ALERT service carries a surcharge with it.

WHERE TO GET HELP ONLINE

When you're stumped with how to use a specific command in an MCI menu, entering HELP followed by the command will generally give you specific information. To see a list of HELP file names, enter HELP INDEX at the main MENU prompt. If you have a way to route incoming information to your computer's disk or a printer, you could print an entire HELP manual by requesting these files one after another. There's a better way, however. If you want to learn more about dealing with MCI Mail, you can get printed documentation from MCI Mail.

IN CONCLUSION

MCI Mail is a valuable communication tool. Because it extends beyond the users of this system, you also have the potential to correspond with people outside the DJN/R subscriber base. For instance, in early 1986 MCI entered an agreement with another information service, CompuServe of Columbus, Ohio, to allow MCI and CompuServe subscribers to exchange electronic letters. For more about that, enter HELP COMPUSERVE at MCI's mail prompt.

This chapter has shown you the basics of MCI Mail, covering what you might need in normal day-to-day usage. There are more special features and services, all outlined in the manuals mentioned above. Or, if you need to talk to a human about them, don't hesitate to call MCI Customer Service and discuss your needs and your problems.

Electronic mail is still in its infancy. MCI, as well as Dow Jones, has made it clear they want your suggestions. If you have comments about the service, let them know what you think and what you need. Sometimes you can even write free letters to a database provider or Dow Jones News/Retrieval itself. These online addresses are listed in the back of the book on page 309. That way, you both gain from the experience.

Chapter 13

MAKING TRAVEL PLANS ONLINE AND MORE

Making travel plans is rarely fun, unless you're planning a dream vacation. Still, Dow Jones News/Retrieval can make travel planning, particularly business travel planning less of a hassle. In fact, it can be downright pleasant.

In this chapter we'll take an online tour of three services, including two that can help specifically in making your travel plans.

• We'll be going into the Official Airline Guide and searching for specific air travel information. That should give us a feel for how the database works.

• Then we'll swing by the "weather bureau," which is actually an up-to-the-minute guide to weather around the world provided by Accu-Weather, Inc.

• Finally, we'll make a brief stop in the Academic American Encyclopedia, so you can see how easy it is to search for topics of interest in this massive online reference work.

At the end of the tour we'll log off for a closer look at all three services, and then examine a very special online service for holders of American Express cards.

TO GET GOING

Right now, log on as you normally do and scroll to the first ENTER QUERY prompt. Go directly to the Official Airline Guide by entering //OAG.

When you arrive at the service (which, incidentally, often is referred to as OAG EE, that is, Official Airline Guide—Electronic Edition), you'll actually be leaving the main DJN/R computers temporarily. OAG EE is furnished to Dow Jones and other information retrieval services as a "gateway."

Your first screen of OAG information should look something like this:

```
WELCOME TO THE OFFICIAL AIRLINE GUIDE
(OAG), COPYRIGHT 1986, OFFICIAL AIRLINE
GUIDES, INC., OAK BROOK, ILLINOIS 60521
: : : : : : : : : : : : : : : : : : :
:        TWO NEW OAG EE FEATURES        :
:      RESERVATIONS AND TICKETING       :
:                  AND                  :
:        HOTEL/MOTEL INFORMATION        :
: : : : : : : : : : : : : : : : : : :
PRESS RETURN FOR SUBSCRIBER BULLETIN
OR ENTER /F, /S, /H, /I, /U
ENTER /M FOR A LIST OF OAG EE COMMANDS
```

Frequent visitors to OAG often press RETURN at this point to see the subscriber bulletin. It outlines new services and changes to the OAG system. However, since the bulletin is likely to be different for you than it was for us when we outlined this tour, we won't take the time to look at it together, though we do commend it to your attention later. The bulletin items are displayed in menu form, making it easy for you to use on your own.

We want you to become familiar right away with the list of major OAG commands you'll be using. To see them, type *one* slash (/) followed by an M. Note the difference—here in OAG, you're using one slash to precede major commands, not the two slashes you've become accustomed to in the main DJN/R system to move between databases.

All together now—enter /M and you should see a list something like this:

```
             ** OAG COMMAND MENU **
Enter:/I FOR INFORMATION AND ASSISTANCE
      /F FOR FARES DISPLAYS
      /S FOR SCHEDULE DISPLAYS
      /H FOR HOTEL/MOTEL DISPLAYS
      /M FOR THIS MENU
      /Q TO EXIT FROM THE OAG EE
      /C TO REVIEW OR CANCEL A RESERVATION
      /U FOR USER COMMENTS AND SUGGESTIONS BOX

ENTER THE COMMAND OF YOUR CHOICE
```

These aren't the only commands you'll have available in OAG. These are the navigation commands necessary to begin searching for specific information, to get online help with the database, to correspond with OAG EE, to review or cancel a reservation, or to log off OAG and go back to the main News/Retrieval system.

To see how OAG works, let's use a scenario. We can pretend that we're going to plan a trip that Charlie and Dave actually took in January 1986, a journey from Huntington, West Virginia, to the home of Dow Jones News/ Retrieval in Princeton, New Jersey. We used OAG to find out how we could get there and back by air.

Before we start, here comes our old disclaimer again—the dates and perhaps some of the specific schedules you see on these pages probably won't match what you see on the screen. Schedules obviously change. However, the commands ought to be the same, so follow along even if the display is a little different.

According to the menu of main commands we just saw, a /S should take us to the section of OAG EE that features scheduling, so now enter /S to see:

```
        ENTER DEPARTURE CITY NAME OR CODE
```

Of course, it has to be a city with an airport. In this case, the departure city is our town, so type Huntington, followed by a comma, followed by WV (and press RETURN, of course).

Next, the system wants to know where we want to go.

ENTER DESTINATION CITY NAME OR CODE

Dave checked with his son who told him the closest airport to Princeton, New Jersey, is Newark, New Jersey. (It was reassuring to see that the kid's geography class was paying off.) So the destination city is Newark. Enter Newark, NJ. Now the system has more questions:

ENTER DEPARTURE DATE
OR PRESS <RETURN> TO USE 15 JAN

Obviously, when you do it, you see today's date rather than 15 JAN. Pressing RETURN at this point (leaving the query blank) will give you flight information for today. This is particularly useful when you're simply browsing to see what flights are *generally* available in preparation for making more specific plans. So press RETURN now to see the next question.

ENTER DEPARTURE TIME
OR PRESS <RETURN> TO USE 600AM

Usually you want to start with the earliest morning flights, so if you're up to traveling as early as 6:00 A.M., press RETURN. Otherwise, enter the earliest time you want to travel. For our tour, we all had our coffee early—press RETURN.

Now OAG does some searching and comes up with the first page of available flights.

```
CONNECTIONS                WED-15 JAN
FROM-HUNTINGTON,WV,USA
 # TO-NEW YORK,NY,USA/NEWARK
  NO EARLIER CONNECTIONS CONSTRUCTED
1  640A HTS   730A CLT PI 745 F28    0
   828A CLT   954A EWR EA 350 D9S B  0
2  640A HTS   730A CLT PI 745 F28    0
   858A CLT  1028A EWR PI  56 72S B  0
3* 700A HTS   743A PIT AL 390 D9S    0
   850A PIT  1005A EWR AL 170 D9S    0
 * THOMAS COOK TICKETING ONLY
ENTER +,X#,F#,RS,B#  (#=LINE NUMBER)
```

Notice the first line says CONNECTIONS. That means there are no direct flights between Huntington and Newark. All flights involve making connections.

Also you may notice that the last line offers some additional commands. These are not navigation commands. Think of them as informational commands that apply only to this particular display. We'll see what most of them do as we go along.

For now, take note of the + symbol in the last line. That means there are more flights to see on yet another page, so enter + and the system will display a second page of flights.

```
          CONNECTIONS       WED-15 JAN
FROM-HUNTINGTON,WV,USA
 # TO-NEW YORK,NY,USA/NEWARK
1* 1145A HTS 1227P PIT AL 402 D9S    0
   100P PIT   209P EWR AL  12 733    0
2  150P HTS   240P CLT PI 741 F28    0
   409P CLT   539P EWR EA 358 D9S S  0
3  150P HTS   240P CLT PI 741 F28    0
   420P CLT   550P EWR PI 336 73S S  0
 * THOMAS COOK TICKETING ONLY
ENTER +,-,0,X#,F#,RS,B# (#=LINE NUMBER)
```

Right away, we see another plus (+) sign, meaning there are even more connecting flights.

The minus (–) sign gives us the opportunity to go back to the previous page, which is the original page of the sequence. If we continued on through several pages and we wanted to get back quickly to the original page, we could type O (that is, capital "o", not zero). That would take us to the top of this sequence quickly.

Okay, we've seen enough flights to get the idea. We want a morning flight, one of those listed back on the first page, so enter either O or minus (–) to take us back one page to the top page of this series of flights.

```
             CONNECTIONS     WED-15 JAN
FROM-HUNTINGTON,WV,USA
 #  TO-NEW YORK,NY,USA/NEWARK
   NO EARLIER CONNECTIONS CONSTRUCTED
1   640A HTS   730A CLT PI 745 F28    0
    828A CLT   954A EWR EA 350 D9S B 0
2   640A HTS   730A CLT PI 745 F28    0
    858A CLT 1028A EWR PI  56 72S B 0
3*  700A HTS   743A PIT AL 390 D9S    0
    850A PIT 1005A EWR AL 170 D9S    0
 *  THOMAS COOK TICKETING ONLY
ENTER +,X#,F#,RS,B#  (#=LINE NUMBER)
```

TRANSLATION, PLEASE

If you're a travel agent or a frequent flyer, you might understand the shorthand in this schedule. But for the rest of us? Well. . . .

Fortunately, the folks at OAG know that the abbreviations used in airline travel sometimes can be confusing. That's why the X command is included. X in this case means "expanded." Entering X followed by the number of a particular flight will get you details, in English no less. Let's take a look at an English narrative of flight number 1. Enter X1 and see something like this:

```
 EXPANDED CONNECTION DISPLAY (1 OF 2)
 LEAVE- 6:40A  ON-15 JAN
 FROM-HUNTINGTON,WV,USA
 PIEDMONT AVIATION FLIGHT 745
 AIRCRAFT-FOKKER VFW F28 (ALL SERIES)
```

```
CLASS-COACH/ECONOMY
ARRIVE- 7:30A   ON-15 JAN
AT-CHARLOTTE,NC,USA

PRESS RETURN FOR 2ND FLIGHT INFORMATION
```

Now, that's better! Now, for the flight from Charlotte to Newark, press
RETURN.

```
 EXPANDED CONNECTION DISPLAY (2 OF 2)
LEAVE- 8:28A   ON-15 JAN
FROM-CHARLOTTE,NC,USA
EASTERN AIR LINES FLIGHT 350
AIRCRAFT-MCDONNEL DOUG. DC9 30-80 SE
CLASS-FIRST/COACH/ECONOMY
MEAL-BREAKFAST
ARRIVE- 9:54A   ON-15 JAN
AT-NEW YORK,NY,USA/NEWARK

TOTAL TRAVEL TIME 3H 14M
ENTER S TO RETURN TO SCHEDULES
ENTER F FOR SELECTED FARES
```

As the note at the bottom of the screen indicates, if we entered F here,
we'd see the fare for this flight. But let's do some schedule comparison first.
Enter S to go back to the schedule page we started from:

```
           CONNECTIONS     WED-15 JAN
FROM-HUNTINGTON,WV,USA
# TO-NEW YORK,NY,USA/NEWARK
 NO EARLIER CONNECTIONS CONSTRUCTED
1  640A HTS  730A CLT PI 745 F28    0
   828A CLT  954A EWR EA 350 D9S B  0
2  640A HTS  730A CLT PI 745 F28    0
   858A CLT 1028A EWR PI  56 72S B  0
3* 700A HTS  743A PIT AL 390 D9S    0
   850A PIT 1005A EWR AL 170 D9S    0
 * THOMAS COOK TICKETING ONLY
ENTER +,X#,F#,RS,B#   (#=LINE NUMBER)
```

Hmmmm. Actually, we aren't used to doing *anything* before 7:00 A.M. Flight number 3 looks a little more inviting to us. Let's check it out by entering 3. That should show you something like this:

```
   EXPANDED CONNECTION DISPLAY (1 OF 2)
LEAVE- 7:00A   ON-15 JAN
FROM-HUNTINGTON,WV,USA
USAIR/ALLEGHENY COMMUTER FLIGHT 390
AIRCRAFT-MCDONNEL DOUG. DC9 30-80 SE
CLASS-COACH/ECONOMY
ARRIVE- 7:43A   ON-15 JAN
AT-PITTSBURGH,PA,USA/GREATER PITTS

PRESS RETURN FOR 2ND FLIGHT INFORMATION
```

This time the layover is in Pittsburgh instead of Charlotte. To get information on the second and final leg of the journey, press RETURN.

```
   EXPANDED CONNECTION DISPLAY (2 OF 2)
LEAVE- 8:50A   ON-15 JAN
FROM-PITTSBURGH,PA,USA/GREATER PITTS
USAIR/ALLEGHENY COMMUTER FLIGHT 170
AIRCRAFT-MCDONNEL DOUG. DC9 30-80 SE
CLASS-COACH/ECONOMY
ARRIVE-10:05A   ON-15 JAN
AT-NEW YORK,NY,USA/NEWARK

TOTAL TRAVEL TIME 3H 05M
ENTER S TO RETURN TO SCHEDULES
ENTER F FOR SELECTED FARES
```

Once again there's the option to check the fare on this flight, but not yet. Let's go back to the original schedule page. (Enter S.)

```
          CONNECTIONS     WED-15 JAN
FROM-HUNTINGTON,WV,USA
# TO-NEW YORK,NY,USA/NEWARK
  NO EARLIER CONNECTIONS CONSTRUCTED
1  640A HTS   730A CLT PI 745 F28    0
   828A CLT   954A EWR EA 350 D9S B 0
2  640A HTS   730A CLT PI 745 F28    0
   858A CLT 1028A EWR PI  56 72S B 0
3* 700A HTS   743A PIT AL 390 D9S    0
   850A PIT 1005A EWR AL 170 D9S    0
 * THOMAS COOK TICKETING ONLY
ENTER +,X#,F#,RS,B#   (#=LINE NUMBER)
```

When comparing fares, this is the best place to do it—from the schedule page. Let's see what the fare is for number 1. Enter F1 (that is the letter "f" followed by the digit "1").

```
NO FARE INFORMATION FOR YOUR SELECTION
ENTER S TO RETURN TO SCHEDULES
```

Whoops! No fare data available. We threw that little ringer in to illustrate that even OAG doesn't know everything. Generally speaking, the flights you'll see marked in the descriptions as Thomas Cook ticketing include fare information (note the asterisk on the previous screen display), and some others do too. As a rule, overseas flights do not include fare information. In those cases you'll have to take a low-tech route and check with your travel agent or the airline itself. However, by using OAG you'll at least go armed with flight schedule information.

Right now, enter S to return to the schedule page from which we've been working.

```
          CONNECTIONS     WED-15 JAN
FROM-HUNTINGTON,WV,USA
# TO-NEW YORK,NY,USA/NEWARK
 NO EARLIER CONNECTIONS CONSTRUCTED
1  640A HTS   730A CLT PI 745 F28   0
   828A CLT  954A EWR EA 350 D9S B 0
2  640A HTS   730A CLT PI 745 F28   0
   858A CLT 1028A EWR PI  56 72S B 0
3* 700A HTS   743A PIT AL 390 D9S   0
   850A PIT 1005A EWR AL 170 D9S   0
 * THOMAS COOK TICKETING ONLY
ENTER +,X#,F#,RS,B#  (#=LINE NUMBER)
```

and let's check the fare for number 3. (Enter F3.)

```
FARES IN US DOLLARS             WED-15 JAN
SELECTED FOR HTS-AL 390 PIT-AL 170-EWR

# ONE-WAY RND-TRP ARLN/CLASS FARECODE
NO LOWER FARES IN CATEGORY
1*  139.00           AL/Y-AL/Y   YH
2   172.00           AL/Y-AL/Y   Y
 NO HIGHER FARES IN CATEGORY
 * ENTER L# TO VIEW LIMITATIONS
ENTER L#,X#,S,RS       (#=LINE NUMBER)
```

Ah, there's something new on the menu. One fare is marked with an asterisk (*), meaning there are limitations. Also note there's a command, L, which is designed to deal with limitations.

To see what it's all about, enter L1 (capital letter "l" and digit one) and see something like:

```
LIMITATIONS DISPLAY          WED-15 JAN
HTS-NYC  AL/Y-AL/Y  FARECODE:YH
USAIR/ALLEGHENY COMMUTER
FARE DESCRIPTION: COACH FARES
BOOKING CODE: Y/YN.
FARE IS ONLY AVAILABLE FOR TRAVEL FROM
```

```
 06:31A THRU 08:59P ON MON THRU FRI.
 FARE IS ONLY AVAILABLE FOR TRAVEL FROM
 12:30P THRU 11:59P ON SUN.
 * END OF LIMITATIONS DISPLAY *
 ENTER F. TO RETURN TO FARE DISPLAY
 ENTER S TO RETURN TO SCHEDULE DISPLAY
```

We can live with those limitations. Let's enter S again to get back to the familiar schedule display.

```
           CONNECTIONS     WED-15 JAN
 FROM-HUNTINGTON,WV,USA
 # TO-NEW YORK,NY,USA/NEWARK
  NO EARLIER CONNECTIONS CONSTRUCTED
 1  640A HTS   730A CLT PI 745 F28    0
    828A CLT   954A EWR EA 350 D9S B 0
 2  640A HTS   730A CLT PI 745 F28    0
    858A CLT 1028A EWR PI  56 72S B 0
 3* 700A HTS   743A PIT AL 390 D9S    0
    850A PIT 1005A EWR AL 170 D9S    0
  * THOMAS COOK TICKETING ONLY
 ENTER +,X#,F#,RS,B#  (#=LINE NUMBER)
```

BRINGING IT ALL BACK HOME

The next command on our list is RS. It means Return Schedule and it's a fast way to check out return flights.

Enter RS and see:

```
 ENTER RETURN DATE
 OR PRESS RETURN KEY TO USE 15 JAN
```

Once again, the date you see will be different. For research purposes, we'll use the same date to check the return schedule. Press RETURN.

```
ENTER RETURN TIME
OR PRESS RETURN KEY TO USE 600PM
```

A late morning flight would be nice. So enter 1100AM. (Pay attention to the style, please—no spaces between the time and AM.)

```
           CONNECTIONS      WED-15 JAN
FROM-NEW YORK,NY,USA/NEWARK
# TO-HUNTINGTON,WV,USA
1* 1255P EWR  206P PIT AL 219 D9S    0
    420P PIT  508P HTS AL 151 D9S    0
2   515P EWR  744P CLT PI 275 73S    1
    935P CLT 1022P HTS PI  46 72S    0
3   626P EWR  808P CLT EA 359 D9S D  0
    935P CLT 1022P HTS PI  46 72S    0
 NO LATER CONNECTIONS CONSTRUCTED
 * THOMAS COOK TICKETING ONLY
ENTER -,X#,F#,RS        (#=LINE NUMBER)
```

What? No cities to enter? That's right. OAG's smart; it remembers your flight plans from Huntington to Newark and is giving you return flight information based on those plans.

To get information about number 1 on the list, enter X1.

```
   EXPANDED CONNECTION DISPLAY (1 OF 2)
LEAVE- 12:55P  ON-15 JAN
FROM-NEW YORK,NY,USA/NEWARK
USAIR/ALLEGHENY COMMUTER FLIGHT 219
AIRCRAFT-MCDONNELL DOUG. DC9 30-80 SE
CLASS-COACH/ECONOMY
ARRIVE- 2:06P  ON-15 JAN
AT-PITTSBURGH,PA,USA/GREATER PITTS

PRESS RETURN FOR 2ND FLIGHT INFORMATION
```

Press RETURN to see the information about the flight from Pittsburgh to Huntington.

```
   EXPANDED CONNECTION DISPLAY (2 OF 2)
LEAVE- 4:20P  ON-15 JAN
FROM-PITTSBURGH,PA,USA/GREATER PITTS
USAIR/ALLEGHENY COMMUTER FLIGHT 151
AIRCRAFT-MCDONNELL DOUG. DC9 30-80 SE
CLASS-COACH/ECONOMY
ARRIVE- 5:08P  ON-15 JAN
AT-HUNTINGTON,WV,USA

TOTAL TRAVEL TIME 4H 13M
ENTER S TO RETURN TO SCHEDULES
ENTER F FOR SELECTED FARES
```

Remember we said fares could be checked from this section as well as the schedule page? Give it a try—enter F to see the fare for this specific *return* flight only.

```
FARES IN US DOLLARS          WED-15 JAN
SELECTED FOR EWR-AL 219 PIT-AL 151-HTS

# ONE-WAY RND-TRP ARLN/CLASS FARECODE
  NO LOWER FARES IN CATEGORY
1*  139.00          AL/Y-AL/Y  YH
2   172.00          AL/Y-AL/Y  Y
  NO HIGHER FARES IN CATEGORY
  * ENTER L# TO VIEW LIMITATIONS
ENTER L#,X#,S,RS   (#=LINE NUMBER)
```

It's the same fare to return, as we expected.

FINDING LODGINGS

Well, now that we have a good idea of the flight schedule information between Huntington and Newark, let's find out about the availability of motels in the Princeton, New Jersey, area.

Seasoned electronic traveler that you are, you no doubt remember what we just said about the navigation commands, the ones preceded by one slash. One of them was /H for hotels. There's no need to go to the top of the schedule sequence or the top of the OAG menu. From this or any other OAG page you can navigate to the top of any other subservice.

So enter /H, and the system will need a little more information:

```
ENTER ANOTHER CITY NAME OR CODE
OR PRESS RETURN TO USE-HUNTINGTON,WV,US
```

Interesting. The system remembers our last inquiry, which made it appear as if we were going to stay in Huntington, so it's ready to give us information on Huntington hotels and motels. But we're looking into spending the night in Princeton, New Jersey, so enter PRINCETON, NJ (remembering to enter the comma and space before NJ).

```
CITY CENTER-PRINCETON,NJ,USA
 #  HOTEL/MOTEL               RATES
       BEGINNING OF LISTINGS
 1  HOLIDAY INN                        2*
    FIRST PLAINSBORO RD.    $57-69
 2  HYATT REGENCY PRINCETON            3*
    102 CARNEGIE CENTER     $90-130
 3  MCINTOSH INN                       NP
    QUAKER BRIDE MALL, RTE. 1,
    (LAWRENCEVILLE)         $29-34
 4  NASSAU INN                         2*
    PALMER SQUARE, BOX 668  $83 UP DWB
 5  RAMADA INN                         NP
    RIDGE RD. & RTE. 1      $85-95
ENTER +,+NAME,X#          (#=LINE NUMBER)
```

The numbers followed by an asterisk are OAG ratings—one star, two star, etc.

The folks at Dow Jones News/Retrieval told us the new Ramada Inn, number 5 on the list above, is only a half mile or so from their headquarters. Let's take an expanded look at that one. Type X5 (meaning "expand the data on number 5").

```
EXPANDED HOTEL/MOTEL DISPLAY

RAMADA INN
RIDGE RD. & RTE. 1
PRINCETON,NJ,USA
ZIP-08540
TEL-609-452-2400
NEW PROPERTY, NOT YET RATED
RATES-DAILY        PLAN-EUROPEAN
$85    LOW SINGLE
$95    HIGH DOUBLE
ROOMS FOR HANDICAPPED
ENTER X# OR H TO VIEW HOTEL MENU
```

To get back to the hotel menu we came from, enter H.

```
CITY CENTER-PRINCETON,NJ,USA
  # HOTEL/MOTEL                 RATES
     BEGINNING OF LISTINGS
  1 HOLIDAY INN                      2*
     FIRST PLAINSBORO RD.    $57-69
  2 HYATT REGENCY PRINCETON          3*
     102 CARNEGIE CENTER     $90-130
  3 MCINTOSH INN                     NP
     QUAKER BRIDE MALL, RTE. 1,
     (LAWRENCEVILLE)         $29-34
  4 NASSAU INN                       2*
     PALMER SQUARE, BOX 668  $83 UP DWB
  5 RAMADA INN                       NP
     RIDGE RD. & RTE. 1      $85-95
ENTER +,+NAME,X#       (#=LINE NUMBER)
```

Here, as in the flight guide, the plus (+) sign means there are more hotels/motels in the Princeton area to be described. For more, enter + and see:

```
CITY CENTER-PRINCETON,NJ,USA
  # HOTEL/MOTEL                 RATES
  1 RED ROOF INN                      NP
     HWY. 1 AT I-295        $28-37
  2 SCANTICON-PRINCETON EXECUTIVE    NP
     CONFERENCE CTR/HTL
     PRINCETON FORRESTAL CENTER
                            $105-300
  3 TREADWAY INN-PRINCETON           2*
     3499 HWY. 1S           $50-58
     END OF LISTINGS
ENTER -,+NAME,O,X#    (#=LINE NUMBER)
```

Many large cities have page after page of listings. If you want to look up a specific hotel in such a list, the +NAME command can be used. Just enter + and the name of the hotel or motel for which you are looking.

We'll talk more about OAG EE at the end of this chapter. Right now, let's leave OAG and go to the Dow Jones weather bureau to check the weather in the area we're flying to.

To leave OAG, the navigation command is one slash (/) and the letter "q," so enter /Q and you'll see this message:

```
YOU HAVE BEEN SIGNED OFF FROM OAG.

TO SEARCH OTHER DOW JONES
NEWS/RETRIEVAL DATA BASES, TYPE
TWO SLASHES FOLLOWED BY THE NAME
OF THE DATA BASE.
  EXAMPLE: //NEWS

OR, TYPE //MENU FOR A DATA-BASE LIST.
```

YOU DON'T NEED A WEATHERMAN

Let's take the express lane to Accu-Weather's report. The command is //WTHR and the first page should look something like this:

```
          DOW JONES NEWS/RETRIEVAL WEATHER REPORT
            COPYRIGHT (C) 1986 ACCU-WEATHER INC.
                  ALL RIGHTS RESERVED.

PRESS FOR
1   Thursday's Forecast: Clouds, Fog
        Throughout Much Of Northwest
2   Northeast Shivers Wednesday
        As Bitter Cold Prevails
3   Weather Guide: Detailed Forecasts
        For Major Metropolitan Areas
4   The Outlook: Mild Temperatures
        Through The Weekend
5   Great Skiing At Eastern Resorts


PRESS N FOR 3-DAY FORECASTS FOR U.S.
CITIES OR F FOR FOREIGN WEATHER TABLES.
```

Princeton is about an hour's drive south of New York City, so it would be getting about the same weather. Enter 3 to look at detailed forecasts for major metropolitan areas. First we get an introductory page:

```
WEATHER 1/15/86                        PAGE 1 OF 1


    Weather Guide: Detailed Forecasts
    For Major Metropolitan Areas
                  ---
Press S (RETURN) for a report of three-day forecasts
for 15 major travel destinations in the U.S.

Forecasts cover the period Wednesday through Friday.
```

Note that the message at the bottom tips you off to the new command, S, to get to the weather menu. Enter S and see something like:

```
1/15/86                                    PAGE 1 OF 3
                    SPECIAL REPORT

PRESS FOR

    1   Atlanta
    2   Boston
    3   Chicago
    4   Dallas
    5   Denver
```

The areas are listed alphabetically. New York isn't on this page, which, we see from the heading, is one of three. So press RETURN to see the next page.

```
1/15/86                                    PAGE 2 OF 3
                    SPECIAL REPORT

PRESS FOR

    6   Detroit
    7   Kansas City
    8   Los Angeles
    9   Miami
   10   New York City
```

The New York City forecast is number 10 on this menu. Enter that number.

```
WEATHER 1/15/86                        PAGE 1 OF 1

   New York City

                        ---
   Quite cold Sunday night, low 18.
   Mainly sunny Monday, afternoon temperatures
moderating to 36.
   Becoming milder Tuesday with increasing clouds. It
may shower late in the day or at night, high 46.
```

Now make a note to yourself to pack the hat and gloves. Princeton may be to the south, but not far enough south to escape that cold blast.

BONING UP ON PRINCETON

Now that we've checked the weather, let's take a side trip to the Grolier's Academic American Encyclopedia. Enter //ENCYC to enter the encyclopedia area.

```
        ACADEMIC AMERICAN ENCYCLOPEDIA
            COPYRIGHT (C) 1986
            GROLIER INCORPORATED

THERE ARE TWO WAYS TO FIND INFORMATION IN THE
ELECTRONIC ENCYCLOPEDIA:

PRESS   TO

1       SEARCH BY THE PARTIAL TITLE OF A SUBJECT
            HEADING
2       SEARCH BY THE COMPLETE TITLE OF A SUBJECT
            HEADING
```

We thought that since we were going to Princeton and had a little extra time, we might tour the area around Princeton University. Let's see what we can find out about that historic institution in advance. We'll search for that entry in the encyclopedia by choosing number 1, a search by the partial title. Enter 1 and see:

```
ENTER ONLY AS MUCH OF THE TITLE AS YOU ARE SURE OF.
INCLUDE ALL PUNCTUATION. ENTER THE LAST NAME FIRST,
FOLLOWED BY A COMMA, A SPACE AND THE FIRST INITIAL.
USE SINGULAR WORDS, NOT PLURAL WORDS.

FOR EXAMPLE, YOU CAN:
ENTER     REAGAN, R  OR REAGAN, RON
TO FIND   REAGAN, RONALD

ENTER     TRADE ASSOCIATION
TO FIND   TRADE ASSOCIATIONS

ENTER QUERY
```

Hey, great instructions. Very clear. Let's see what entries the encyclopedia has for Princeton. Enter PRINCETON (of course it doesn't have to be uppercase) and the system should display something like:

```
      PAGE 1 OF 1
PRESS  FOR

 1    PRINCETON
 2    PRINCETON THEOLOGICAL SEMINARY
 3    PRINCETON UNIVERSITY
-----------------------------------------------------
       PRESS <RETURN> TO VIEW THE SELECTIONS
         AGAIN OR ENTER A NEW QUERY.
```

We have the option of reading about the community of Princeton, Princeton Theological Seminary, or Princeton University. For this tour we're primarily interested in the university, so enter 3 to see the first page of the Grolier article.

```
Princeton University
Established in 1746 as the College of New Jersey by a
charter from King George II and given its present
name in 1896, Princeton University (enrollment:
6,160; library: 3,000,000 volumes) is a private,
coeducational, liberal arts institution in Princeton,
N.J. A member of the Ivy League, it has a graduate
school, schools of engineering and applied sciences
and of architecture and urban planning, and the
Woodrow Wilson School of Public and International
Affairs (1930). Research in plasma physics, aerospace
and
```

That's the end of the first page of the three-page article.

At this point, our tour has ended. If you want to see the remainder of the article on Princeton, press RETURN, then RETURN again at the end of the next page.

When you're finished, log off—the DISC command, of course—and get comfortable. We have some more information to give you about some of the things you've just seen.

MORE ABOUT OAG EE

The Official Airline Guide is a mighty database for travelers who want more control of their itineraries.

Because of its flexibility, it is a bit complex, but not incomprehensible. Lots of online help about the program is available. In addition, there's a 24-hour phone helpline. For help within the continental United States and Hawaii, dial 1-800-323-4000. In Illinois dial 1-800-942-3011. Outside the continental United States dial 312-654-6808.

The United Kingdom/Continental Europe help desk is available from 9:00 A.M. until 5:30 P.M., London time. The number is 01-930-2915.

We showed you the navigation commands, the ones that are preceded by a single slash. Think of these commands as taking you to various "departments" of OAG—the Fare Department with a /F, the Schedules Department with a /S, the Hotel/Motel Information Department with a /H, the Information Department with a /I, and the Reception Desk (for a general menu) with a /M.

There are other commands at the bottom of the screens, which are used to obtain specific information. There is a complete list of them in the Online Survival Kit in the back of the book, beginning on page 313.

Finally, inexperienced OAG users might find the idea of booking flights through OAG EE a bit frightening. As with most online ordering services, however, there is a lot of help and plenty of places in the ordering sequence for you to correct errors or even cancel the entire order.

When you are ordering tickets online, it's necessary to begin the procedure by letting OAG know the exact date you are leaving and returning. You can start the booking procedure from several different places in the schedule/fare sequences. You start it by entering B. During the ordering procedure you're likely to be prompted for the type of trip (one-way or round-trip), the class of service (if more than one class is offered), your name, seat preference, phone number, and, depending on the ticketing method, perhaps your credit card number. OAG EE accepts all major credit cards.

Before ordering tickets online, it's a good idea to scan option 9 from the Information and Assistance Menu. It's called Reservations and Ticketing and includes a sample ordering session. It's an excellent way to preview the procedure before ordering tickets.

MORE ABOUT WEATHER

When we took the tour to the weather forecast area, we chose an option where three-day forecasts for the 15 major travel destinations are featured. There are other places in /WTHR to get forecasts from other cities in the United States and around the world.

At the bottom of the main weather menu were instructions for getting these forecasts.

```
PRESS N FOR 3-DAY FORECASTS FOR U.S. CITIES OR F FOR
FOREIGN WEATHER TABLES.
```

If you enter an N at this point, you'll see a menu featuring forecasts for Northeastern cities, Middle Atlantic cities, Southeastern cities, South Central cities, Midwestern cities, Plains States cities, Rocky Mountain cities, and West Coast cities.

If you enter F, you'll see another menu for European cities, Canadian cities, Latin American cities, Middle Eastern cities, and Asian cities.

In addition, the main menu usually has several articles about weather in general throughout the United States, including reports about weather upcoming in the next two or three days.

AMERICAN EXPRESS ADVANCE

If you're an American Express cardholder, there's a special service just for you on Dow Jones. You can access American Express ADVANCE on Dow Jones by entering //AXP from the bottom of most screens.

By using American Express ADVANCE, cardholders can order items from the American Express Merchandise Shop or they can request travel brochures or reservations from the American Express travel service. American Express ADVANCE offers card account information as well, including statement details for the previous two months and a balance for the previous six months.

Those who hold American Express cards need a personal identification number before they can see account details, and you can apply for one by calling 1-800-CASH NOW.

If you don't have an American Express card, you can still see a demonstration of how card account information works by selecting either 2 or 3 at the //AXP main menu.

Chapter 14

AT HOME
WITH DOW JONES

Time to leave the world of business temporarily. In this chapter we'll look at some of Dow Jones News/Retrieval's offerings that aren't directly tied to the world of finance.

For a long time now the computer industry's seers have been predicting that eventually computerized information retrieval services would find as much use in the home as in the marketplace. We've already found some examples of services that might have application in the home—the Academic American Encyclopedia (//ENCYC), Accu-Weather (//WTHR) and the various news and sports databases. And there are many more.

In this on-line tour, we'll:

• Stop in at Comp-U-Store, where you can shop for thousands of items from the comfort of your own home (or office).

• Take a look at the Cineman Movie Reviews, where information about literally thousands of films, new and old, waits to be gathered at the touch of the keyboard.

• See how to use the Medical and Drug Reference section, an online medical encyclopedia written specifically for database retrieval to get instant medical information.

• Use another interesting reference work, Peterson's College Selection Service, a great tool for choosing a college to fit your own plans or the college plans of others.

That puts a lot on our plate for this chapter, so this will be one of our longer tours. This will help us in several ways. In addition to illustrating a number of new services, the tour itself should resolve any lingering doubts you might have about your ability to navigate across the system and figure out the various menus you come across.

SHOPPING IN THE COMP-U-STORE

Log on to the system as you normally do. When you arrive at the first ENTER QUERY prompt, head directly for Comp-U-Store by entering //STORE to see:

```
          COMP-U-STORE ONLINE
           COPYRIGHT (C) 1986
     COMP-U-CARD INTERNATIONAL, INC.
            STAMFORD, CT.

PRESS  FOR

1   SHOPPING AND ORDERING FOR MEMBERS

2   SHOPPING FOR NON-MEMBERS

3   ONLINE MEMBERSHIP APPLICATION
```

Some of your fellow DJN/R subscribers haven't explored Comp-U-Store because they think on-line shoppers have to be members of "the club" to use the databases. Not true. You can browse all you'd like in the same databases where members shop. It's only if you want to order items that you have to be a member. Let's see—enter 2 at this menu.

```
          YOU ARE NOW BEING SIGNED ON TO
                  COMP-U-STORE

              FOR CUSTOMER ASSISTANCE,
            PLEASE CALL COMP-U-STORE'S
                 TOLL-FREE NUMBER

          IN CONTINENTAL UNITED STATES:
                 (800) 843-7777

             PRESS <RETURN> TO CONTINUE
```

After pressing RETURN, there may be a brief pause while you see the following message:

```
             PLEASE WAIT WHILE YOUR
             COMP-U-STORE SIGN ON
                IS BEING PROCESSED

          YOUR SIGN ON HAS BEEN COMPLETED
             PRESS <RETURN> TO CONTINUE
```

Why is the log-on to Comp-U-Store different from that of other services you've seen on Dow Jones News/Retrieval? Comp-U-Store is a separate entity from Dow Jones. In fact, Comp-U-Store is found on several information services as a "gateway," just as the Official Airline Guide is a gateway. What that means is that when you call Comp-U-Store from DJN/R, you are being connected to the main Comp-U-Store database.

When the connection is complete and you press RETURN, you'll see an introductory message promoting one of the Comp-U-Store services, something like this:

```
New shop on Comp-u-Mail - the Virginia Veal Farms.
Look in the Gourmet Food Shoppes to order quality
veal.
Press Return/Enter to continue
```

Press RETURN to see the main directory.

```
******* MAIN DIRECTORY *******
   1) What's New
   2) SHOPPING
   3) Auctions & Amusements
   4) The Information Booth
   5) CONSUMER SERVICES
   6) Member Sign-up/Address Change
Enter Selection #
```

We'll look at some of the highlights of //STORE. If we don't cover an option on this menu that looks interesting to you, plan to make a return visit on your own.

On this leg of the tour we'll do a little comparative shopping for a small TV set, the kind you might put beside your bed or on a kitchen counter. So, let's go to the SHOPPING area by entering 2. That should lead you to a menu like this one:

```
            *** Shopping ***
 1) Comp-U-Store & Best Buys
 2) Comp-U-Mail - Specialty Shops
 3) The Drugstore
 4) Home Furnishing Store
 5) Discount Travel
 6) American Travel Association
 7) Warehouse Outlet
 8) Return to Main Directory
Enter Selection # >
```

We are met with a menu of choices. Note the many special areas for shopping, from items you might find in a drugstore to bargain travel. But for real comparison shopping, the place to be is number 1, so enter the number for the option called "Comp-u-store & Best Buys."

```
       ** Comp-u-store **
 1) Shopping & Ordering
 2) Best Buys (Databasement)
 3) Process a stored order
 4) Return to Shopping Directory
Enter Selection # >
```

Notice the "databasement" where you can find some great buys. As with any bargain basement, items come and disappear quickly. Note, too, that if you have stored an order, you would choose number 3 on this menu to complete the ordering process.

Right now let's continue on our way to the shopping area. Type 1 and press RETURN.

```
Enter:
 Product Type
 (LISt) for Product Listing
```

Let's assume this is your first time in Comp-U-Store and you could use a little assistance. Enter LIS to see the types of merchandise Comp-U-Store offers.

```
 #         Categories
 ---    --------------------
 1   Major appliances
 2   Small appliances
 3   Stereo & audio equipment
 4   Tv & video equipment
 5   Computers & accessories
 6   Phones & communications
 7   Cars, car stereo & tires
 8   Cameras & optical equip.
 9   Sports, exercise & health
```

```
10   Home & office equipment
11   Home furnishings
12   Silverware and cutlery
13   China, crystal & gifts
14   Luggage, watches & clocks
15   Tools & lawn equipment
16   Musical instruments
Enter a Category # >
```

Since we're looking for a TV set, (option 4 in our example) enter that number to see a listing of codes for TV and video equipment.

```
Code        Product
--- -------------------------
AVDK  Laserdisk/cd players
AVSY  Audio/video component systems
MOVI  Videotape movies
TVAC  Tv/video accessories
TVBW  Black & white televisions
TVCC  Video camcorders
TVCL  Color televisions
TVCM  Video cameras
TVCR  Video cassette recorders
TVDK  Video disk players
TVMN  Video monitors
TVPA  Pro video accessories
TVPC  Pro video cameras
TVPJ  Color projection televisions
TVPO  Video cassette (player only)
TVPR  Pro video recorders
Press Return/Enter to continue
or enter selection >
```

This is a list of codes unique to Comp-U-Store. You need to jot down any of the four-letter codes that look promising. For instance, our code is TVCL (color televisions). Enter that, and the system should respond with:

```
Enter:
 Brand name
 (NP) No preference
 (LISt) Brand listing
 >
```

If you entered LIS now, you'd see the TV brands offered in Comp-U-Store. But let's assume we have no preference because our main purpose here is comparison shopping. So, enter NP.

```
Screen size in inches/style?
(NP) No preference
 (1) Up to 11" portable
 (2) 12"-13" portable
 (3) 14"-17" portable
 (4) 19" table with remote
 (5) 19" table no remote
 (6) 20"-25" table with remote
 (7) 20"-25" table no remote
 (8) 25" oak console with remote
 (9) 25" oak console no remote
(10) 25" pecan console with remote
(11) 25" pecan console no remote
(12) 25" pine console with remote
(13) 25" pine console no remote
(14) 25" other console with remote
(15) 25" other console no remote
(16) 26"-27" table with remote
(17) 26"-27" console with remote
Press Return/Enter to continue >
>
```

We're looking for a small TV. So choose 1 from this menu.

```
Stereo broadcast capable?
(NP) No preference
(1) Decoder included
(2) Decoder required
(3) No stereo capability
>
```

Enter NP.

```
Ship-to State
(necessary for quote)
>
```

Don't let this one scare you. As the parenthetical line says, the system needs to know where you live in order to calculate the shipping charges. Entering the information does *not* commit you to ordering anything.

So enter your own state's two-letter postal code. We entered our state, West Virginia, which is WV, and the system asked us to confirm that:

```
WEST VIRGINIA (Y or N) >
```

The system is merely double checking your last entry (and perhaps showing off a bit). Enter Y if the state is correct. Now the system says:

```
What's the most you will spend?
>$
```

Like a good salesperson, Comp-U-Store wants a ballpark figure in order to direct you to merchandise you're likely to want.

So we all stay together, enter 250 (the dollar sign isn't necessary). The list ought to appear something like this.

```
Color televisions Page 1 Of 3
   #   Mfg    Model      FDC
   1  EMRS  EC10R       213.31
   2  EMRS  EC11W       213.31
   3  EMRS  PC5         213.31
   4  EMRS  TC7         225.15
   5  GE    80904       162.16
   6  GE    80955       183.56
   7  HTCH  CT0911      233.91
   8  MGVX  CE3925SL    227.75
   9  PANA  CT1123      240.06
  10  PANA  CTF1011     229.36

Enter Selection #, or
p# for that page >
```

You should notice right away from the first line that there are three pages of TVs that meet our criteria. This is the first page. To get to the next page, press RETURN.

```
Color televisions Page 2 Of 3
   #   Mfg    Model       FDC
  11  PANA  CTF1013     248.23
  12  PANA  CTG1000     217.16
  13  PHLC  C1910SSL    215.00
  14  QASR  RP2137WW    228.62
  15  QASR  WP2145XH    222.80
  16  QASR  WP2145XL    222.80
  17  QASR  WP2145XU    224.28
  18  QASR  WP2145XX    222.80
  19  RCA   ELR295S     219.73
  20  SHRP  9KS05       221.66

Enter Selection #, or
p# for that page>
```

To see the third and final page, press RETURN again.

```
Color televisions Page 3 Of 3
  #  Mfg    Model        FDC
 21 SHRP  9KS15        221.66
 22 SHRP  9KS25        221.66
 23 SMSG  C5101MA      201.54
 24 SYLV  CZD102SL     230.50
.
Enter Selection #, or
p# for that page >
```

There are the choices. Let's say we saw a model on the first page that looked like what we wanted. To get back to page 1, enter P and the page number, that is P1.

```
Color televisions Page 1 Of 3
  #  Mfg    Model        FDC
  1 EMRS  EC10R        213.31
  2 EMRS  EC11W        213.31
  3 EMRS  PC5          213.31
  4 EMRS  TC7          225.15
  5 GE    80904        162.16
  6 GE    80955        183.56
  7 HTCH  CT0911       233.91
  8 MGVX  CE3925SL     227.75
  9 PANA  CT1123       240.06
 10 PANA  CTF1011      229.36
.
Enter Selection #, or
p# for that page >
```

Number 9 looks interesting and quite close to our $250 limit. To read more about it, enter 9.

```
            Color televisions
Brand:PANASONIC      Model: CT1123
List:         369.95
Price:        230.06
With shipping and  CUBucks:       230.06
```

```
handling:    240.06 Color:WG
SAVE:        139.89
--------------Description---------------
10" COLOR PORTABLE TV WITH WIRELESS REMOTE TUNING.
HAS AUTO FINE TUNING, BRIGHTNESS CONTROL, EARPHONE
JACK, DETACHABLE ANTENNAS AND CARRY HANDLE. WOODGRAIN
PLASTIC CABINET.
Want to order: (Y or N) >
```

Unless you're a member, you couldn't order if you wanted to, but give the system a break and don't try to confuse it. Simply enter N. You'll return to the list page from which you started.

```
Color televisions Page 1 Of 3
   #  Mfg      Model       FDC
   1  EMRS     EC10R       213.31
   2  EMRS     EC11W       213.31
   3  EMRS     PC5         213.31
   4  EMRS     TC7         225.15
   5  GE       80904       162.16
   6  GE       80955       183.56
   7  HTCH     CT0911      233.91
   8  MGVX     CE3925SL    227.75
   9  PANA     CT1123      240.06
  10  PANA     CTF1011     229.36
.
Enter Selection #, or
p# for that page >
```

Okay, we've seen how easy it is to use Comp-U-Store. If you decide to become a member, you'll be charged an annual membership fee (at this writing it's $25). For the fee, you'll receive a Comp-U-Store password and user guide (which lists many of those four-letter product codes, incidentally) and the opportunity to order merchandise of all kinds and charge it to a major credit card. There also many other features, such as online auctions and special "open house" promotions with gifts and contests. For more information, you can reach the Comp-U-Store people at a toll-free number, 800-843-7777. Be sure to tell them you're a Dow Jones News/Retrieval subscriber.

Even if you don't become a member, it's useful to have Comp-U-Store available for browsing. We know people who use Comp-U-Store to get an idea of a "good" discount price for merchandise before hitting the local shopping mall or discount house.

Time to move on. Hmmm—how do we get out of here? No visible exits. Remember the first rule of computers: When in doubt, type HELP. Do that now.

```
                    --- HELP ---

TO MAIN:     To go to the Main Directory
TO NEW:      To see What's New
TO SHOP:     To go to Shopping Directory
TO STORE:    To go to Comp-u-store
TO BEST:     To go to Best Buys
TO MALL:     To go to Comp-u-mall
TO DRUS:     To go to The Drugstore
TO HOME:     To go to Home Furnishings
TO TRAVEL:   To go to Discount Travel
TO OUTLET:   To go to Warehouse Outlet
TO GAMES:    To go to Amusements Directory
TO STAKES:   To go to Comp-U-Stakes
TO INFO:     To go to Information Booth
TO CONSUMER: To go to Consumer Services
TO MEMBER: To go to Member Sign-up
TOP:         Returns to top of Directory
Press Return/Enter to continue
or enter selection >
```

These commands can be used from nearly any prompt in Comp-U-Store to go to any other area quickly. But there are more commands, so press RETURN again to see them.

```
HELP:     Displays all commands
EXIT:     To log off Comp-u-store
Press Return/Enter to continue
or enter selection >
```

There's one more HELP screen, which you ought to review quickly before we leave, so press RETURN again.

```
                --- HELP ---
*The list displays products which meet your
 specifications.
*Enter a specific item # to see a description of that
 product.
*If more than one page is indicated at the top of the
 list, type p and the page number to see more
 choices.
*Type CHA to change your answers to the questions.
*Type ORDER to process a stored order.
Press Return/Enter to continue
or enter selection >
```

At this prompt, enter **EXIT.**

```
THANK YOU.

PRESS   TO

1       BROWSE COMP-U-STORE
2       SEARCH OTHER DOW JONES NEWS/RETRIEVAL
            SERVICE DATA BASES
-----------------------------------------------------
TO SIGN OFF, PLEASE TYPE DISC

ENTER QUERY
```

AT THE //MOVIES

The next stop is the movie library. From this prompt enter //MOVIES.

```
            Cineman Movie Reviews
      Copyright (C) 1986 Cineman Syndicate

Press  For
  1 New Releases: BRAZIL, THE CLAN OF THE CAVE BEAR,
      IRON EAGLE, THE JOURNEY OF NATTY GANN, TROLL
  2 Current Films
  3 Movies: 1926-1986
  4 Coming Attractions
  5 Top Box Office Hits
  6 Trivia Quiz
```

This menu will appear differently on your screen; it's updated regularly with the new releases. Notice that you can check reviews of new releases, see reviews of films currently making the rounds, get a preview of coming attractions from Hollywood, see a list of current box office hits, and even play a movie trivia game. But the lion's share of this database is devoted to the thousands of movie reviews in number 3. Let's see how these films are displayed. Enter 3.

```
            MOVIES; 1926-1986

ENTER ONLY AS MUCH OF THE TITLE AS YOU ARE SURE OF,
INCLUDING PUNCTUATION.

FOR EXAMPLE, YOU CAN:

ENTER      ABSENCE
TO FIND    ABSENCE OF MALICE

ENTER MOVIE TITLE
```

First, let's check for one of Dave's favorite movies of all time—*The Blob*. Given half a chance, Dave will go on for minutes on end about how this is a science fiction masterpiece (and illustrate again why he's not a nationally recognized film critic).

To see what Cineman has to say about this movie, all you need do is enter the word BLOB at the prompt. You should see:

```
MOVIES                                        P 1 OF 2


                    THE BLOB
                    (FAIR)
                    (1959)
                     ---
     Slimy goo from outer space invades a small town,
and a young Steve McQueen comes to the rescue. This
puffed-up sci-fi nonsense is primarily aimed at
adolescent audiences. There are, however, a few scary
scenes scattered here and there, and Steve McQueen
makes the most of the situation.
     Also cast are Olin Howlin and Earl
```

Press RETURN to see the second and last page.

```
MOVIES                                        P 2 OF 2

Rowe and Aneta Corseaut. The film spawned a sequel
called "Beware! The Blob," also known as "Son of
Blob."
     Director -- Irwin S. Yeaworth, Jr.
83 minutes
```

Finding all the movies that contain the same word is just as simple. And you don't need to go back to the top, or beginning of the //MOVIES program. For example, let's say you want to see a list of all the *Friday The 13th* movies, but you don't remember how many there were. Enter FRIDAY to see the list.

```
FRIDAY                                          P 1 OF 1
PRESS    FOR

   1   FRIDAY FOSTER (POOR)
   2   FRIDAY THE 13TH (FAIR)
   3   FRIDAY THE 13TH - THE FINAL CHAPTER (POOR)
   4   FRIDAY THE 13TH - A NEW BEGINNING (POOR)
   5   FRIDAY THE 13TH - PART III (BORING)
   6   FRIDAY THE 13TH - PART II (BORING)
```

Friday Foster doesn't belong in the *Friday The 13th* saga, of course, but typing FRIDAY shows you the scope of the *Friday the 13th* series, including what Cineman (and most viewers) thought of the series. From this menu, of course, you could enter a number to see the particulars of any of these movies. (We'll spare you that experience.)

Cineman has been popular since the early days of online services. It's handy to have around for a quick review of an old flick on the cable (the database reviews films all the way back to 1926), as well as to get a handle on a new release playing in the neighborhood theater. In addition, with the excitement in home videocassette recorders these days, Cineman has found a new audience—those wanting to compare films before rushing out to make some weekend rentals.

ON TO THE DOCTOR'S OFFICE

Now it's on to another database, one that can be of considerable comfort when a member of the family is ill. We're talking about //MEDX, the medical service supplied by International Medical Reference, Inc.

Let's assume that your child has come down with a case of tonsillitis and you'd like to find out a little more about the condition beyond what the doctor told you.

To get to the medical database, enter //MEDX. That should lead you to this opening menu:

AT HOME WITH DOW JONES

```
                           MEDX
                   COPYRIGHT (C) 1986
          INTERNATIONAL MEDICAL REFERENCE INC
PRESS FOR

1 MEDICAL AND SURGICAL INFORMATION

2 INFORMATION FROM THE ESSENTIAL GUIDE TO
  PRESCRIPTION DRUGS, HARPER & ROW, PUBLISHERS, INC.
-----------------------------------------------------
PRESS <RETURN> FOR AN EXPLANATION OF THE MEDX SERVICE
AND A LIST OF ITS EDITORIAL BOARD OF CONTRIBUTING
PHYSICIANS
```

As the title page tells you, if you press RETURN, you'll be shown an overview of the database and some instructions on how to use it. Or you can go directly to the medical and surgical information, as we'll do. Enter 1.

```
ENTER ONLY AS MUCH OF THE NAME OF THE ILLNESS,
MEDICAL CONDITION OR BODY PART AS YOU ARE SURE OF.

FOR EXAMPLE, YOU CAN:

ENTER      BACK
OR         LOWER BACK

TO FIND  LOWER BACK PAIN

ENTER REQUEST
```

The subject was tonsillitis. So enter TONSILLITIS.

```
MEDX                                    PAGE 1 OF 1
PRESS  FOR

  1   GENERAL INFORMATION
  2   INFLAMMATION - TONSILLITIS
  3   SURGERY - TONSILLECTOMY
```

//MEDX has three discussions of tonsillitis. Let's see the specific information about the condition. Enter 2.

```
MEDX                                    PAGE 1 OF 1
PRESS   FOR

  1   SWOLLEN TONSILS - TONSILLITIS
  2     SYMPTOMS
  3     CONTAGION
  4     SPECIAL DANGERS AND PRECAUTIONS
  5     TREATMENT
  6     RELATED TOPICS IN MEDX DATABASE
```

Notice that number 1 appears as if it's a major topic and 2–6 are indented as if they are subtopics. That's the way it's organized. If you typed 1 and pressed RETURN at the bottom of each subsequent screen, you'd see all the information under numbers 1 through 6. Or, if you like, you can skip any part of the total entry and jump right to what you want to read.

Let's assume your main concern is special dangers and precautions and treatment of the condition. You can go directly to those subtopics by entering 4. Do that now.

```
MEDX                                    PAGE 1 OF 3

SPECIAL DANGERS AND PRECAUTIONS
    Acute tonsillitis, if not adequately treated, may
develop into a chronic condition. The child may then
become infected repeatedly with colds and sore
throats, low grade fevers, and ear infections.
```

    Acute tonsillitis, if not adequately treated, may
result in rheumatic fever or kidney infection. In
adults, it may lead to arthritic condition.
    It is for these reasons that troublesome tonsils
and adenoids were at one time removed almost

Press RETURN to see page 2. When it scrolls to the end of that page,
press RETURN to see page 3.

It says this is the last page of three pages. True enough, but if you
press RETURN at this point, you'll go immediately into the subsection on
treatment.

MEDX   PAGE 1 OF 3

TREATMENT
    Acute tonsillitis should be brought to the
attention of a physician at once. Antibiotics will
usually be prescribed, in order to counteract the
infection as well as to prevent the development of
more serious disease. Supplementary treatment is
also recommended:
    1. Aspirin to relieve pain.
    2. Large quantities of water, fruit juices, or
       other fluids.
    3. Bed rest.
    4. Ice cream, cold drinks-

Press RETURN to see page 2. When the screen stops scrolling, press
RETURN to see page 3.

Remember the sixth selection from the main tonsillitis menu? When you
press RETURN again, you'll be taken straightaway to this last subsection. Do
that now.

MEDX   PAGE 1 OF 1

RELATED TOPICS IN MEDX DATABASE
    For further information see the following sections
of the MEDX database:

```
        Medical Database
     ARTHRITIS
     KIDNEY INFECTION
     RHEUMATIC FEVER
     TONSILLECTOMY
```

From this list, you could type one of the related topics and get information on that condition as well.

//MEDX offers medical and drug information covering more than a thousand illnesses and their medical and surgical treatment, providing no little amount of details; it has some 40 entries that deal with cancer and more than 100 about various skin conditions.

Of course, it's intended as a *nondiagnostic* reference work—your computer isn't ready to take over the doctor's job—but it's as handy as having a detailed medical encyclopedia on your desk.

To leave //MEDX, we could simply type two slashes (//) and the name of another Dow Jones service. However, let's take this opportunity to practice with a navigation command and "back out" of the database using the M command. Entering M in this database, and many others around the system, allows you to return to the menu you previously saw. For example, enter M now.

```
MEDX                                          PAGE 1 OF 1

PRESS  FOR

   1   SWOLLEN TONSILS - TONSILLITIS
   2     SYMPTOMS
   3     CONTAGION
   4     SPECIAL DANGERS AND PRECAUTIONS
   5     TREATMENT
   6     RELATED TOPICS IN MEDX DATABASE
```

Enter M again to get back to the first page of the medical and surgical information section of //MEDX.

Now enter M one more time to see the main menu.

By using M we have taken the menu road to get back to the beginning of the database.

GOING TO //SCHOOL

The time comes in most parents' lives when the youngsters start exploring the possibilities for higher education. Dow Jones News/Retrieval comes to the rescue again with a searchable database that allows you to find the college or university that suits your own child's needs.

Let's suppose your high school age son has asked you to help him find a college or university where he can get a degree in registered nursing, a profession in great demand these days. You think of Peterson's College Selection Service on Dow Jones. To get there, enter //SCHOOL.

```
   PETERSON'S COLLEGE SELECTION SERVICE
           COPYRIGHT (C) 1986
      PETERSON'S COLLEGE GUIDES, INC.

COLLEGE DESCRIPTIONS ARE SUPPLIED BY THE SCHOOLS.

THERE ARE TWO WAYS TO FIND INFORMATION:

PRESS    TO SEARCH BY

 1 COLLEGE NAME FOR DETAILED INFORMATION ABOUT
   SPECIFIC SCHOOLS

 2 YOUR INDIVIDUAL REQUIREMENTS TO FIND THE RIGHT
   SCHOOLS FOR YOU
```

Notice there are two functions in this service. If you choose number 1, you could simply enter the name of a college or university and get information about it. But you need to search for a school that suits your son's needs, so choose number 2.

```
       THE COLLEGE SELECTION SERVICE

Press  For
1   The College Selection Service
2    Type Of College: 2-Year, 4-Year
```

```
3    Coed, Men Only, Women Only
4    Entrance Difficulty
5    Geographic Location
6    Campus Setting
7    Total Enrollment
8    Costs: Tuition, Fees, Room & Board
9    Areas of Study
---------------------------------------------------------
Press 1 for all selections. Or enter your choices
separated by commas.
                    EXAMPLE: 4,5,7
```

Here's how you can search for the school of your choice. If you choose number 1, you'll get to narrow your search by answering questions 2 through 9. So, let's go through the entire list to see what happens.

```
                    TYPE OF COLLEGE

Press  For

1    Two-Year Colleges
2    Four-Year Colleges with No Graduate Programs
3    Colleges or Universities with Graduate Programs
4    Upper-Level Institutions Starting with the Junior
     Year
---------------------------------------------------------
Enter your choices separated by commas.
               EXAMPLE: 2,3.
Press return if you have no preference.
```

You son needs a four-year institution to become a registered nurse. But let's say it doesn't matter to you whether the school has graduate programs. The options would be either 2 or 3 so enter 2,3 (that is, the digit 2 followed by a comma and then the digit 3).

```
                COED, MEN ONLY, WOMEN ONLY

Press   For

1   Coed Schools and Coordinate Schools with Separate
       Campuses For Men and Women but some Shared
       Classes and Activities
2   Men Only
3   Women Only
--------------------------------------------------------
Enter your choices separated by commas.
                      EXAMPLE: 1,2
```

Your son insists on going to a coeducational school. He's so insistent, in fact, that *he* punches in number 1 for you.

```
                  ENTRANCE DIFFICULTY
Press   For
1   MOST DIFFICULT Average Scores
       1350+ on SAT, 32+ on ACT;
       Class Rank Top 10%
2   VERY DIFFICULT Average Scores
       1150+ on SAT, 26+ on ACT
       Class Rank: Top 20%
3   MODERATELY DIFFICULT Average Scores
       1000 on SAT, 20+ on ACT
       Class Rank: Top 50%
4   MINIMALLY DIFFICULT Average Scores
       SAT Under 900, ACT Under 21
       Class Rank: Lower 50%
5   NON-COMPETITIVE Virtually All Students Accepted
```

You figure your son ranks in about the middle of his class. So enter 3,4 to get both MODERATELY DIFFICULT and MINIMALLY DIFFICULT entrance levels.

```
                    GEOGRAPHIC LOCATION

You can select as many as 3 college locations by
region and state. Enter the region codes and 2-letter
state abbreviations separated only by commas. For
example, you can:

        Enter: PA,CO,1

        To Select: Pennsylvania
                   Colorado
                   New England States
------------------------------------------------------------
Press return for a list of region codes
```

Let's look at the regions the search program defines. Press RETURN.

```
                    GEOGRAPHIC LOCATION

Press For Regions    State Abbreviations

   1 New England     CT,ME,MA,NH,RI,VT
   2 Mid Atlantic    DE,DC,NJ,NY,PA
   3 S. Atlantic     FL,GA,MD,NC,SC,VA,PR
   4 Great Lakes     IL,IN,MI,OH,WI
   5 Plains          IA,KS,MN,MO,NE,ND,SD
   6 E S Central     AL,KY,MS,TN,WV
   7 W S Central     AR,LA,NM,OK,TX
   8 Mountain        AZ,CO,ID,MT,NV,UT,WY
   9 Pacific         AK,CA,HI,OR,WA
  10 Canada          (All Provinces)
------------------------------------------------------------
Enter up to 3 choices. EXAMPLE: PA,CO,1
```

As it said on the preceding screen, you can simply type the postal code for a specific state if you're interested in one or two states rather than an entire region. Or, you can type a combination of states and regions. Your son is interested primarily in the East South Central states. Enter 6.

CAMPUS SETTING

```
Press  For

 1    Major Metropolitan Area
 2    Near a Major Metropolitan Area
 3    Small to Medium-sized City
 4    Small Town
 5    Rural Area
-----------------------------------------------------
Enter your choices separated by commas.
                  EXAMPLE: 2,3
Press return if you have no preference.
```

The boy wants to go to a college in a big city. You want him to go to school in a small town. You compromise and choose options 2 and 3 (small to medium, perhaps *near* a metropolitan area). Enter 2,3 and see:

TOTAL ENROLLMENT
(Includes Graduate Students)

```
Press  For

 1    VERY SMALL: Under 1000 Students,
        Like Wells, Goucher and Haverford
 2    SMALL: 1000-4999 Students,
        Like Brandeis and Johns Hopkins
 3    MEDIUM: 5000-9999 Students,
        Like Yale, Brown and Duke
 4    LARGE: More than 10,000 Students,
        Like Cornell and Ohio State
-----------------------------------------------------
Enter your choices separated by commas.
                  EXAMPLE: 1,2
Press return if you have no preference.
```

He's thinking about a reasonably large institution, maybe not huge but certainly more than 5,000 students. So enter 3,4.

```
                        COSTS
Press  For
                    In-State Students
   1   $0-$2,500
   2   $2,501-$5,000
   3   $5,001-$7,500
   4   $7,501-$10,000
   5   $10,001-$12,500
   6   $Over $12,500
                  Out-of-State Students
   7   $0-$2,500
   8   $2,501-$5,000
   9   $5,001-$7,500
  10   $7,501-$10,000
  11   $10,001-$12,500
  12   Over $12,500
```

Ah, now we're down to the nitty-gritty. You estimate you can handle costs up to $7,500, so enter 8,9.

```
                  AREAS OF STUDY

The next screen lists general Areas of Study like
Business, Foreign Languages and Engineering &
Computer Sciences.

Please select the single general areas in which
you're the most interested.
-----------------------------------------------------
Press return to pick a general area of study.
```

Here's where you'll begin specifying general study areas. Press RETURN for some options:

```
Press  For
  1   Architecture
  2   Arts
  3   Business
  4   Communications
  5   Education
  6   Engineering & Computer Sciences
  7   Foreign Languages
  8   Health-Related Professions
  9   Humanities & Religion
 10   Library & Information Sciences
 11   Sciences
 12   Social Sciences
 13   Social Services & Home Economics
 14   Vocational Program: 2-year
 15   Preprofessional Sequences: 4-year
```

Nursing should be under the health-related professions studies, so choose 8.

```
                        MAJORS

The next screen lists specific Majors in the general
Area of Study you chose.

Please limit your choice to no more than 3 Majors. If
you select too many majors, most colleges will have
at least one of them. By narrowing your search, you
will be able to focus on schools most likely to meet
your needs.
-------------------------------------------------------
Press return to select your majors.
```

Press RETURN to specify the major you're looking for.

HEALTH-RELATED MAJORS

Press For

```
1  Animal Hospital Technologies
2  Dental Services
3  Dietetics & Nutrition
4  Medical Technologies
5  Nursing & Physician's Assistant
6  Optometry
7  Pharmacy & Pharmaceutical Sciences
8  Speech Therapy, Speech Pathology & Audiology
9  Therapies: Occupational, Physical,
     Rehabilitation, Respiratory
```

Finally, we've arrived at the place to specify "nursing"— it's option 5 on this menu. Enter that, and there may be a brief pause as the system performs the search. Then it should report something like this:

```
20 COLLEGES MEET YOUR CRITERIA.

PRESS    TO
  L        LIST THE COLLEGES FOUND
  C        CANCEL AND START A NEW SEARCH
(RETURN) VIEW YOUR REMAINING SELECTIONS
```

Here you have an opportunity to review your selections. Press RETURN to see what selections you have made from the previous menus.

YOUR SELECTIONS

```
4-YEAR COLLEGES WITH NO GRAD WORK
UNIVERSITIES & 4-YEAR COLLEGES WITH GRAD WORK
COED
MODERATELY DIFFICULT
MINIMALLY DIFFICULT
EAST SOUTH CENTRAL STATES
```

```
   20 COLLEGES MEET YOUR CRITERIA.

PRESS    TO
   L        LIST THE COLLEGES FOUND
   C        CANCEL AND START A NEW SEARCH
```

This is only the first page of your selections. Press RETURN again to see the remainder of your selections.

```
                  YOUR SELECTIONS

CITY
SMALL TOWN
MEDIUM (5,000 - 9,999)
LARGE (10,000+)
$2501-$5000 FOR NONRESIDENTS
$5001-$7500 FOR NONRESIDENTS
NURSING (REGISTERED)
PRESS    FOR                              * MORE *
```

Now comes the list of 20 colleges and universities that meet your specifications. Press RETURN.

```
1    AUBURN UNIVERSITY
     Auburn University, AL 36849
2    AUBURN UNIVERSITY AT MONTGOMERY
     Montgomery, AL 36193
3    AUSTIN PEAY STATE UNIVERSITY
     Clarksville, TN 37044
4    EAST TENNESSEE STATE UNIVERSITY
     Johnson City, TN 37614
5    MARSHALL UNIVERSITY
     Huntington, WV 25701
6    MIDDLE TENNESSEE STATE UNIVERSITY
     Murfreesboro, TN 37132
```

This is the first of more than three screens full of schools. However, one of this list has caught Dave's eye—it's his Alma Mater, Marshall University—and he wants to see what Peterson's has to say about it. Enter 5.

```
PRESS    FOR
  1   CAPSULE PROFILE
  2   GENERAL INFORMATION
  3   STUDENT BODY CHARACTERISTICS
  4   FRESHMAN ACADEMIC DATA
  5   ADMISSIONS REQUIREMENTS
  6   EXPENSES & FINANCIAL AID
  7   SPECIAL ACADEMIC PROGRAMS
  8   CAREER SERVICES
  9   CAMPUS LIFE & HOUSING
 10   ATHLETICS
 11   MAJOR FIELDS
 12   ADMISSIONS OFFICE CONTACT
 13   ANNOUNCEMENTS
 14   COLLEGE'S OWN IN-DEPTH DESCRIPTION
```

Choose number 1.

```
SCHOOL                                   PAGE 1 OF 21

GENERAL INFORMATION State-supported coed university.
Founded 1837. Awards A (college transfer and
terminal), B, M, D. Institutionally accredited by
regional association; programs accredited by NLN
(nursing), NCATE (teacher education); candidate for
program accreditation by NASM (music). City setting;
50-acre barrier-free campus. Total enrollment:
11,323. Faculty: 514 (361 full-time, 153 part-time);
57% have doctoral degrees; graduate assistants teach
a few undergraduate courses. Calendar:
```

Note: the "capsule" profile section isn't *really* 21 pages long. Actually, the profile is divided into sections which begin with general information. In other words, you could choose any number through 13 to see a part of the capsule profile. Number 14, the college's own self-description, is separate. (Administrators of more than 700 of the same 3,000 universities described here have written essays of up to 2,000 words about their institutions.)

Right now, enter M (for menu) to go back to the main menu for Marshall University.

```
PRESS    FOR
   1   CAPSULE PROFILE
   2   GENERAL INFORMATION
   3   STUDENT BODY CHARACTERSTICS
   4   FRESHMAN ACADEMIC DATA
   5   ADMISSIONS REQUIREMENTS
   6   EXPENSES & FINANCIAL AID
   7   SPECIAL ACADEMIC PROGRAMS
   8   CAREER SERVICES
   9   CAMPUS LIFE & HOUSING
  10   ATHLETICS
  11   MAJOR FIELDS
  12   ADMISSIONS OFFICE CONTACT
  13   ANNOUNCEMENTS
  14   COLLEGE'S OWN IN-DEPTH DESCRIPTION
```

Perhaps you want to look at the section on athletics. Without reading through all the other sections, you can enter 10 to go directly to the athletics section. Do that now.

```
SCHOOL                                    PAGE 1 OF 2

ATHLETICS Member NCAA (Division I).
Intercollegiate sports: baseball/softball M(I), W(I);
basketball M(I,s), W(I,s); bowling M,W; cross-
country running M(I,s), W(I,s); football M(I,AA,s);
golf M(I), W(I); riflery M(I), W(I); soccer (M(I);
swimming and diving M(I,s); tennis M(I,s), W(II,s);
track and field M(I,s), W(I,s); volleyball M(I,s),
W(I,s). Intramural sports: badminton, baseball/
softball, basketball, bowling, cross-country running,
fencing, field hockey, football, golf,
```

By now, you should have a good idea of how to use the service.

By the way, it's sometimes so easy to use these electronic versions of reference works that we forget just how massive the collection of information is. Peterson's is a good example. If all the information available online here were printed out, as it is in Peterson's paper edition of the guide, it would amount to a 2,500-page, two-volume reference work. The database has detailed information on more than 1,900 four-year and 1,400 two-year colleges and universities in the United States and Canada.

Enjoy a browse through this database, and when you're finished, DISConnect and join us on the other side of the subheading called . . .

IN RETROSPECT

We've seen a lot of different databases on this tour, and a lot of similarities among them. All of them guide you through the mazes with menus or questions. Several of them have the same types of navigation commands.

We didn't show you all the commands you can use in these databases, of course. You can get a better idea of some of them in the Online Survival Kit at the end of the book. We urge you to review the commands in each area before you enter again just to refamiliarize yourself with the database's concept and function.

You might not use any of these databases on a daily basis— they're not as timely as the Current Quotes and the daily news features—but it's nice to know they're available when you need them. All of them can give you an edge in handling your daily affairs and keep you from wasting time running in circles looking for information that is as close as your computer.

Chapter 15

... AND THAT'S NOT ALL YOU GET

We've now seen the major online features of Dow Jones News/Retrieval, the databases that have made this system famous. If that's all there were, it would be more than sufficient to win Dow Jones a place in the online hall of fame. But, as the guys on television say, that's not *all* you get.

DJN/R has broken new ground in the electronic information game by providing some remarkable offline support for its online customers. There's top-flight software that helps you analyze the data you retrieve. There are in-person seminars for subscribers to sharpen their online skills. There's even a new service that lets you use the resources of Dow Jones when you're not at your computer keyboard.

In this chapter we'll take a few minutes to look over what else is available to you as a subscriber to Dow Jones News/Retrieval.

SOFTWARE THAT MAKES A DIFFERENCE

One of the earliest criticisms of electronic information services was that they were too complicated to use. Many of those in positions to change things reacted by adding more menus to their services, by reevaluating the language used in their commands to see if they could make it clearer, and by rewriting the software in the spirit of that phrase professional programmers have grown to hate—"user friendly."

Meanwhile, another front has opened up—development of sophisticated, powerful, "friendly" software that you can use on your end of the connection to communicate.

In the early days of News/Retrieval, desktop computers were in their infancy. When communicating online, they weren't much more than "dumb terminals," able to display what was being transmitted by the host system and maybe print it out, but not much more.

Since about 1980, however, the power of personal computers has grown dramatically. So much so, in fact, that using a modern desktop system as a dumb terminal these days is akin to having a Ph.D. teach a class by simply reading the textbook aloud.

DJN/R publishes a line of remarkable software that harnesses the new powers of small computers. With these packages, you can press the "Go Button" to automatically log on to the system, retrieve preselected quotes, current or historical, and log off automatically in minutes. Then you can have the software help you analyze what you've found, drawing graphs and charts, or letting you run the figures through your favorite spreadsheet.

The software is so good that we've been anxious to tell you about it, but we decided to rein ourselves in until Chapter 15 for several reasons.

First, this software is not exactly cheap; it's a one-time investment of a hundred to several hundred dollars for each package. Of course, if you're using Dow Jones in your business, it's probably a tax-deductible business expense.

More to the point, we felt it was important that you learned how to navigate the system on your own before you considered turning over much of the responsibility to a program. (That's an attitude shared by many at Dow Jones News/Retrieval too, incidentally.) It just makes good sense to have the skills to find information for those special occasions. Once you do, you might want to invest in a package that can handle the day-to-day needs for particular quotes and reports. In other words, use these fine programs as part-time helpers, not full-time chauffeurs.

Oh, and by the way, News/Retrieval recently introduced a project that lets you review its top software packages before deciding whether to buy them. You now can rent any Dow Jones Software program for a monthly fee—$10 to $30, depending on the program—at a one-month minimum. The shipping charges will be waived and you'll also receive another free DJN/R password as part of the deal. If, after at least one month of renting, you wish to buy the program,

Dow Jones will credit you with 50 percent of the rent you've already paid toward the purchase price. If you want more details on the rental program, call the software telemarketers at Customer Service, 1-800-257-5114 (in New Jersey the number is 609/452-1511).

Those are also the numbers to call to order any of the software packages we discuss here.

So, now that you've learned to drive DJN/R in standard shift, let's see what's available in a sleek automatic.

THE BIG THREE

The three most popular Dow Jones Software packs are The Market Manager, Market Analyzer PLUS, and Spreadsheet Link. They're all available for the IBM PC and true compatibles as well as the Apple IIe & IIc and the Apple Macintosh family. Watch //INTRO for other developments.

All of them provide automatic log-on and work with files that you can prepare offline. They also offer an "E-Z Terminal mode" which acts as a simple communications program for touring the system on your own.

In addition, these, and most of Dow Jones's software, come with outstanding user's manuals that simplify the operations considerably. With most, spending an hour or two running through the sample sessions in the manuals is all the training you'll need to run the programs.

Here's a rundown:

The Market Manager PLUS

This program lets you create and manage numerous portfolios (up to 26 on a floppy disk-based system and 255 on a hard disk).

The software automatically values stocks, bonds, Treasury issues, options, and mutual funds. At its core is a tax-lot accounting feature that records and maintains details on each security transaction. The system actually matches sell transactions with existing positions to minimize tax liability. It also keeps track of broker commissions, dividends, interest, stock splits, and the portfolio's cash balances.

One nice option is a "price alert" feature which, when used online, keeps you abreast of rapid changes in an active portfolio. Another is a "security alert" to help you identify expiring options, stocks going long-term, and any of your bonds that are about to mature.

At tax time the software can save you hours, because after tracking dividends and interest, it records their tax-exempt status, separating totals into federal-, state-, and municipally exempt categories. Also it updates holdings by portfolio, by security, by gain and loss calculations, and by cash transactions.

At this writing, the suggested retail price was $249 and there were versions available for IBM-compatible systems, the Apple IIe and IIc, and the Apple Macintosh.

The Market Analyzer PLUS

If you're a fan of charts and graphs to get the Big Picture, you'll want to consider this one. It's a great tool for serious investors.

The Analyzer allows you to specify offline what securities you want to follow. Then it logs on to the system and builds a database of historical quotes on each company. After that it will routinely update those databases each day you tell it to log on.

After the software saves the historical information to disk, it can construct a number of standard technical analysis charts to track individual companies or compare several of them. Among the charts are stock bar and comparison charts, relative strength charts and trend lines, moving averages, and oscillator and price/volume indicator charts.

If your system uses floppy disks, the software can store data for up to 600 trading days on 40 stocks or 120 trading days on 200 stock per floppy. If you use a hard disk, you can keep up to 520 trading days on 500 stocks.

The suggested retail price is $349. At this time, versions supported IBMs, the Apple II family, the Texas Instruments Professional Computer, and the Tandy Model III.

Spreadsheet Link

Here's a unique idea. What if you could pick up data from Dow Jones and then run it through analyses with your favorite spreadsheet program, whether it's Lotus 1-2-3, Multiplan, or VisiCalc? Well, that's precisely what this program does.

With Spreadsheet Link, you begin offline specifying the data you want to retrieve (from either //CQE, //HQ, //EARN, //DSCLO, or //MG), simply placing special symbols in the rows and columns of your spreadsheet. Then you tell the software to log on and read the script you've written for it.

After it's logged off again, you enter your spreadsheet and pick up the data file and, presto, it's saved you the tedious task of data entry.

Spreadsheet Link comes with a half dozen sample templates for common applications, and, of course, you can build your own.

Suggested retail price: $249. Versions: IBM and compatibles, the Apple II family. The Apple Macintosh version retails for $99 and requires Straight Talk, a communication and information software package from Dow Jones.

SOME OTHER PROGRAMS TO CONSIDER

In addition to these main entries, Dow Jones Software has other programs you may be interested in. For instance:

Straight Talk: If you're using an Apple Macintosh to access the system, you really should take a look at this one. It's only $95 and it does some beautiful things with DJN/R, particularly letting you use your mouse pointing device and its pull-down menu system. It also makes use of the Mac's notepad convention to indicate what information you want retrieved, as well as the machine's Scrapbook and Clipboard features.

E-Z Access: A "plain vanilla" communications program for Apple IIc and IIe and IBM Computers, this one is only $29.95.

Home Budget: This is a $139 package for IBM systems for offline maintenance of home financial records and taxes. It does not access the system.

DOWPHONE—A NEW FRONTIER

All of what you've seen so far in our tours can be generically defined as *videotex*, computer-based services that display their information on your screen, services that are interactive. In other words, you're not a passive observer; you interact with the system to inform it about what data you wish to view.

Dow Jones also is a pioneer in a new field of interactive information—

audiotex, which delivers the goods not to your eye, but to your ear. You don't even have to use a computer to access it; all you need is a standard push-button telephone.

In April 1984 Dow Jones & Co. introduced DowPhone, through which subscribers can call access numbers and punch in four-digit codes to hear up-to-the-minute business and financial news and to access the latest stock quotes (delayed 15 minutes from the exchanges, just like those available online through //CQE).

DowPhone even has facilities for building and storing individual portfolios in which you can keep symbols for up to 100 companies so that you can get news and quotes about them with a minimum of numeric codes.

You can see why *InfoWorld* magazine once dubbed a subscription to DowPhone as one of the "status symbols among business executives."

Dow Jones maintains three local numbers for access in New York City and New Jersey (area codes 212, 201, and 609) as well as an 800 number for those outside the area.

To sign up for DowPhone, you're charged an annual subscription fee (at this writing it's $25), plus a connect fee (usually 50 cents a minute) for the time you're on the line. If you call long-distance to the New York-New Jersey area DowPhone numbers, you will, of course, also be accountable for the phone bill. Or you can use the 800 number at a charge of $1 a minute.

So, what do you get for the money?

DowPhone subscribers are provided with a "passport," that is, an individual numeric access code, and a list of the four-digit codes for the various news categories and stock quotes available. (DowPhone has been adding services regularly since the 1984 startup. The subscribers' *Dowline* magazine regularly publishes lists of newly added codes.)

A routine DowPhone call goes something like this:

• You pick up the phone and dial one of the four access lines (the 800 number or one of the New York-New Jersey numbers) and hear a voice that says, "Enter your DowPhone passport number, please."

• You punch in your seven-digit access code, and a recorded voice begins reciting headlines of the top business and financial news of the hour. (To make the recordings, Dow Jones has a staff of five veteran broadcasters.) Each story is followed by its own four-digit code. If you need to know more about any of the stories, you can enter its codes following the headlines.

• After the headlines, you hear a tone which signals that DowPhone is awaiting a single digit to indicate what you want to hear now. For example, if you wanted to hear more news for specific industry groups, you would punch the 7 button, followed by a four-digit industry group or topic, such as 9002 for stock market updates, 9003 for the latest Dow Jones Average, 9071 for stocks splits, and so forth. Or if you wanted to check the latest stocks for a specific company, you would punch 6 followed by the company's unique code (such as 5012 for Apple Computer, 4188 for IBM, 8125 for Texas Instruments). Or you could check the companies listed in your portfolio, or even hear a 30-second market analysis of individual companies from Innovest Systems, Inc.

As a time-saver, DowPhone provides a "break key" of sorts. Pressing the asterisk button (*) at any point interrupts a broadcast and lets you punch in a new command.

All of this happens pretty fast; DowPhone can tell you the quotes of six stocks in a minute. Also it's quite transportable; DowPhone will work from virtually any push-button phone, even most cellular phones installed in automobiles. And Dow Jones can set up multi-user accounts so that a number of people in the same organization can use the same passport.

If you're interested in pursuing this, give a call to the Customer Service Department, 800-257-0437. You also can get a free demonstration of the system by calling that number. It would be a good idea to have in mind several industry news areas that you'd like to hear about, as well as a stock or two. Then you'd just tell the Customer Service people you'd like to hear the day's report on, say, personal computers and telecommunications, and also the latest stock quotes on IBM and Apple. During the demonstration, Customer Service will take care of running DowPhone from its end, then come back on the line to answer any questions you might have and sign you up if you're ready.

Chapter 16

GOING AHEAD
ON YOUR OWN

Now that we've finished the walking tour of Dow Jones News/Retrieval, our challenge—showing you how the system looks and works today—is almost done. On the other hand, yours—staying current with it and rolling with the changes that occur down the pike—is just beginning.

We've made no secret of the fact that News/Retrieval, like every other vital, active electronic information service, still is evolving. New features come online frequently. Old features get facelifts as the systems people figure out better and easier ways for them to work. No one in the electronic data world has yet found the *perfect* system, because no one's ever done this before. We're all still in the first few pages of what will be an illustrious chapter in the history of communications.

Some people find it annoying to try to work with a system that is constantly changing. They're stymied when they find that an old, comfortable database suddenly has a new appearance or has been augmented or has been supplanted by a more powerful but different database.

All of us can offer them sympathy—and little other comfort. At this time, change is the only thing any of us can predict about this animal. When we began this adventure together, we talked about the kind of people who take advantage of new technology, and self-reliance emerged as a big part of the picture.

But we're preaching to the wrong congregation, aren't we? You're now a leg up on the other fellow, because you've seen the system from the inside. You've learned not only the commands for the various features, but the ideas behind the commands, giving you a historical perspective. Now if an individual database's operation changes tomorrow, you're going to make an easier transition because you already know how it used to work. And while the commands might change, the object of those commands won't.

As we've told you, that's the big secret. Commands and structure evolve; the goals and functions usually are more stable. It's a lot like language. Words change every day, but the ideas behind them are constant. Progressing from one dialect to another doesn't mean you have to learn how to think all over again, just how to find new words to express those old thoughts.

Being concept-oriented is going to help you deal with new services as well as changes in old ones. For instance, if News/Retrieval were to introduce a new searchable text feature today, it might not use the same commands you learned in the Text-Search Services (//TEXT). You can bet, though, that it would use many of the same central ideas for defining what it is you're looking for. So knowing how to "speak" //TEXT is going to reduce the time it takes you to pick up a new local dialect.

WHERE TO LOOK FOR THE WINDS OF CHANGE

An ancient rule of public speaking, and writing, and every other kind of communications you can think of, is:

Tell 'em what you're going to tell 'em.

Tell 'em.

Then tell 'em what you told 'em.

Dow Jones takes that adage to heart by forecasting its changes long before it implements them, and you can pick up on those signals in messages both online and offline.

In the first tour we took together, you met a database called //INTRO, which has developed into a kind of "Welcome Wagon" for the system. It's an electronic newsletter that's ideal as a first stop for new arrivals—it was designed with them in mind—but that's not its only purpose. //INTRO also is a central clearinghouse for news of all new features on the system. About once a week or so DJN/R adds files to //INTRO. So even now that you're an old pro in these parts, we suggest you make the free //INTRO a regular stop.

You also met a database called //DJ HELP, which functions as your electronic "owner's manual." It usually contains about 25 screens of information, from specific commands to overviews of searching techniques. It's very basic, which means that if you're heading off into less familiar waters, it's a good first stop for a refresher course on what lies ahead.

Remember, too, that every feature on Dow Jones has its own help files and many of a database's newest features are discussed there. To read help messages about a specific database, just append the word HELP to the usual command—//DJNEWS HELP or //TEXT HELP or //SP HELP.

News/Retrieval also provides offline help in using new and old features. The best of the lot is *Dowline*, a slick magazine published six times a year and delivered by mail to every subscriber. *Dowline* is filled with articles about how to make better use of existing features, what features are coming up for the service, and the like. Also popular are its regular "Investing" articles that give tips on how to use the data accessible through DJN/R in real-life situations. Another goodie is "Input/Output," a detailed question-and-answer column in every issue.

In addition, Dow Jones & Co. conducts regular subscribers' seminars around the country to give firsthand training on how to use some of the more sophisticated databases. You can find a schedule of upcoming conferences offline in *Dowline* and online in the //INTRO databases.

Finally, if none of these features answers a particular question you have, remember that you're just a toll-free call away from News/Retrieval's Customer Service Department. For most of us, the number is 1-800-257-5114. For those of you in Dow Jones's home state, New Jersey, the number is (609) 452-1511. All dial-up information services have customer service representatives, but few go to the lengths that DJN/R does. Their representatives have been given a minimum of three-months' intensive training on the system before they ever answer a call. In addition, the department has specialists on hand to deal with some topics, such as software and hardware-related issues.

We advise you to try first to solve your problems yourself, but if you're stuck, don't hesitate to call in an expert.

WHAT'S ON DECK FOR DOW JONES?

What new features does the future hold for Dow Jones News/Retrieval?

Well, understandably, Dow Jones is no more likely to give us a detailed list of new subjects than CBS is going to leak its fall lineup or GM is going to preview its new cars.

However, we can tell a lot about where News/Retrieval is going by where it's been recently.

For instance, we probably can expect continued emphasis on the integration of news and statistical databases. After all, two of the system's newest features—//CQE and //TRACK—do just that. And, as we've seen, Dow Jones Software puts a high priority on using //DJNEWS as a tool in making business decisions by making it easy to use one database in concert with another.

Also, because of News/Retrieval's roots in the publishing business, we can expect news of the day to continue as a high priority. We look for more enhancements to //TEXT, and perhaps additional electronic editions to join *The Wall Street Journal* and *The Washington Post*. Also it's likely that the systems people will try to come up with an option that will allow you to search all the //TEXT databases at the same time with a single set of queries.

And, while we're guessing, we expect Dow Jones to continue looking for features that give us a quick overview of the business day, a sort of day-long business update with one stop, providing the hot news from other databases around the system.

That feature would appeal particularly to the prime-time (daytime) customers, fitting nicely with a long-term goal of the company. DJN/R officials have said publicly that they expect to put more emphasis on services for daytime subscribers who are linking up from business offices. That doesn't mean Dow Jones is turning its back on the home audience; that's still a major part of the subscriber bases. It does mean, though, that we should see more features that summarize the news and business developments that are happening *right now*.

SO LONG—NOT GOODBYE

Now that you've learned the mechanics of using News/Retrieval, it's up to you to decide what to do with that knowledge. It would be perfectly understandable if you decided to keep your wisdom to yourself and guard it as part of your business savvy.

However, we hope you will share your enthusiasm with your friends and colleagues. You've seen the sheer mass of new information available online every day. Chances are that if you can't use a particular feature in your work, the fellow in the next office can.

Some offices these days are appointing information specialists to use these dial-up services, one person to log in with Dow Jones every day to pick up the vital information for the whole office. Others set up an overnight system—staffers note which features they want and then a colleague logs on from home in the evenings when the rates are lower and picks up the data to bring to work the next day.

The next section of the book, the Online Survival Kit, has some lists and tables that might help in that connection, particularly the chart on page 317, which reports the times at which each database is updated.

We'd be interested in hearing about it if you come up with new ways to use these resources in your life. Our MCI Mail online addresses also are reported in the back pages of the Survival Kit. If you're so inclined, drop us a line sometime. After all, no matter where you are, we're within the sound of your new electronic voice.

ONLINE
SURVIVAL KIT

It's time to fill up your glove compartment for your online travels through Dow Jones News/Retrieval. This section contains road maps for quick reference—major commands we've learned along the way, addresses of important databases, pointers on getting help when you need it, and more.

We've divided the Online Survival Kit into several parts:

I. Making Connections: log-on procedures, communications parameters, and the like

II. Troubleshooting and Getting Help

III. Electronic Address Book

IV. Command Compendium

V. Where and When to Access

VI. Symbols and Codes

VII. Some Definitions

VIII. Telecomputing Bookshelf

IX. Reaching Us

I. MAKING CONNECTIONS

You can reach Dow Jones News/Retrieval through five different systems: Tymnet, Telenet, Uninet, DataPac, and Dow Jones's own DowNet system. Here are the log-on instructions for each.

Tymnet

1. After connection, the system will display PLEASE TYPE YOUR TERMINAL IDENTIFIER. (At 1200 baud, this message sometimes is garbled.) Enter the letter identifying your terminal type (in most cases, this is "a") and do not press RETURN.

2. After the system displays PLEASE LOG IN:, press CONTROL R, then enter DOW1;; or DOW2;; (without pressing RETURN). Note that the second semicolon will not display.

3. Now the system will display, WHAT SERVICE PLEASE????? Enter DJNS <RETURN>

4. Finally the system will ask ENTER PASSWORD. Type in your password and press RETURN. (The password will *not* display on your screen as you type it.)

Note: In step 2 of this explanation, pressing CONTROL R prior to entering DOW1;; or DOW2;; is not strictly necessary. However, it's a good habit to get into with Tymnet, because the CONTROL R signals the network that you want to "enable" certain control codes (notably Control S and Control Q).

Telenet

1. After connection, press RETURN twice.

2. The system will display a message something like, TELENET XXX XX TERMINAL=. Press RETURN

3. Telenet's prompt—an @ sign—will appear. Type C 60942 and press RETURN

4. The system will display 60942 CONNECTED. WHAT SERVICE PLEASE????? and you should type DJNS <RETURN>

5. Then Telenet will display ENTER PASSWORD, at which you type in your password.

Uninet

1. After you place the modem call, Uninet will display "L?" and you should press RETURN, a period, and another RETURN—that is, <RETURN>. <RETURN>

2. The next message from Uninet is UNINET PAD XXXXXX PORT YY SERVICE: Now type PROF3 RETURN

3. Uninet then displays SERVICE:, at which you should enter DOW <RETURN>

4. The system now says something like U001 000 CONNECTED TO 609000006 WHAT SERVICE PLEASE????? and you should enter DJNS <RETURN>

5. Finally, you should receive the password prompt.

DataPac

1. Following the modem connection, enter three periods— ...<RETURN> and the system will respond with DATAPAC:TERMINAL ADDRESS:

2. If you want to access through Tymnet, enter 13106,DOW1;; <RE-TURN>. If you're connecting through Telenet, type 131060900042 <RETURN>

3. The system then will report DATAPAC: CALL CONNECTED. HOST IS ONLINE. WHAT SERVICE PLEASE????? Enter DJNS <RETURN> and you'll be prompted for your password.

DowNet

The log-on sequence for DowNet (available at this writing in New York City, Chicago, Denver, Houston, and Princeton, New Jersey) is identical to the procedure used with Tymnet.

Communications Parameters

Here is the "standard setting" for communicating with Dow Jones News/Retrieval. If you're unsure how to set your equipment for these parameters, check your user's manuals or consult your computer dealer.

full duplex

no parity

one stop bit

one start bit

eight data bits

XON/XOFF to "off"

II. TROUBLESHOOTING AND GETTING HELP

Getting online help is a piece of cake on News/Retrieval. All you need to do is enter the double slash command (//) followed by the name of the database you're curious about, then a space and the word HELP. For instance, for help on the Text-Search Services (//TEXT), you'd enter //TEXT HELP.

Also remember that //INTRO often features helpful articles online about new features and commands in specific databases. It's a good idea to stroll by //INTRO once every week or two to see if there's any new material.

//DJHELP also contains information on new features and gives online guidance to using the major features.

Sometimes, though, you want to speak to another live human being. Then call the Customer Service hotline. For most of the country, it's 1-800-257-5114. (The only exception is for New Jersey residents, who should call 609-452-1511.)

On Monday through Friday the department is open from 8:00 A.M. to midnight Eastern Time. On Saturday it's open from 9:00 A.M. to 6:00 P.M. Closed on Sundays.

Customer Service can help with a myriad of specific problems—hardware- or software-related—interpreting information in a specific database, changing a password, and so on.

For help with DowPhone, the number is 1-800-257-0437.

For help with MCI Mail, call that company's toll-free number, 1-800-424-6677 (in Washington, D.C., 833-8484).

Some MCI addresses:

Speaking of MCI, you also can reach many helpful folks through MCI Mail (//MCI). Here are some handy addresses to which you can send letters at no charge:

To send a letter to DJN/R and to the editor of *Dowline* magazine, address a letter to **DOW JONES NEWS RETRIEVAL** or **DJNR FREE COMMENT.**

To write to those who put together the Cineman movie reviews (//MOVIES), address the message to **CINEMAN.**

For the **DISCLOSURE ONLINE** database folks, write to **DSCLO.**

For the providers of the Money Market Service (//MMS), address it to **MMS.**

To the providers of the Corporate Earnings Estimator (//EARN), write to **ZACKS** (that is, Zacks Investment Research).

III. ELECTRONIC ADDRESS BOOK

Through the tours you saw that the massive resources of Dow Jones News/Retrieval are subdivided into slightly under 40 individual databases. The command for reaching those databases is the double slash.

Here's the list of the major players.

Help in using the system:

//MENU, the "top" of DJN/R, a list of the databases in menu form.

//DJ HELP, online guide to the databases, with news of new features.

//INTRO, a free online newsletter, with database announcements, software news, etc.

//COPYRT, DJN/R's "banner headline" which provides information on important breaking news and service announcements.

//SYMBOL, a database of stock symbols, industry groups, and other useful codes for the Current Quotes and Dow Jones News Features.

//DEFINE, a comprehensive dictionary of 2,000 financial words and phrases, handy for interpreting information retrieved from the financial analysis databases.

Business and investing facts and figures:

//CQE, the enhanced Current Quotes database, which provides the delayed stock quotations on companies you specified. //CQE (unlike the older //CQ) also provides flash reports if there's breaking news about a company you've looked up. (Search with codes retrieved from //SYMBOL.)

//DJA, Dow Jones Average, the daily high, low, close, and volume for the Dow Jones industrials, transportation, utilities, and 64 stock composites. It's a historical database.

//FUTURES, quotes from the commodity exchanges around the country, with delayed prices on more than 80 commodities.

//HQ, Historical Quotes, with monthly summaries back to 1979 and quarterly summaries back to 1978. (Search with codes retrieved from //SYMBOL.)

//RTQ, Real-Time Quotes, that is, stock quotations with no delay, features the news flashes, like //CQE. It's an extra-cost service. (Search with codes retrieved from //SYMBOL.)

//FIDELITY, an electronic brokerage service that can take orders for stocks and options online.

//TRACK, the Dow Jones Tracking Service that, for $5 extra a month, lets you create up to five profiles of 25 companies each for easy tracking through //CQE and //DJNEWS.

Analyses for business decisions:

//DSCLO, the DISCLOSURE ONLINE database that provides company documents, such as 10-K extracts, business profiles, SEC filings, balance sheets, financial ratios, etc.

//EARN, in which top Wall Street analysts forecast the latest earnings-per-share for 3,000 widely followed public companies.

//MG or //MEDGEN, the Media General financial databases on 4,300 companies and 180 industries, giving revenue, earnings, dividends, volume, ratios, and price changes.

//MMS, a weekly survey of economic and foreign exchanges from money market dealers at 50 leading financial institutions, including median forecasts of domestic monetary and economic indicators, weekly consensus analysis, and forecasts of foreign exchanges.

//SP, Standard & Poor's, profiles of more than 4,600 companies, with financial overviews, projected earnings, dividends, and company operations reviews.

News and current events:

//NEWS, top national and foreign news of the hour, compiled by the DJN/R staff from the Associated Press.

//SPORTS, stories, standings, statistics for most major sports, professional, major college, and top amateur teams.

//WTHR, national weather summaries and forecasts by geographic region, tables for more than 50 major cities, provided by Accu-Weather, Inc.

//DJNEWS, up-to-the-minute business news from *The Wall Street Journal*, *Barron's*, and the Dow Jones News Service Broadtape, with a backlog of 90 days' worth. (Search with codes retrieved from //SYMBOL.)

//TEXT, full-text searchable database of articles from *The Wall Street Journal* and *The Washington Post* (back to 1984) and *Barron's*, the Dow Jones News Service, and the selected WSJ stories (back to 1979).

//KYODO, the Japan Economic Daily from Kyodo, offering same-day coverage of major business, economic, and political news, including Japanese financial market wrap-ups.

General services:

//MCI, electronic mail service by MCI, offering electronic and hard-copy delivery. No per-minute charges and no fee to receive mail.

//OAG, the Official Airline Guide, including 820,000 schedules for domestic and international flights, with fare information for major North American and international flights, and options for ordering tickets online.

//AXP, American Express ADVANCE, a cardholder's billing information service, providing statements for the previous two months, balances for the previous six months, travel-planning information, and catalogs.

//ENCYC, the Academic American Encyclopedia, offering 32,000 articles searchable by keywords, updated quarterly.

//STORE, Comp-U-Card's online shopping feature, Comp-U-Store, with more than 60,000 products that can be ordered through the system.

//MEDX, a nondiagnostic reference for medical and drug subjects, covering more than a thousand illnesses and their medical and surgical treatments. Information on drug side effects, food interaction, and precautions.

//MOVIES, Cineman Movie Reviews, including thousands of titles from 1926 to the present, updated weekly, with previews of coming attractions and lists of current box office hits.

//SCHOOL, the Peterson's College Selection Service, a guide to undergraduate studies, searchable by geographic location, major, enrollment, entrance difficulty, and specific college name.

IV. COMMAND COMPENDIUM

In most of Dow Jones News/Retrieval's databases, several one-letter commands can be used to navigate. You can check the HELP sections of each database to make sure these commands apply. (For example, //DJNEWS HELP will give you helpful information about that feature.)

Here are the commands that work in most databases:

\<RETURN\> to reach the next page of a document

R to back up (or reread) one page

T to go to the "top" menu of that particular database

M to go to the previous menu (that is, the last menu you saw in that database)

DISC to log off (disconnect) from the system

Beyond these, some features have some extra navigation commands available, generally specified on the first menu of the database. For instance, many of the databases use P and a page number to go to a specified page number in the database (for example, P34 to go directly to page 34).

Here are some special navigation commands available in major services:

World Report (//NEWS)

N to display additional national news headlines
F to see more foreign news

Japan Economic Daily (//KYODO)

N to retrieve more news
F to retrieve financial news
P to retrieve a list of the four previous editions

Official Airline Guide (OAG)

Basic navigation commands:

/I to receive additional information

/F to retrieve a fares' display

/S to get a schedules' display

/H to get to hotel/motel information

/M to return to the commands menu

/U to access the user comment area (the suggestion box)

/X (number) to get expanded information on a specified flight

/F (number) to retrieve a fare display on a specified flight

/L (number) to get fare limitation information

RS (no slash preceding) to retrieve return schedule information

Other commands are *not* preceded by a slash. Here are some of them and when they can be used:

CX: When viewing a list of direct flights between two airports, CX can be used to view connecting flights between the same airports.

DX: When viewing a list of connecting flights between two airports, DX can be used to see the direct flights between the same airports.

F#: Displays the fare for the flight on a specific line # when you are in the schedule area.

S#: Displays a schedule for a fare on a specific line # when you are in the fare area.

X#: Use X followed by a number to expand a display (interpret the shorthand) in the schedule, fare, or hotel/motel area.

L#: Used to display the limitations for a fare on line #. If there are limitations, the fare will be marked by an asterisk.

R#: Used to display the return schedules on line # when in the fare area.

B#: Used to begin a reservation booking for a flight on a specific line #.

RS: Displays return schedules.

RF: Displays return fares.

M: When in the fares area, returns you to the fares menu. In the hotel/motel area, it returns you to the location menu.

C: Used to cancel a booking session. No reservation will be made.

B: Used in a booking sequence to make a reservation from an expanded display.

When you are viewing an expanded schedule, fare, or fares limitations of an expanded hotel/motel display, you can use the following commands.

S: to display or return to schedules.

F: to display or return to fares.

M: to display hotel/motel location menu.

In addition, there are three commands that will help you move from one screen to another in a display sequence. They are:

+: Scroll to the next sequential screen.

−: Scroll to the previous sequential screen.

O: Immediately scroll to the original screen in the sequence.

Academic American Encyclopedia (//ENCYC)

Q to enter a new query

Comp-U-Store (//STORE)

LIST to list products
NP to indicate you have no brand preference
HELP for assistance within the database
BACK to go back to the previous question
MAIN to return to the opening menu
TOP to view the "top" menu
CHANGE to change product features previously selected

Sports Report (//SPORTS)

N to retrieve more sports news
F to retrieve full results, standings, and statistics

Weather Report (//WTHR)

N to get a two-day national forecast at any time
F to access weather reports for foreign cities

MCI Mail (//MCI)

SCAN to summarize the letters in your mailbox
READ to view the messages
PRINT to display the message without pauses
CREATE to write an MCI letter
DOW JONES to leave MCI and return to DJN/R
ACCOUNT to adjust your terminal settings in MCI Mail
HELP and HELP followed by a command to receive additional information
MENU to return to the main menu

Control Codes

Control Codes help you control the flow of information from Dow Jones News/Retrieval to your computer screen. Enter them by pressing the "Control" key and the specified letter. Do not use the <RETURN> key. Here are the most commonly used control codes.

CONTROL S to "freeze" the display

CONTROL Q to "unfreeze" the display, that is, to cancel Control S

CONTROL X to send a "break" signal to DJN/R (not available on all networks)

CONTROL R to redisplay the last line you entered (not available on all networks)

CONTROL H to backspace (not available on all networks)

V. WHERE AND WHEN TO ACCESS

Getting the latest from DJN/R is simply a matter of logging in and asking for it. However, you can be assured of the absolute latest if you know *when* the service updates its various databases. Here's a list that might help (all times are Eastern Standard Time):

Daily Updates

//COPYRT: Various times through the day to reflect breaking news and announcements

//CQE: 8:00 A.M. to 7:00 P.M. (Mutual funds are updated at 6:00 A.M. each business day, Treasury issues at 7:00 P.M.)

//DJA: 5:00 P.M.

//DJNEWS: 7:00 A.M. to 7:00 P.M.

//FUTURES: 8:45 A.M. to 5:15 P.M.

//HQ: 6:00 A.M.

//KYODO: 8:00 A.M.

//NEWS: 6:30 A.M. to 2:00 A.M. (also updated on Saturdays and Sundays from 10:00 A.M. to 2:00 A.M.)

//OAG: 6:00 A.M.

//RTQ: 10:00 A.M. to 6:00 P.M.

//SPORTS: 6:30 A.M. to 2:00 A.M. (also updated on Saturdays and Sunday from 10:00 A.M. to 2:00 A.M.)

//SYMBOL: 6:00 A.M. (to add new ones)

//TEXT: 6:00 A.M. (There is a 36-hour delay after online publication in //DJNEWS.)

//TRACK: 7:00 A.M. to 7:00 P.M.

//WTHR: 10:00 A.M. to 7:00 P.M. (also updated on Saturdays and Sundays at 11:00 A.M.)

Weekly Updates

//INTRO: At least weekly, more often as needed

//MCI: Weekly updated newsletter containing announcements (Type HELP NEWS at the MCI menu.)

//MG (//MEDGEN): 6:00 A.M. on Mondays
//MMS: 7:00 P.M. on Fridays
//MOVIES: 6:00 A.M. on Wednesdays
//DSLCO: 6:00 A.M. on Saturdays

Less Frequent Updates

//AXP: Individual accounts updated monthly, travel updated continuously, and shopping updated bimonthly
//DEFINE: Annually
//DJ HELP: Updated as needed to reflect changes and additions to the system
//ENCYC: Quarterly, in January, April, July, and October
//MEDX: Annually
//MENU: As needed to reflect new databases available
//SCHOOL: Annually, in the fall
//STORE: As needed by the staff of Comp-U-Store to list new products

Finding Regular Statistics

Statistics are the life blood of business, and News/Retrieval can be your regular contact for daily, weekly, monthly, and quarterly figures through its //DJNEWS features.

Here's a rundown of the major statistical groups and their category codes. To retrieve any of them from //DJNEWS, simply enter a period and the letter I, followed by a slash (/), the category code, a space, and the symbol 01. For instance, to retrieve the daily dividend reports, the command would be:

.I/DIV 01

Daily Statistics

Type	Code
Dividend reports	DIV
Foreign exchange rates	MON
Stock market reports	STK
Dow Jones Averages	DJA
Earnings reports	ERN
Commodity prices	CMD
Bond market	BON
Treasury bill rates	BON
Money rates	MON and FIN

Weekly Reports

Type	Code	Day Published
Federal Reserve data	EMI	Mondays
Treasury bill auction	BON	Tuesdays
Money supply	EMI	Fridays

Monthly Reports

Type	Code	Day Published
Building awards	CON	First day of the month
Leading indicators	EMI	First day of the month
Manufacturers' profits	EMI	First week of the month
Mortgage rates	BNK,REL,CON,FIN	First week of the month
Automobile sales	AUT	Fifth day of the month
Employment figures	EMI	Monday of second week of the month
Consumer credit	EMI	Second week of the month
Retail sales	EMI	Second week of the month
Inventories	EMI	Middle of the month
Industrial production	EMI	Middle of the month
Producers Price Index	EMI	Third Monday of the month

Capacity utilization	EMI	Third week of the month
Housing starts	EMI	Between 17th and 20th
Personal income	EMI	Third week
Durable goods orders	EMI	Thursday or Friday of next-to-last week
Balance of trade	EMI	Between 25th and 28th
Machine tool orders	EMI	Last Monday of the month
Consumer Price Index	EMI	Fourth week of the month
Federal budget reports	EMI	Fourth week of the month
Federal budget analyses	TAXES, ECO	Fourth week of the month

Quarterly Reports

Type	Code	Day Published
Corporate profits (WSJ)	ECO	One month after close of first quarter
Corporate profits—US Commerce	EMI	20 days after WSJ survey
Balance of payments	EMI	Between 18th and 20th
Gross National Product	EMI	20th of the month
Productivity	EMI	Last day of the month

VI. SYMBOLS AND CODES

Many of the databases on News/Retrieval require some special codes and symbols to make them do their stuff.

The majority of the codes, the symbols for companies you might look up in //CQE or //DJNEWS, can be located in the //SYMBOL databases. Others are included in the user guides you receive with your membership.

Here are some of the more commonly used codes for various databases around the system.

//DJNEWS, Industry, and Subject Symbols

Throughout the Dow Jones News/Retrieval system you have opportunities to search databases for information on specific stocks or industry groups. Here is a list of symbols for some of the common searches. With the //DJNEWS feature, enter a period, followed by the symbol. (For example, .I/PUB would seek news from the publishing world.)

I. *General News, Domestic and Foreign*

Current-day general news	I/GEN
All current-day ticker news	A/
Barron's news	BRRNS
Daily calendar	I/CAL
Executive changes	WNEWS
Headlines of the hour	I/HOH
"Hot" business news	H/
Labor news	LABOR
General foreign news	FORGN
Africa	AFRIC
Canada	CANDA
Europe	EUROP
Far East	FREST
Japan	JAPAN
Latin America	LATAM
Mideast	MDEST

II. *Economic and Stock Market News*

General economic news	I/ECO
General market news	I/STK
Active stocks	I/ACT
Bankruptcies	I/BCY
Block trades	I/BLK

Bond market news	I/BON
Buybacks, swap offers	I/BBK
Chief Executive Officers	I/CEO
Commodities news	I/CMD
Dividend actions	I/DIV
Dow Jones averages	I/DJA
Dow Jones interview	I/CEO
Earnings reports	I/ERN
Economic indicators	I/EMI
Heard on the Street	I/HRD
Initial equity offerings	I/INI
Monetary news	I/MON
Stock indexes	I/NDX
Tender offers, mergers, and acquisitions	I/TNM
Financial markets roundup	MARKT

III. Government News

General government news	GOVMT
Congressional news	G/CNG
Executive branch news	G/EXE
Agriculture Department	G/AGD
Civil Aeronautics Board	G/CAB
Defense Department	G/DEF
Energy Department	G/ERG
Environmental Protection Agency	G/EPA
Federal Communications Commission	G/FCC
Federal Reserve Board	G/FED
Federal Trade Commission	G/FTC
Food and Drug Administration	G/FDA
Internal Revenue Service	G/IRS
Interstate Commerce Commission	G/ICC
Justice Department	G/JUS
Labor Department	G/LBR
Securities and Exchange Commission	G/SEC

Supreme Court	G/SUP
Taxes	TAXES
Transportation Department	G/TRN
Treasury Department	G/TRE

IV. Major Industries

Accounting	I/FIN
Acquisitions	I/TNM
Advertising	I/MKT
Aerospace	I/ARO
Airlines	I/AIR
Apparel	I/TEX
Appliances	I/ELE
Autos, auto parts	I/AUT
Bankruptcies	I/BCY
Banks	I/BNK
Broadcasting	I/TEL
Casinos and gambling	I/CNO
Chemicals	I/CHM
Computers	I/EDP
Construction, materials	I/CON
Cosmetics	I/FAB
Electric, electronics	I/ELE
Environment	I/ENV
Farm equipment	I/FAR
Farm products	I/CMD
Financial	I/FIN
Food and beverage	I/FAB
Foreign exchange	I/MON
Gold	I/PCS
Hospital supplies	I/PHA
Household products	I/FAB
Industrial equipment	I/IND
Insurance	I/FIN
International money, trade	I/MON
Land development	I/REL

Leasing	I/FIN
Machine tools	I/IND
Marketing	I/MKT
Mergers	I/TNM
Mining, metals (nonprecious)	I/MIN
Movies	I/FLX
Mutual funds	I/FIN
Natural gas, pipelines	I/LNG
Nuclear power, fuel	I/NUK
Office equipment	I/OFF
Packaging (all types)	I/PUL
Petroleum	I/PET
Pharmaceuticals	I/PHA
Photography	I/PIX
Plastics	I/CHM
Precious metals, stones	I/PCS
Publishing	I/PUB
Pulp, paper	I/PUL
Railways	I/TRA
Real estate,	I/REL
Records, recording studios	I/FLX
Restaurants	I/FAB
Retailing	I/RET
Rubber	I/RUB
Securities industry	I/SCR
Ship lines, builders	I/TRA
Supermarkets	I/FAB
Telecommunications	I/TEL
Telephone, telegraph	I/TEL
Tender offers	I/TNM
Textiles	I/TEX
Thrift institutions	I/BNK
Tobacco	I/FAB
Transportation (not airlines or cars)	I/TRA
Truck lines	I/TRA
Utilities	I/UTI

Quotes: For //CQE (and //CQ), //HQ and //RTQ

The prices you receive from the quotes databases are generally composite quotes. However, you can receive quotations from specific exchanges if you precede the stock symbol with one of these numeric codes:

1 for the New York Exchange

2 for the American Exchange

3 for the Pacific Exchange

4 for the Midwest Exchange

Specifying issues other than common stock:

In //CQ, //CQE, and //RTQ you can seek quotes on investment opportunities other than common stock if you precede the symbol with one of these codes:

Prefix	Means
+	Mutual Funds
/	Corporate and Foreign Bonds
#	U.S. Treasury Bonds and Notes
−	Stock options

//DJA Codes:

Speaking of //DJA, indexes are available for industrials, transportation, utilities, and 65 selected stocks. Use these codes for the desired index:

IND for Industrials

TRN for Transportation

UTL for Utilities

65 for the 65 active stocks

Commodities Symbols

As we discussed in Chapter 5, //FUTURES tracks the commodities markets around the continent. To use the system, you have to be aware of a number of diverse codes. Here are the codes currently being employed in //FUTURES:

Contract Month Codes

January	F	July	N
February	G	August	Q
March	H	September	U
April	J	October	V
May	K	November	X
June	M	December	Z

Abbreviations of Commodity Exchanges

CBT	Chicago Board of Trade
CME	Chicago Mercantile Exchange
CRCE	Chicago Rice & Cotton Exchange
CSCE	Coffee, Sugar & Cocoa Exchange
CMX	Commodity Exchange, NY
FINEX	Financial Instrument Exchange
IMM	International Monetary Market
KC	Kansas City Board of Trade
MCE	Midamerica Commodity Exchange
MPLS	Minneapolis Grain Exchange
CTN	New York Cotton Exchange
NYFE	New York Futures Exchange
NYM	New York Mercantile Exchange
PBT	Philadelphia Board of Trade
WPG	Winnipeg Commodity Exchange

Commodities Symbols and Their Exchanges

Symbol	Future (Exchange)
DC	Bank CDs (IMM)
WB	Barley (WPG)
AB	Barley, Alberta (WPG)
BP	British Pound (IMM)
XP	British Pound (MCE)
CD	Canadian Dollar (IMM)
XD	Canadian Dollar (MCE)
FC	Cattle, Feeder (CME)
LC	Cattle, Live (CME)
XL	Cattle, Live (MCE)
XQ	Copper (MCE)
XC	Corn (MCE)
C	Corn (CBT)
NO	Cotton (CRCE)
ED	Eurodollar (IMM)
WF	Flaxseed (WPG)
FR	French Franc (IMM)
M	GNMA Mortgages CDR (CBT)
WG	Gold (WPG)
XK	Gold, New York (MCE)
KI	Gold, One Kilo (CBT)
LH	Hogs (CME)
XH	Hogs (MCE)
JY	Japanese Yen (IMM)
XJ	Japanese Yen (MCE)
MV	KC Mini Value Line Futures (KC)
KV	KC Value Line Futures (KC)
MB	Long-Term Municipal Bond Index (CBT)
LB	Lumber (CME)
MX	Major Market Index (CBT)
BC	Major Market Index, Maxi (CBT)
MP	Mexican Peso (IMM)
ND	Nasdaq 100 (CBT)
OX	National OTC Index (PBT)

Symbol	Future (Exchange)
YX	NYSE Composite Futures (NYFE)
O	Oats (CBT)
WO	Oats (WPG)
XO	Oats (MCE)
XU	Platinum (MCE)
PB	Pork Bellies (CME)
RS	Rapeseed (WPG)
NR	Rough Rice (CRCE)
WR	Rye (WPG)
SX	S&P 100 Futures Index (CME)
SP	S&P 500 Futures Index (CME)
OT	S&P OTC 250 (CME)
SL	Silver (WPG)
XY	Silver, New York (MCE)
XI	Silver, Chicago (MCE)
AG	Silver (CBT)
XX	Soybean Meal (MCE)
SM	Soybean Meal (CBT)
BO	Soybean Oil (CBT)
XS	Soybeans (MCE)
S	Soybeans (CBT)
XF	Swiss Franc (MCE)
SF	Swiss Franc (IMM)
XT	Treasury Bills (MCE)
TB	Treasury Bills (IMM)
XB	Treasury Bonds (MCE)
TR	Treasury Bonds (CBT)
TY	Treasury Notes (CBT)
XM	West German Mark (MCE)
DM	West German Mark (IMM)
XW	Wheat (MCE)
KW	Wheat (KC)
W	Wheat (CBT)
WW	Wheat (WPG)
MW	Wheat (MPLS)
NW	White Wheat (MPLS)

Understanding //FUTURES' Price Quotes

COMMODITY	DISPLAYED PRICE	READ AS
Bank CDs	9063	90.63, a yield of 9.37%
Barley	11620	116.20 Can. dollars a ton
British Pound	12605	$1.2605 per Pound
Canadian Dollar	7506	$.7506 per Can. dollar
Cattle	7095	70.95 cents per pound
Copper	6070	60.70 cents per pound
Corn	2734	273½ cents per bushel
Cotton	7840	78.40 cents per pound
Eurodollar	8992	89.92, a yield of 10.08%
Flaxseed	35650	356.50 Can. dollars a ton
French Franc	10975	$.10975 per French franc
GNMA CDR	6803	68 3/32, yield of 13.581%
Gold	35650	$356.50 per troy ounce
Hogs	5182	51.82 cents per pound
Japanese Yen	4127	$.004127 per yen
KC Mini Value Line Futures	18230	182.30 times 100
KC Value Line Futures	18230	182.30 times 500
Long-Term Municipal Bond Index (CBT)	8301	83 1/32 times 1000
Lumber	15230	$152.30 per 1,000 bd. feet
Major Market Index	2454	245½ times 100
Major Market Index, Maxi	26350	263.50 times 250
Mexican Peso	467	$.00467 per peso
Nasdaq 100	16179	161.79 times 250
National OTC Index	16179	161.79 times 500
NYSE Composite Futures	10355	103.55 times 500
Oats (CBT and MCE)	1872	187¼ cents per bushel
Oats (WPG)	12450	124.50 Can. dollars a ton
Platinum	34580	$345.80 per troy ounce
Pork Bellies	6950	69.50 cents per pound
Rapeseed	40530	405.30 Can. dollars a ton
Rough Rice	803	$8.03 per cwt.
Rye	14600	146.00 Can. dollars a ton

COMMODITY	DISPLAYED PRICE	READ AS
S&P 100 Futures Index	16520	165.20 times 500
S&P 500 Futures Index	16670	166.70 times 500
S&P OTC 250	16179	167.19 times 500
Silver	7580	758.0 cents per troy ounce
Silver (WPG)	603	$6.03 per troy ounce
Soybeans	6194	619½ cents per bushel
Soybean Meal	15150	$151.50 per ton
Soybean Oil	2675	26.75 cents per pound
Swiss Franc	4105	$.4105 per Swiss franc
Treasury Bills	9116	91.16, a yield of 8.84%
Treasury Bonds	7015	70 15/32, yield 11.901%
Treasury Notes	7910	79 10/32, yield 11.540%
West German Mark	3395	$.3395 per mark
Wheat	4182	418¼ cents per bushel
Wheat (WPG)	16380	163.80 Can. dollars a ton
White Wheat	3876	387¾ cents per bushel

About //TEXT

In Chapters 10 and 11 we took a long, hard look at Text-Search Services (//TEXT) and saw how to use it for detailed searches of *The Wall Street Journal*, *The Washington Post* and the Dow Jones News Service. Here's some back-pocket information about //TEXT:

Section Codes in Documents

AN: The story's unique identification number

HL: The headline of the story (In *The Wall Street Journal* and *The Washington Post* databases the HL section also includes the byline of the writer.)

DD: Document date

IN: The industry group code, again the same as you could find in //SYMBOL

TX: The actual text of the story

CO: The Dow Jones company code

SO: The source of information used in the story

Regarding the SO (source) section, //TEXT uses these codes to identify sources:

T   the story comes from the "broadtape" of the Dow Jones News Service.

B   *Barron's*

J   *The Wall Street Journal*

N   the News/Retrieval Service

W   *The Wall Street Journal* and the Dow Jones News Service.

Washington Post Sections

In //TEXT, *The Washington Post* is making creative use of the source (SO) section; it can identify various sections of the *Post*. Here's a list of the *Post's* sections, their codes, and the date they're updated. To use a *Post* section in a //TEXT query, include the name of the section followed by a period, the letters SO, and another period. For instance, searching the food section in a query would be "FOOD.SO." Be sure to type in the codes just as they appear in the first column.

Section Code	Updated
A Section	Daily
Editorial	Daily
Op/Ed	Daily
Metro	Daily
Style	Daily
Business	Daily
Sports	Daily
Style Plus	Daily
Weekend	Friday

Section Code	Updated
Religion	Saturday
Food	Wednesday and Sunday
Real Estate	Saturday
Show	Sunday
Washington Home	Thursday
Travel	Sunday
Outlook	Sunday
Post Magazine	Sunday
Book World	Sunday
TV Week	Sunday
Health	Wednesday

VII. SOME DEFINITIONS

The financial world has its own lexicon. During our online forays you learned about a great database called //DEFINE that gives you the definitions of some 2,000 business terms and phrases. In addition, here are some commonly used terms you'll see in some databases.

Major Terms Used In the Media General (//MG) Reports

Price

P/E Ratio Current: Based on the latest closing price (bid) and the trailing 12 months' earnings per share. In an effort to eliminate distortions, any calculations involving P/E ratios to determine industry averages ignore those companies with P/Es greater than 50. Any stock with a current or five-year average P/E greater than 50 will show an NC in that field.

P/E Ratio-5-Year Average High (Low): Based on the high (low) price in each of the previous five years and the fiscal year earnings for the five years.

Price to Common Stock Equity: The latest closing price (bid) per share divided by the current estimated common equity per share.

Price to Revenue Per Share: The latest closing price (bid) per share divided by the current estimated common equity per share.

Relative Price Index: Calculated on this formula:

Relative Price Index =
300 (latest closing price)

---

a (Common Equity Share) – b (Latest 12 Mos. EPS) + c (Ind. Div. Rate)

Where:
a = Price/Equity ratio of stocks on database
b = Price/Earnings ratio of stocks on database
c = Price/Dividend ratio of stocks on database

Price Movement

Beta Co-Efficients: This co-efficient is a measure of how much a given stock tends to change in price relative to the market as a whole. A beta co-efficient of 1 means that the market and the stock move the same. A 5 percent move in the market would produce a 5 percent movement in the stock. A co-efficient of 2 suggests that the stock tends to fluctuate twice as much as the market. If the market moves up 5 percent, then the stock tends to move up 10 percent. A co-efficient of 0.5 means that the given stock will move one-half as much as the market either up or down.

Up Market: The betas for up markets are calculated on the last eight upward moves of 5 percent or more in the Media General Composite Market Index. At the eighth point, once a 5 percent swing has been attained, the beta is recalculated at a new moving high point as the market move continues until a 5 percent reversal has occurred. When there is only a partial record of a given stock's price, a minimum of four swings of 5 percent or more are required for the beta calculation.

Down Market: Same as above except the betas are calculated on the basis of 5 percent downswings in the composite index. The calculation itself is an unweighted average of the stock's percentage change during a "swing period" divided by the market's percentage change during a "swing period." The co-efficient is noted by an asterisk where the beta is at least as large as its probable error (i.e., 6,745 times the standard error of its mean).

Volume

Shares: The stock's reported total volume for the last full trading week.

Dollars: The above volume figure times the latest closing price (bid).

% of Shares Outstanding: The latest weekly volume as a percentage of the company's latest reported shares outstanding.

Liquidity Ratio: A measure of how much dollar volume was required during the same recent time period to move the stock's prices up or down by one percentage point. This ratio is calculated by accumulating the daily percentage changes of each issue for each trading day of the month, whether they are plus or minus, and then dividing this total percentage figure into total dollar volume for the month.

On-Balance Index: Relates the up market volume of the stock during the previous four weeks to its change in price through a complex equation. This index will vary upward depending on whether upward price moves are accompanied by high and increasing volume. These moves are regarded by many as favorable signs.

Revenue and Earnings

Note that 12-month figures are trailing ones, calculated from figures shown in the latest interim reports and the latest fiscal year reports, when appropriate. Fiscal figures are reported by the company. Interim figures are based on cumulative data. All earnings are from continuing operations, per-share figures are fully diluted ones, and calculations based on them reflect such dilution. The footnote under "Earnings Last 12 Mos." governs all revenue and earnings figures; s, first six months; n, first nine months; and f, fiscal year.

Five-Year Growth Rate: The five-year growth in fully diluted earnings per share arrived at through the least squares method, brought up to date through each interim by time-weighing the first and sixth points.

Dividends

Dividends are the latest indicated rate, and the yield is based on that amount and the latest close.

Five-Year Growth Rate: This figure is arrived at by the least square method, using dividends actually paid for the first five years and the indicated rate for the sixth point.

Ratios

Profit Margin: The profit margin of the company based on the latest 12 months' revenue and earnings.

Return of Common Equity: Latest annual earnings from continuing operations divided by common stock equity.

Return on Total Assets: Based on the latest 12 months' total earnings and the total assets as reported in the company's latest fiscal year balance sheet.

Revenue to Assets: Revenues divided by total assets.

Debt to Equity: The total long-term debt of a company as a percentage of the total common equity of the company, both from the latest annual balance sheet.

Interest Coverage: Profit before taxes plus interest, divided by interest, taken from the latest annual income statement.

Current Ratio: Current assets divided by current liabilities.

Shareholdings

Market Value: Latest reported shares outstanding times the latest closing price-per-share of common stock.

Latest Shares Outstanding: Latest reported shares outstanding, adjusted for any subsequent stock splits or dividends.

Insider Net Training: Net change in insider holdings—purchases vs. sales—based on the latest SEC report. 0 means there were no transactions or transactions netted out to 0; +0 means the transactions netted to purchases of fewer than 500 shares; –0 means transactions netted to sales of fewer than 500 shares.

Short Interest Ratio: Short interest for the latest month's report divided by the average daily volume for the month corresponding to the report. The figure shows the number of days it would take to cover the short interest if the trading rate continued at the rate of the month covered by the report.

Footnotes

NA: Item not applicable to this stock
NE: Negative earnings invalidate calculation
NC: Data required for calculation not available
q: Based on first quarter information
s: Based on first six months information
n: Based on first nine months information
f: Based on fiscal year information
*:   When applied to 12-month earnings, an asterisk indicates an actual amount for the interim period, other than a quarterly multiple, resulting from a fiscal year change. When applied to beta figures, an asterisk denotes a coefficient at least as large as its probable error (i.e., 6,745 times the standard error of its mean).
G: Value calculated greater than allowed range
L: Value calculated less than allowed range
a: Under current dividend yield, indicates a stock dividend
b: Indicates cash plus stock dividend when applied to dividend yield column
Z: Indicates coverage greater than 99.9 times
X: No interest

SEC Public Documents Described in Disclosure ONLINE (//DSCLO)

Registration Statement (abbreviated in //DSCLO as REGST): A document that must be filed before securities can be offered for public sale.

Prospectus (PRSPCT): The final version of the Registration Statement; must be filed on the date the public offering is made.

Shelf Registration (SHELF): Filed before the securities can be offered; registers the securities expected to be sold within the next two years.

10-K (10-K): An annual summary of a company's management and financial position; must be filed 90 days after the firm's fiscal year ends.

10-Q (10-Q): A quarterly report offering a continuing view of a firm's financial position, filed 45 days after the close of its fiscal quarter.

20-F (20-F): For companies headquartered outside the United States, the same as a 10-K; must be filed 180 days after the end of the fiscal year.

8-K (8-K): A periodic document reporting any events deemed important to the shareholders of the SEC; filed no more than 10 days after the event.

Annual Report to Shareholders (ARS): *Not* an official SEC document, but usually provided to the shareholders by the company at the end of the fiscal year.

Proxy Statement (PROXY): A firm's official notification to shareholders of matter to be brought to a vote at the company's annual meeting; filed between the end of the fiscal year and the meeting.

13-F (NA): A quarterly report of stockholdings, filed by institutions 45 days after the close of the calendar quarter.

13-D (SCH 13D): Records sale, purchase, or change of intention by 5 percent of the owners of a company's stock; filed 10 days after the event.

13-G (SCH 13G): An annual report of stockholders, filed by 5 percent of the owners of a firm's stock 45 days after the close of the calendar year.

14D-1 (SC 14D1): Filed by those making a tender offer which would result in 5 percent ownership of a company's stock; filed the date the offer is made.

14D-9 (SC 14D9): A company's recommendation to shareholders in the event of a tender offer; filed within 10 days after the offer is made.

13E-4 (SC 13E4): Filed when a company wants to repurchase its own shares; filed on the date the offer is made.

13E-3 (SC 13E3): Filed by a company offering to repurchase its own shares for the purpose of "going private"; filed on the date the offer is made.

Form 3 (NA): The initial statement of ownership by the officers, directors, or 10 percent of the principal stockholders; filed 10 days after the security is first acquired.

Form 4 (NA): The statement of a change in ownership by the officers, directors, or 10 percent of the stockholders; filed 10 days after the end of the month during which the action occurred.

Standard & Poor's Online

Following are the definitions of terms used in Standard & Poor's Online as well as an explanation of the footnotes found in the Standard & Poor's Online database.

Average Daily Volume: Average daily trading volume for current month.

Beta: The measure of price volatility relative to the general market.

Book Value Per Share: Computed by dividing total of stockholders equity less intangible assets and preferred shares at liquidation value by number of shares outstanding at end of year (or period).

Current Ratio: The ratio of current assets to current liabilities as of the most recent date for which information is available.

Dividends: Dividends shown are total payments, including extras made in the indicated calendar year.

EPS: Earnings per share, shown on a "Primary" basis as reported by company, including discontinued operations but excluding extraordinary items.

Ex-Date: The date on which stock sells "ex-dividends"; that is, the date it sells without the right to receive the latest declared dividend.

Five-Year Growth: The compounded annual rate of per-share earnings growth for the previous five years.

High and Low Prices: For calendar years; bid prices used for OTC stocks.

Interim Share Earnings: For the longest accounting interval since the last fiscal year-end and compared with those for the year-earlier period.

Last Dividend: Last dividend payment and the frequency of payment as indicated by M(monthly), Q(quarterly), S(semi-annually), or A(annually).

Long-Term Debt: Shown in millions of dollars; includes funded debt, long-term bank loans, deferred compensation, etc.

P/E Range: Price/Earnings ratio range obtained by dividing the annual earnings into the high and low market price for the year; banks' and insurance companies' operating earnings are used.

Last 12 Months: Indicates 12 months' EPS through latest interim period.

Net Income: Shown in millions (M) of dollars, after deduction of expenses, taxes, and fixed charges, but before extraordinary (except as noted) items and all dividends.

Paydate: Payable date is the date of disbursement of the latest payment; if an extra or stock dividend also is being paid, it is so footnoted.

P/E Ratio: Derived by dividing price by estimated new year earnings, or last 12 months' earnings if no estimate is available.

Percent Institutional Holdings: The percentage of shares held by financial institutions.

Range: The high and low price since a specified date.

Rate and Yield: A projection of payments for the next 12 months based on the latest payment and the percentage obtained by dividing that rate by the current price of the stock.

Shares Outstanding: Excluding treasury stock in millions (M).

Revenues: Shown in millions (M) of dollars as indicated.

S&P Footnote Explanations

Here are the footnote letters you might see in the Dividends section of Standard & Poor's and what they mean:

c   Based on last year's payment
d   Dividend paid in Canadian funds
e   Excluding extras
f   Pro forma
g   Previous record (if any) not available
h   Canadian funds
j   Stock of another company
k   Includes extras
n   Also stock
p   Dividend paid a/c arrears
r   Less tax country of origin
s   Dividend from capital gains
t   Excludes capital gains distribution
u   Includes extras and stock

Here are the footnote letters you may find in the Earnings section and what they mean:

a   Net investment income
b   Before depletion
c   Company only
d   Deficit
e   Estimate
f   Pro forma
g   Fully diluted earnings
i   Currency of country of origin
k   Interim periods one year earlier than column heads
l   Interim not comparable with annual earnings
n   Net asset value
o   Combined various classes
p   Preliminary
r   Primary earnings with dilutive common equivalent
s   Before tax loss carryforward

t   Partial year
u   Net gain from operations
w   Excluding extraordinary income
x   Including extraordinary income
y   Excluding extraordinary charges
z   Including extraordinary charges

If you see footnote letters in other S&P sections, here is what they mean:

b   Giving effect to new financing
c   Based on last year's payment
d   Converted to U.S. funds
e   Excluding extras
f   Pro forma
g   Previous record (if any) not available
h   Canadian funds
i   Currency of country of origin
j   Stock of another company
k   Includes extras
n   Also stock
o   Combined various classes
u   Includes extras and stock
v   Nonvoting

VIII. TELECOMPUTING BOOKSHELF

Books on computer communications abound. Here are some that are on our bookshelves.

How to Get the Most Out of CompuServe, 2nd edition, by Charles Bowen and David Peyton, Bantam Books, $16.95. Recently updated tutorial on the largest consumer information service around.

How to Get the Most Out of The Source, by Charles Bowen and David Peyton, Bantam Books, $14.95. An online tour guide to that popular information service.

Smarter Telecommunications, by Charles Bowen and Stewart Schneider, Bantam Books, $12.95. A general guide to the wonders of information services, databases, and computer bulletin boards.

The Complete Handbook of Personal Computer Communications, by Alfred Glossbrenner, St. Martin's Press, $14.95. One of the first commercial books devoted to dial-up services, available in an excellent updated edition.

Using and Applying the Dow Jones Information Services, by Donald R. Woodwell, Dow Jones-Irwin. A guide to problem solving and interpreting data retrieved from the service.

The Dow Jones-Irwin Guide to On-Line Investing, by Thomas A. Meyers, Dow Jones-Irwin, $25. A guide to using on-line services in investment decisions.

Omni Online Database Directory, by Mike Edelhart and Owen Davies, Collier Books, $10.95. Directory and evaluation of more than 1,000 databases.

The Computer Data and Database Source Book, by Matthew Lesko, Avon Books, $14.95. Encyclopedia of commercial and public databases.

The Joy of Computer Communication, by William J. Cook, Dell Books, $5.95.

IX. REACHING US

Now that you're an old pro at the ins and outs of Dow Jones News/Retrieval, we hope you'll feel free to drop us a line sometime and let us know how you're getting along. We're just an MCI Mail away.

Charlie is registered as Charles Bowen (MCI ID 224-5135). Dave is listed as David A. Peyton (MCI ID 162-9244).

INDEX

ABOUT THE AUTHORS

CHARLES BOWEN and DAVID PEYTON have been writing about the electronic community since 1982. They have written *How to Get the Most Out of CompuServe, 2nd edition* (Bantam Books, 1986) and *How to Get the Most Out of The Source* (Bantam Books, 1985), and have written articles and columns for an assortment of computer magazines and journals.

Bowen also was coauthor with Stewart Schneider of *Smarter Telecommunications* (Bantam Books, 1985). He is a freelance writer and a former newspaper editor. He and his wife Pamela live in Huntington, West Virginia.

Peyton is a feature writer and columnist for the Huntington Publishing Co., where he has worked for twenty years. He also is a columnist for Gannett News Service. He lives in Huntington with his wife Susan and their fifteen-year-old son, Davy.